The Master Musicians

New Series Edited by Eric Blom

WEBER

Carl Maria von Weber

WEBER

by

WILLIAM SAUNDERS

Illustrated

London   J. M. Dent and Sons Ltd
New York   E. P. Dutton and Co. Inc.

All rights reserved
Made in Great Britain
at The Temple Press Letchworth
for
J. M. Dent & Sons Ltd
Aldine House Bedford St London
First Published 1940

PREFACE

THERE is probably not one of the great nineteenth‑century composers about whose life so meagre a body of source material exists as does about Carl Maria von Weber's. Apart from his correspondence, which is not extensive, and the brief autobio‑graphical notes that are included in his literary works, the complete authorities still remain: (1) the biography written by his son, Baron Max Maria von Weber; (2) the small volume entitled *Weber* by Sir Julius Benedict; and (3) the admirable volume by F. W. Jähns, *Carl Maria von Weber in seinen Werken*. The Life written by his son exists in an English version, but the translation is bad and full of errors, and this applies even to a greater extent to Lady Wallace's translation of Nohl's *Musiker‑briefe,* in which Weber's letters to Gänsbacher are included. Benedict's work, on the other hand, although originally written in English, is not so much a biography as a bare series of annals, based on Max von Weber's work up to the day on which Benedict became a pupil of Weber, and thereafter it becomes less of a biography than a description of the author's friendship with the composer and their personal relations. Both works are valuable up to a point, but they must be used with caution. Jähns's volume, however, is invaluable and a *sine qua non* to every serious student of Weber's life and works. In compiling this volume I have made considerable use of these three works, but, so far as I was able, I have verified all statements of fact derived from them. I have, of course, also worked over most of the later books on Weber, and where I made use of them, I have acknow‑ledged my indebtedness in the text. For the reasons I have given above, I believe the present work to be the first complete biography of Weber that has ever been written directly in English.

Preface

For scores of Weber's operas I have to thank Messrs Novello & Co. Ltd, whose editions are still the best in existence. I am also indebted to C. F. Peters Verlag, Leipzig, for works published by them, and to Messrs Anton Böhm & Sohn, Augsburg, for their exquisite score of the *Grosse Jugendmesse*. Through the kindness of Dr Mary Grierson and Dr Hans Gál I was permitted to borrow from the University of Edinburgh Music Library the rare first editions of *Sylvana* and of the *Sechs Lieder* (Op. 30), which, with first editions of the pianoforte Sonatas, are the only Weber rarities this library possesses; but, even with only these, its affluence, compared with most other libraries in the country, is inestimable. No one who has done work for the art of music so long as I have in Edinburgh can pretend a lack of indebtedness in almost any branch of musical activity on which one may be engaged to the late Professor Frederick M. Niecks and to Professor Sir Donald F. Tovey, and I gratefully acknowledge all that I owe to them which may have gone to the making of this book.

W. S.

EDINBURGH,
    August 1939.

vi

CONTENTS

ILLUSTRATIONS

ix

CHAPTER I

THE ANCESTRAL BACKGROUND

THE musical editor of the *Journal de Paris*, in an article which appeared in that periodical on 8th December 1824, the day after the *première* of the adaptation of *Der Freischütz* by Castil-Blaze, produced at the Odéon under the title of *Robin des bois,* writes: 'I seek Weber in our most recent biographical works; I seek him in our dictionaries of music; nowhere Weber.'

If this composer's position is not quite so insecure as that to-day, there is still a vast amount of unnecessary and inexcusable ignor-ance regarding the life, work and influence of one of the most significant figures in the history of music and in the development of music-drama in the nineteenth and twentieth centuries.

Carl Maria Friedrich Ernst von Weber was born in a house in the Lübecker Strasse, No. 26, at Eutin, a beautiful little town, charmingly nestling in a veritable grove, about midway between Lübeck and Kiel, in the Grand-Duchy of Oldenburg. This was on 18th December 1786. He was descended from a race of landed proprietors in the upper Rhenish districts of the Holy Roman Empire, and music, of a more or less exalted character, seems to have run in the family, as indeed it did in most of the Upper German and Austrian families, of any social standing at least, during the seventeenth and eighteenth centuries. Not-withstanding the plebeian surname, Weber (i.e. Weaver), which the family carried, no doubt from an earlier occupational source, it must have been one of considerable importance by the beginning of the seventeenth century, for we are informed that in 1622 the Emperor Ferdinand II bestowed the title of *Freiherr* (or baron) upon a certain Johann Baptist Weber. This individual, who is described by a French biographer of the composer[1] as 'a faithful factotum' of the emperor, is said to have been an elder brother of Joseph Franz Xaver Weber, the great-grandfather of Carl Maria; but the German biographers are all very reticent on this subject when they are not altogether silent.

With the reputed younger brother of this ennobled factotum, however, we find ourselves on more solid genealogical ground. Joseph Franz Xaver Weber was undoubtedly the great-grand-father of our hero. He was a miller, and is said to have been a great lover of music and the drama, and to have had a small theatre and concert-room built on his estate. But Europe was just then in the throes of the Thirty Years War and, apart from the fact that all the Webers were staunch Catholics, it was Germany that had to bear the brunt of the war, and, considering the condition in which the Peace of Westphalia left that vast expanse of territory and the dwellers thereon, they were lucky to lose nothing more than their lands. But these they certainly did lose, and, the restitution clauses of the Peace of Westphalia notwithstanding, they were never recovered. Their patent of nobility seems to have lapsed, or been held in suspense, for we read that 'the title of the elder brother was not transmitted till 1738,' when it must have been revived in the person of Fridolin, the son of Joseph Franz Xaver, who died in 1754. It must be said here that there is some difficulty in reconciling the relationships between Freiherr Johann Baptist and Johann Franz Xaver and his son Fridolin with the dates recorded in all the biographies which mention them at all. This will at once be apparent when it is noted that the first-named is said to have received his title of nobility in 1622, while his younger brother became the father of the last-mentioned, who died in 1754. It is not entirely impossible for this to have been the case, of course, but the probabilities are all against its having been so, more especially as we have no records of any of the earlier members of the family having shown undue precocity, or of having

---

[1] André Cœuroy, *Weber* ('Les Maîtres de la Musique,' Paris, 1925), p. 1.

survived well beyond the normal span of life. This, no doubt, is one of the chief reasons why the German authorities are all so reticent in connection with the matter.

Fridolin Weber was *Amtmann*, or factor, to the Freiherr von Schönau-Zella, near Freiburg-im-Breisgau, and he was an enthusiastic and skilful musical amateur, being a good vocalist and an adept at playing the violin and organ. He had three sons, Joseph Anton, Fridolin and Franz Anton, by a wife in whose veins flowed French blood. The eldest of the three brothers, Joseph Anton, became a good citizen of Freiburg, where he lived out his placid days, and beyond the mere fact of his having existed he does not come under consideration here. To Fridolin, however, more than merely passing reference must be made. He was born at Zell in 1733 and, like his father, he was an excel-lent singer and violinist, but preferred the reflected glory of being the father of professional musicians to the first-hand fame of being one himself. He succeeded his father in the management of the Schönau-Zella estates, and appears to have dropped the outward manifestation of nobility—the prefix *von*—probably as a matter of policy. He finally became a member of the famous chapel of the Elector Carl Theodor at Mannheim, however, and in 1756 he married Marie Caecilie Stamm of that city. By her he had four daughters, all of whom became notable singers in their time. They were all more or less connected with Schikaneder's theatre, and one has an uncomfortable feeling that they were kept dangling around there by their rather unprincipled mother for such gains as the matrimonial—or not always too strictly matrimonial—market might offer. Josefa, the eldest, and Aloysia, the next in age, were both gifted with coloratura voices of good quality and extraordinary flexibility. Mozart met them when the former was only nineteen years of age and the latter barely sixteen, and he fell head over ears in love with Aloysia. Why Fridolin had left Schönau-Zella has not transpired, but for whatever reason he may have done so the change to Mannheim had not been advan-tageous, and there is no doubt that when Mozart came upon the scene the Webers were extremely poor. Fridolin was making a bare living by taking small singing engagements and working precariously as a copyist and prompter at the Opera. It was early in December 1777 that Mozart arrived in Mannheim, and the first mention of Fridolin Weber we find in Mozart's letters to his father appears in one dated 17th January 1778, where he tells of his having copied four airs which he proposed to present to the Princess of Orange, with whom, a few days later, he was going to spend some time at Kirchheim-Boland, knowing that she was 'a great lover of song.' Immediately afterwards every letter he wrote to his father was full of praises of the talents of the Webers and commiseration with them for their poverty. His enthusiasm for this family soon sent his father into a panic, and after two months of tense and hysterical correspondence the young composer capitulated and left Mannheim and the Webers, for a time at least. What happened between this departure and his settling down with the family in Vienna three years later, and what we know about the scheming of Marie Caecilie, belongs entirely to the biography of Mozart; but the eventual outcome of it all was Mozart's marriage to—not his first love, Aloysia, who had long before spurned him and married an actor named Lange— but the third of the Weber girls, Constanze. For Josefa, it may be noted, he wrote the part of the Queen of Night in *Die Zauberflöte*, for Aloysia he composed several arias at various times,[1] and the soprano part in the unfinished C minor Mass was intended for Constanze. All four of Fridolin's daughters inherited a pro- portion, more or less extensive, of their father's and grandfather's vocal gifts.

The youngest son of Fridolin, the *Amtmann* Franz Anton, retained his title of nobility, but displayed very little of that high-sounding quality either in his life or character. Like his father and brother Fridolin he owed much of his cultural de- velopment to the higher education he had received at Freiburg.

[1] K. 294, 316, 383, 416, 418, 419, 538.

As a child he had been inherently clever and brilliant, but entirely lacking in control; his mind was incorrigibly crooked and he was boastful, unsteady and swift to anger. By reason of his rank he had the reversion of an appointment in the service of the Bishop of Hildesheim. This he took up, in 1758, after he had served the Elector of the Palatinate, Carl Theodor, in the strange dual capacity of director of the opera at Mannheim and ensign in the elector's guard. Such an anomalous position, however, was obviously untenable for any length of time, and as he rose in favour with the commander of the elector's forces, General Baron von Weichs, his enthusiasm for music proportionately cooled. Eventually, he threw it entirely aside and followed his leader into the imperial army. There he led the jovial life of a soldier of fortune until 1756, when he fought against Frederick the Great at the battle of Rosbach, where he was slightly wounded. It may have been for this reason that he left the army shortly afterwards and entered the service of Clemens August, the Elector of Cologne and Bishop of Hildesheim, in the capacity of steward. Here he met the daughter of the chief financial councillor of his department, the beautiful Maria Anna von Fumetti. They soon became lovers, and in 1758, after the death of the lady's father, they were married. Franz Anton not only succeeded to the latter's lucrative appointment as court councillor at Steuerwald, but to his fairly large fortune as well. But the monotony of business soon became too much for the highly strung, ambitious and utterly unstable Franz Anton, and in order to vary it, he plunged again, with an ardour bordering almost on fanaticism, into the practice of music. As a performer on the violin, viola and double bass he had few equals in his time, and so enamoured did he become of his art again that he was seldom seen in the streets or in the fields without one of these instruments, on which he would play as he walked, followed by his numerous family. He soon became, on this account, the standing joke of the place, but worse than that was the fact that he gradually lost all interest in the business side of his office and eventually neglected it altogether. So long as the easy-going Clemens August lived matters were allowed to drift, but on the death of the elector and appointment of his successor, the Prince-Bishop Friedrich Wilhelm, the inevitable reckoning had to be made. Hare-brained musicians found no favour with this high potentate, and while apparently Franz Anton Weber could not be altogether deprived of his emoluments, he could be forced to retire with a pension, and this was the procedure adopted by the new prince-bishop. But Franz Anton did not leave Hildesheim immediately on his retirement: he was probably compelled to remain in residence in order to retain the lien on his pension. Whether that was so or not, however, the fact remains that he followed his art there, in a more or less haphazard fashion, and worked towards the musical education of his children till 1773, in the hope of realizing the aim of his life by sending one or more of them into the great world as the musical wonder or wonders of his age. He also contrived to spend the greater part of his wife's fortune.

Again, however, the restless spirit of Franz Anton must find a wider outlet than was possible in a dull provincial German cathedral town, and in the year in question he set out with the whole of his family as a wandering troupe of actors and musicians. No trace of them can be found, from the time of their leaving Hildesheim until he turns up again, acting in the capacity of violinist-conductor and composer at Lübeck, as to the manner born, in 1778. And, in April 1779, he became *Kapellmeister* to the Lord Bishop of Eutin at a salary of 400 thaler. But he did not hold this position long either. The toil, fatigue and constant exposure to every sort of weather, to say nothing of the loss of self-respect, which continually attended the life of a travelling showman, proved to be too much for the proud, high-born and once beautiful Maria Anna von Fumetti, who, heart-broken and worn out with child-bearing, is known to have consistently opposed her husband's bohemianism and general mode of life. She must have fallen into a state of chronic sickness soon after the family left Hildesheim. After a long period of suffering she

WEBER'S BIRTHPLACE AT EUTIN

eventually died in 1783, in her forty-seventh year, leaving her husband with five children on his hands.

This event seemed to revive all the *Wanderlust* in Franz Anton's restless spirit and, in the following year, we find him again on his way to Vienna in order to secure musical tuition for his sons, Fritz and Edmund, from Joseph Haydn. He still had in view the pet project of making musical prodigies of them. In Vienna they found accommodation in the house of a family called von Brenner, and there the impressionable Franz Anton fell violently in love with the daughter of the house, Genofeva, who, according to his grandson, Baron Max von Weber, was 'a mild, fair, pretty girl of sixteen years.' This writer, however, is not famed for too strict a degree of accuracy in many of his statements, and later research seems to have established her age, at this time, as being nearer twenty-two than sixteen. Nevertheless it is an un-doubted fact that there was great disparity between their ages, and the girl, being none too strong, was altogether unsuited to the life she would be expected to lead with Weber. The remainder of Franz Anton's story, up to the point where the present actual biography should necessarily open, may best be told in the words of his grandson, as translated by J. Palgrave Simpson:

By what magic the middle-aged and needy musician won the maiden's heart and, still more, the consent of the father, is not apparent. The scarcely well-assorted pair were married on the 20th August 1785; and, shortly afterwards, Franz Anton von Weber took back his young and lovely bride to his only home at Cutin (*sic*).[1] His appointment as musical director of the prince bishop had been relinquished; but as *Stadtmusikus*, or salaried and privileged leader of all the music of the town on festive occasions, he still contrived to obtain a scanty sub-sistence. That the pride of the ambitious artist was deeply wounded

---

[1] This is an obvious error, the translator having apparently mistaken the Gothic capital letter 𝕰 for the somewhat similar ℭ, in the original. The actual name of the town is Eutin, but Mr. Simpson calls it Cutin throughout the whole of his translation.

CHAPTER II

CHILDHOOD AND YOUTH

EARLY in 1787 a series of operatic performances were given at the episcopal court of Eutin, and there is every likelihood that Franz Anton von Weber, as *Stadtmusikus*, had something to do with the production of the works, if he did not actually conduct them. It has been suggested that this event may have been the means of effecting a revival of his *Wanderlust*. Whether or not this was the case, it is a fact that once again, in May 1787, he took to the road with the 'von Weberschen Schauspielergesellschaft,' consisting of himself, his poor, feebly protesting young wife, his three grown-up daughters, one son and, if one may be permitted to give him a place in the company, the six-months-old infant, Carl Maria. They were to remain on the road for some years. One feels a certain repugnance at the thought of this child of tender age being carried hither and thither in the train of that tawdry and scarcely respectable band of strolling players, and at the idea of the long, weary nights he must have spent keeping his little mind amused and alert in the draughty wings of pro-vincial theatres, while the older members of the family were performing. From birth he was a very delicate child and, as was later discovered, he suffered from a disease of his right thigh-bone which caused him to limp all through his life. But this strolling life tended to sharpen his wits and at a very early age taught him self-confidence and insight into the characters of those with whom he came into contact. Nor was he lacking in affec-tion, although that natural instinct must have been consistently curbed and suppressed by the harsh treatment he received, doubt-less enough with the best intentions, from his fanatical father. His love for his mother was lifelong, and the earliest known

9

writing that he has left is the rather pathetic inscription in the old album of a certain Elise Vigitill, which reads: 'Dearest Elise, always love your sincere friend Carl von Weber; in the sixth year of his age; Nuremberg, 10th September 1792.'

The obsession in Franz Anton Weber's mind that one of his children should, like the young Mozart, become a musical prodigy, had so far failed to materialize, but, nothing daunted, he visualized a means of bringing it into effect in his latest born. Not content with allowing any talent the child might possess to develop of its own accord, he immediately introduced a forcing process which caused the boy untold misery and nervous derangement. Since the birth of Carl Maria the Weber company had wandered over and through practically the entire length and breadth of the German lands, and, during the first decade of the boy's life no stone was left unturned to make him the prodigy his father had set his mind upon. Franz Anton himself first took him in hand, but the earliest systematic tuition he received was from his elder brother Fridolin, but with so little success that one day, in a fit of temper, the latter exclaimed: 'Carl, you may become anything else you like, but a musician you never will be!'

During this period Franz Anton also contrived to have him taught the arts of drawing, painting in oils and pastel, as well as engraving, in which, as existing specimens of his work show, he acquired a fair degree of skill. But his mother's health was by this time steadily on the decline, and about the year 1796, probably on this account, the company's circuit had become restricted to the Nuremberg and Erlangen districts. During a visit to Hildburghausen Genofeva became so ill that she was unable to accompany the troupe further, so she, Franz Anton, his sister— the gentle and kindly Adelheid—and the boy Carl Maria were left behind in a humble lodging and with very little money.

Here Franz Anton made the acquaintance of Johann Peter Heuschkel, a noted oboist and organist, and the orchestral conductor to the residing Duke Friedrich of Meiningen. Taking a fancy to the young Carl Maria, this fine musician asked to be allowed to give him instruction on the piano and in thorough-bass. Here at last was a teacher whose methods were based on science and pure pedagogical principles. His first task was the difficult one of making his pupil unlearn all the faults of technique and style he had imbibed from the not too competent Franz Anton and Fridolin.

His [the boy's] rambling hands were bound down to the severest precision. He was made to tread the dry, dusty road of thorough-bass, step by step, ploddingly and slowly, on that wearing and weary pilgrimage, which can alone lead to the true shrine of art; and many were the tears shed by the poor child on his ungenial and dreary path. But the affection he soon learned to entertain for his amiable young master supported him on his way; and, sooner than might have been expected, the child himself began to discover the power this severe discipline would place within his grasp.

In his autobiography Weber himself pays a fine tribute to this admirable musician from whom he had received the 'best possible, indeed the only true, foundation of the pianistic art; powerful, expressive and full of character, with the equal cultivation of both hands.'

For about a year the Webers remained at Hildburghausen,[1] and there is no doubt that this was one of the happiest of the boy's childhood years. But his father's restless spirit once more began to trouble him, and very soon the call of the open road and the nightly glare of the footlights were to prove irresistible. His wife's health had somewhat improved; the theatrical company was at Salzburg and soon to depart thence upon an extended tour of Bavaria, Baden and the Palatinate; so, in the autumn of 1797, Hildburghausen, with all it had held for the young Carl Maria, was abandoned, and at Salzburg the company again received the absentees. But ill-luck seemed to dog the footsteps of the

[1] It is amusing to find Professor Elwart, of the Imperial Conservatoire of Paris, citing Hildburghausen as one of Weber's early masters, in his *Histoire des concerts populaires* published in 1864.

wandering play-actor, wherever he went. He found Salzburg in a
state of political ferment, which very soon reacted so injuriously
upon the fortunes of the theatrical venturers that it was not long
before they were compelled to close down. And on 13th March
1798 the poor, long-suffering Genofeva died. But in the January
of that year, Franz Anton, still with a view to making Carl Maria
the prodigy on which he had set his heart, had been successful
in placing him in a training-school for young choristers, conducted under the Salzburg archiepiscopal auspices, and here the
boy was again fortunate in finding special favour with the director
of the establishment, who was no less a personality than Michael
Haydn, the brother of the great Joseph Haydn. Michael Haydn,
although he possessed very little of his illustrious brother's creative
faculty, was a good musician and teacher, but he was then sixty
years of age and rather out of touch with modern trends. He was
a formalist and perhaps a little pedantic, and the child failed to
learn under him with anything approaching the pleasure he had
felt when studying under the capable and enthusiastic Heuschkel.
Nevertheless, although, as he said later, he 'had learned little under
great stress' from Haydn, the latter seems to have been satisfied with
the progress he had made and particularly with *Six Fughettas for
Pianoforte Solo* the boy had composed under his immediate observation. Carl Maria's father was so delighted with these that
he had them printed in score with the following dedication:

To Herr Edmund von Weber, in Hessen-Cassel, my beloved
brother, from Karl Maria von Weber in Salzburg. To you, as con-
noisseur, musician, teacher and, finally, brother, in the eleventh [!]
year of his age, these first-fruits of his musical labours, by your tenderly
oving brother. Salzburg, 1st September 1798.

These pieces, being more or less mere exercises in composition,
set by his master, probably bore little trace of the pianistic style
of the Weber of later days, and the themes may have been suggested, if not actually composed, by Haydn. Still, they demonstrate, even at that early date, Weber's love for tonal purity and

also, practically the whole of the boy's early compositions were accidentally destroyed by fire in Senefelder's workshop.

It was in May 1799 that the Webers left Munich. Little is known of their itinerary during the remainder of that year, except that they made a short sojourn at Carlsbad in the course of their wanderings. There the boy attracted the attention of the Chevalier von Steinsberg, that manager of the local theatre who entrusted to him an opera libretto entitled *Das stumme Waldmädchen* (*The Dumb Girl of the Forest*), which he had written himself. It is not improbable that an arrangement whereby young Weber should set it to music was then made. Neither is it without the bounds of probability that Weber made public appearances as pianoforte soloist during this period, although none can actually be traced.

In 1800, however, the family had again settled down, this time at Freiberg in Saxony, and during the summer of that year Carl Maria undoubtedly played in concerts at Erfurt, Gotha and Leipzig with conspicuous success. And in the autumn of the same year he renewed his relations with the Chevalier von Steinsberg who had made his appearance, with his own theatrical troupe, at Freiberg. This company was far above the level of touring theatrical companies of the time in ability and attainment, but all agog for some novelty that would keep its enterprise high in the public estimation, and Weber required little urging to get on with the score of his opera, which was completed by the month of October. He states in his autobiography that, 'seduced by the anecdotes of miracles achieved by celebrated *maestri*,' he had written 'the whole second act in ten days.'

For some unexplained reason the opera had its first performances at Chemnitz, in the month of October, 'by another troop,' says the composer's son; but I am not convinced that that was the case. It was announced as '*The Dumb Girl of the Forest*, a grand romantic comic opera;—the music by C. M. von Weber, thirteen years of age, a pupil of Haydn.' This, and a similar announcement which heralded the performances given at Freiberg a month later, i.e. on 24th November, were obviously written by Franz Anton, who again understated the composer's age, and no doubt purposely omitted to give the Christian name of Michael Haydn. What reception the opera received at Chemnitz is not known, but it was lukewarmly received in Freiberg, where it was described by a newspaper critic as 'a mere blossom of genius, which promises better and riper fruit.' And then followed a bitter and acrimonious journalistic controversy, started by Franz Anton in his son's name, which did neither of them any good and, making their further stay in Freiberg somewhat uncomfortable, drove them on to the roads again. The youth himself had no delusions regarding the value of the opera, which he afterwards described as 'a very crude work, but not wholly without inventive power.'

That he had not been neglecting his researches in connection with the lithographic processes while in Freiberg, is proved by a letter he wrote from that town to Artaria of Vienna, on 9th December 1800, in the following terms:

I believe that I shall not make your celebrated firm, as music and print-sellers, an unwelcome offer and proposal, if I submit for your acceptance the hereafter described *arcanum*, being an apparatus highly to be recommended, on account of the rapidity with which it works, combined with a *small outlay*, and which shall become your sole property on the subjoined conditions:

1. I can engrave music on stone in a manner not to be surpassed by the finest English engraving, which the accompanying specimen testifies.

2. A workman in winter is able to complete two or three plates, and in the long summer days three or four.

3. A plate of this kind can be used afresh thirty times, that is, polished up.

4. Two men can in one week print off as many thousand sheets as can be printed with ordinary type.

5. The whole stock of the machinery does not exceed 100 thaler. I await your reply to the enclosed address.

Further, of the musical works I completed while studying under Michael Haydn, I can offer you:

TITLE-PAGE OF WEBER'S FIRST PUBLISHED WORK

Three easy trios for violin, viola and violoncello, for dilettanti; six variations for the pianoforte; six ditto; three ditto, pianoforte sonatas; six ditto, variations on the song *Lieber Augustin*.

I ask six copies of each work and a moderate sum, which I leave you to propose with your usual fairness. In the expectation of a favourable answer on both points, I am, etc.[1]

To this letter no reply was ever received.

At what precise date the Webers left Freiberg is not known, although a recent German writer [2] states confidently, but without giving his authority, that it was in March 1801, and that the wanderers passed through Chemnitz [3] and Munich, ultimately reaching Salzburg in November. It was probably during this period, of which we know so little, that the fourteen performances of *The Dumb Girl of the Forest* in Vienna, the successful representation of the opera in St Petersburg, and its translation into the Czech language for Prague, of which Weber also speaks in his autobiography, took place.

At Salzburg the young composer renewed his relations with old Michael Haydn, and as the Webers remained in that sadly troubled town until the summer of 1802, he was able to profit considerably from the further instruction he there received. Here, during this year, he also composed his third opera, *Peter Schmoll und seine Nachbarn* (*Peter Schmoll and his Neighbours*). It was a comic opera in two acts, based on a novel by Cramer, and although the score has never been published the most essential musical numbers have survived, and we have it on the authority of Michael Haydn, who was never too lavish in distributing praise, that it was not without merit, even in his eyes. 'In all truth, with full conviction, and with the best judgment,' he wrote, 'I attest

---

[1] Nohl's *Musiker-Briefe*, Lady Wallace's translation, 1867, p. 207.

[2] Erwin Kroll, *Carl Maria von Weber* ('Die grossen Meister der Musik'), 1934, p. 6.

[3] Philipp Spitta, writing in Grove's *Dictionary of Music and Musicians*, states that we have letters dated 24th April and 7th May, written by Franz Anton from Chemnitz.

that this opera has been composed in the truest rules of harmony, with much fire, great delicacy, and appropriate feeling.' While in Salzburg at this time, Weber composed *Six Petites Pièces à quatre mains,* made up of a Sonatina, a Romance, a Minuet, an Andante with Variations, a March and a Rondo, which he was successful in having published by Gombart of Augsburg, as his Op. 3. His second opus was a collection of *Sechs Variationen fürs Klavier oder Piano Forte,* which he had lithographed and published himself in Munich.

On leaving Salzburg for the second time the Webers, father and son, seem to have turned their steps to Augsburg, where Franz Anton's eldest son, Edmund, who had left his father's theatrical company in 1798, was in residence. He there had employment partly in the service of Clemens Wenzeslaus, Prince-Bishop of Augsburg, and partly as conductor of the local theatre orchestra. The production of *Peter Schmoll,* under Edmund's direction, was doubtless the main purpose of their visit, but it was not immediately realized, and the wanderers did not tarry there very long. The autumn of 1802 saw them making a tour of north Germany, visiting Meiningen, Eisenach, Sondershausen, Brunswick, Hamburg, Hildburghausen, Coburg and the boy's birthplace, Eutin, where he met Johann Heinrich Voss, who was to supply him with many beautiful lyrics for musical setting, and who probably first turned his thoughts in the direction of song composition. His first real song was *Die Kerze* (*The Taper*), which he composed in Hamburg in October 1802, while on this tour, and with this and the songs that were to follow Carl Maria von Weber made his first direct appeal to the hearts of the German people. The mighty surge of romance that his later operas were to send abroad throughout the entire artistic world was already well begun in the songs, which exerted a softening and civilizing influence upon all classes of the Teutonic people.

In December of this year the travellers were again at Augsburg, concerned about the forthcoming production of *Peter Schmoll.* It is on record that, while waiting for this, many pleasant evenings were spent in the characteristic German fashion of that leisurely age, playing chamber music for their own gratification and for the artistic pleasure and edification of any guests who happened to be present. During the northern tour, and while awaiting the outcome of their efforts at Augsburg, the young composer also did a considerable amount of study. He read several philosophical works and studied the writings of Carl Philipp Emanuel Bach, Agricola and Kirnberger on the theory of music. He derived great benefit, too, from his friendships with Thaddäus Susan, a student of law and a flautist in the Salzburg orchestra, and with a certain Dr Munding, who led him into discussions and expressions of opinion which he criticized and corrected when they were not in strict accordance with fact or reason.

At last the first performance of *Peter Schmoll* took place at Augsburg, but it does not appear to have created much impression, favourable or otherwise. The opera was a characteristic example of the *Singspiel*, a form to which Weber remained faithful in all of his music-dramas except *Euryanthe*. Only the overture has been published and the spoken dialogue has disappeared, but enough of the music has survived to show the point of the remark made by the archbishop's concert-master, Joseph Otter: 'Erit mature ut Mozart.' The music, indeed, is essentially Mozartian in character, if not actually in style, with all the delicious freshness of youth that is so completely in keeping with the traditional manner of the German *Singspiel*.

It may have been the lack of success of *Peter Schmoll und seine Nachbarn*; or perhaps, as has been suggested, the realization by Franz Anton and Carl Maria that the latter had still much to learn regarding operatic technique and the elements necessary to ensure success in the creation of such works; or, what is perhaps most probable of all, it was the unappeasable and ineradicable *Wanderlust* that remained the torment and pleasure of Franz Anton during practically the whole of his life that sent the Webers yet again on their travels. This time their objective was Vienna, at that period still the musical capital of the whole world, and there they arrived in the summer of 1803. As a teacher Joseph Haydn was no longer in question, although he was still alive at the age of seventy-one, Beethoven was rapidly rising towards the height of his fame, but he was living in semi-retirement, and others were hardly more attainable as teachers for the youth, even if they were perhaps a little more approachable. There can be little doubt that it was Haydn they had in view, however, for they came armed with recommendations from his brother Michael and from Edmund von Weber, who had been one of the master's favourite pupils. But none of the greater luminaries being available, a smaller but no less scintillating star, the Abbé Vogler, was eventually chosen, and Carl Maria was placed under his tutorial guidance.

Much has been said and written about Vogler, whose import-ance in the realm of music has been vastly overrated in Great Britain owing to Browning's poem bearing his name. The value of this poem, as a whole, may perhaps best be judged by the concluding lines of the twelfth and last stanza:

> Give me the keys. I feel for the common chord again,
> Sliding by semitones, till I sink to the minor,—yes,
> And I blunt it into a ninth, and I stand on alien ground,
> Surveying awhile the heights I rolled from into the deep;
> Which, hark, I have dared and done, for my resting-place is
>   found,
> The C Major of this life: so, now I will try to sleep.

But perhaps, the position has never been better summed up than it was by Sir Donald Tovey in his programme-note on the overture to *Euryanthe*:

Weber was consumptive from his birth: he had no time to lose, and no disposition to lose it. Throughout his thirty years of life, his time was lost for him by fools and humbugs. His master, Abt Vogler, to whom he always remained loyal, was one of the most devastating of musical humbugs. He has been described for all time, not by Brown-ing's poem (to which Browning gave the wrong name on purpose), but by that great classical scholar, Otto Jahn, who, in his life of Mozart,

characterizes Vogler as one of those musical philosophers who disguise
their lack of solid musical schooling in a vast ostentation of general
culture. Vogler's other great pupil was Meyerbeer. It is a pity the two
pupils did not exchange their physical constitutions.[1]

It was through an acquaintance which Carl Maria made with
a young and somewhat dissolute officer, Johann Baptist Gänsbacher, to whom he had been presented in the house of Count
Firmian, that he first came into contact with Vogler. Gänsbacher had recently retired from the army in order to satisfy his
inordinate passion for music by studying under the abbé, and very
soon he had Weber sharing in his studies, as unfortunately he also
had him sharing his youthful follies and indiscretions. But whatever harm the latter may have done the lad, and they certainly did
him no good, there is reason to believe that, all Vogler's charla-
tanism notwithstanding, he gained a great amount of valuable
musical instruction and experience, not to mention discipline,
from his association with the abbé. He certainly acquired from
him new methods of study and greater powers of theoretical concentration than he had ever previously known, and the romantic
glitter and glamour that was largely inherent in his nature he
found vastly accentuated and even exaggerated in the life and work
of his master. Thus, essentially congenial to each other as they
were, the mutual attraction was immediate, and the pupil derived
an inspiration to follow his art with ever-increasing enthusiasm and
a stimulation to create works which should embody all the bril-
liancy and charm of his particular style. Vogler was then working on the score of his opera *Samori*, making a great secret of the
fact by whispering it to all who were willing to lend their ears for
the purpose. Behind closed doors and with a great show of

[1] *Essays in Musical Analysis*, vol. iv, p. 54. Tovey adds a footnote to
this, as follows: 'I have been reproached for the "savagery" of this
wish. It does not seem savage to Weber; and Meyerbeer can afford to
put up with it ever since the gentle Rossini said to the composer of a
funeral march for that master: "Would it not have been better if you
had died and Meyerbeer had written your funeral march?"'

mystery he played the overture to Weber and then commissioned him to prepare the pianoforte score of the entire work. Vogler's operas were of little account musically, and they are now as dead as the dodo, but one or two of them had a certain vogue in their day, and there cannot be any shadow of doubt regarding Weber's having benefited from his work upon them. In addition to the pianoforte arrangement he composed *Eight Variations on a Theme from Vogler's 'Castor und Pollux'* and *Six Variations on a Theme from 'Samori.'* Vogler, with all his faults, was not insensible to all that Weber had done in assisting at rehearsals of *Samori* and in accomplishing so much of the editorial drudgery in preparing it for the press, and when Professor Rhode, the director of the Breslauer Komödienhaus, wrote to the abbé to ask him whether he could recommend a conductor for the orchestra of that important theatre, Vogler immediately and unhesitatingly put forward the name of Weber, who was engaged entirely on the strength of this recommendation.

It was not without a struggle and considerable searching of heart, however, that Weber was able to tear himself away from Vienna. In the preceding year Franz Anton had left the lad there and had returned to Salzburg. For the first time in his life, freed from the paternal control and left pretty much to his own devices, he had very readily come under the baneful influence of the gay and dissolute Gänsbacher, who introduced him into the kind of society that was only too ready to receive a handsome young genius whose charm of manner and ability to sing beautiful songs, many of which were of his own making, to play the guitar with surpassing delicacy, and to ruffle it with the most roistering Viennese of them all more than compensated for the poverty of his estate. Although no details have come to light, it has been said that he had here met his first love and formed his earliest romance with a lady of rank who was somewhat older than himself, but who loved him ardently. A song, *Jüngst sass ich am Grabe der Trauten allein*, composed immediately after his leaving Vienna, is said to have been inspired by this affair.

CHAPTER III

MANHOOD AND APPROACHING MATURITY

THE Breslau appointment marked the opening of a new epoch
for Carl Maria von Weber. His long apprenticeship to the art
of music was now practically at an end; he was more or less free
from the control of his father, to whom, however, he still looked
up with filial respect and admiration; and he had passed into a
condition of maturity and responsibility that soon proved to be
far in advance of his actual years. Between the date of his leaving
Vienna and that of his taking up his duties in Breslau there lies
one of those tantalizing hiatuses that are so common in the lives
of the Webers. He is known to have visited Salzburg on the
way and picked up his father there. He also met his old friend
Thaddäus Susan again and, on 4th June, in his room, composed
a 'schwärmerisches Lied' entitled *Wiedersehen* in celebration of the
reunion. But where or how he spent the five months between
that date and the day of his taking over his duties in Breslau
seems to be unknown or, at the least, entirely in doubt. The
writer of the article on Weber in Grove's *Dictionary of Music and
Musicians* [1] says that 'if his biographer is correct in stating that
Weber did not enter upon his post at Breslau before November
1804, he must either have been living there for more than three
months without occupation or have been touring about as an
artist from June to October. But there is no indication of his
having taken either of these courses.' Yet Erwin Kroll states positively that he arrived in Breslau on 11th July 1804. He also
states, on the authority of an entry in the diary of young Eichendorff, who was then a senior student in the Catholic Refectory

[1] Philipp Spitta.

School of St Joseph, that Weber began his duties in the opera house on 1st August, with a performance of Mozart's *Titus*.

Breslau was then, as it is to-day, the second city of Prussia. It was a place of great military and industrial importance, but although it had a good opera, its cultural standards were not high. The 'pillars of society' were chiefly drawn from the army officer and landed *Junker* classes, with a sprinkling of university professors, all with their wives and female relations. And, like all such cities, the place was thus a veritable hotbed of intrigue, jealousies and scandal. It was not, therefore, a bed of roses that the eighteen-year-old Carl Maria von Weber was destined to lie upon when he betook himself to the ancient city on the Oder. While his artistic abilities were all in his favour, and the management of the theatre, under the highly skilled directorship of Professor J. G. Rhode, was sympathetic, practically everything else was against him. He was considered presumptuous on account of his youth; the burghers mistrusted him because of his nobility; while the nobles despised him for having so far degraded his rank as to follow the profession of a mere musician. The older members of the orchestra also resented the dictation of one who, though only a boy in years, was yet obviously possessed of a knowledge infinitely greater than their own. Yet though several, including J. Schnabel, the leader and first violin of his band, a distinguished and able musician, resigned, causing him a considerable degree of pain, others remained loyal. And one particularly bright spot in his sojourn at Breslau was the friendship he formed with the afterwards renowned musical theorist, teacher, and pianoforte, organ and clarinet player Friedrich Wilhelm Berner, although, as we shall presently see, it was not unmixed with tragedy. Berner was about six years older than Weber, who made his acquaintance through a letter of introduction he had brought to him from Vogler. Notwithstanding the difference in age, the two musicians found they had much in common and soon became fast friends. In company with Berner Weber was soon singing and dancing, drinking and love-making in the whirl of the Breslau *jeunesse dorée*, as he had so recently been in that of the gayer city from which, only a few months earlier, he had taken his departure. But there was a difference. Berner was a man of greater solidity than Gänsbacher and, while, on occasion, he entered into the gaieties of the place with all the zest of youth and effervescing high spirits, his first love was his art and he never lost sight of the need for deep concentration and constant work in order to keep abreast of the times and to achieve the ultimate aim he had in view. The influence he exerted upon the younger musician was thus as much to the good as otherwise. Even so, Weber's indiscretions very soon brought him into a dangerous situation, aggravated both by the voice of scandal and the more overt machinations of his enemies. Knowing the character borne by the society of Breslau, Weber ought to have been even more than ordinarily circumspect in his conduct, instead of plunging head over ears into all that was certain to set tongues wagging, even if it had no worse consequences.

From the aesthetic point of view, however, Breslau owed a great deal to Weber. When he arrived in the city, he found the opera personnel, thanks to the enlightened policy of Professor Rhode, not too bad, although, owing to lack of funds, remuneration was poor and the company—singers and instrumentalists—consequently impermanent and fluctuating. The backbone of the operatic repertory consisted of works by Mozart, Dalayrac and Vogler, which were performed creditably. But there was, of course, room for improvement, and the young conductor took his first step in that direction by drastically reorganizing the distribution of his orchestral forces. At Breslau, in 1804, the eighteenth-century idea of the operatic orchestra still prevailed. From the Bach-Handel period, or earlier, musical taste seemed to favour massive effects rather than pure tone-colour, and wood-wind players were usually as numerous in an orchestra as were those of strings. Weber therefore found this craze for loudness of tone in the long-established custom of arranging the wind instruments in front of the strings, whose tone was thus more or less strangled before it reached the ears of the audience. His sense of colour and romantic effects was naturally offended by this arrangement, and he at once set about the distribution of his players in order that more delicate and picturesque nuances of light and shade and richer and more mellow tone-patches might be obtained when required by the sentiment expressed by the music or by the action on the stage. The result was an orchestra arranged with the strings to right and left of the conductor and the other instruments behind, or partially intermingled, more or less on the principle that is in common practice at the present day.

Strange as it may seem to us, this innovation aroused a perfect tornado of opposition, both in the orchestra and among the public. Complaints were loud and long and, while Weber courteously listened to all of them and considered them carefully, he nevertheless could find no reason to retract. It was then that Schnabel resigned and became the leader of an opposition that was eventually to effect Weber's downfall at Breslau. This was accelerated by an unfortunate accident, which resulted in Weber's losing his beautiful singing voice and all but cost him his life.

In the midst of his conducting and wild night-orgies and jollifications, he still found time to compose a number of works characterized by elements of that spiritual cast which later was to become the dominating factor of his creations. It was at Breslau that the *Overtura chinesa*—the *Chinese Overture*—which he afterwards adapted as an overture to Schiller's German adaptation of Gozzi's strange play, *Turandot*, was composed, and also the *Romanza siciliana* for flute and orchestra, specially written for the admirable amateur flautist Jacob Lahn. He further began the composition of an opera entitled *Rübezahl*, the book of which had been written by his constant friend and director, Professor Rhode. Only three numbers of this were ever written, in addition to the overture, which the composer long afterwards remodelled and published as *Der Beherrscher der Geister* (*The Ruler of the Spirits*).

One day, immediately after the completion of the overture, Weber invited his friend Berner to come and hear him play it over. It was night when Berner arrived at the composer's dwelling and, although a light at the window showed that the house was occupied, he got no response to his knocking at the door. Justly fearing that something was wrong, he pushed open the door and entered. A lamp was burning on the table and the piano was open, but to his horror he found Weber recumbent and unconscious on the floor, with a broken bottle by his side. He shouted for help and Franz Anton, who was again unsuccessfully carrying on his engraving business at Breslau, rushed in from an adjoining room. He saw at once that the composer had drunk the contents of a bottle of *aqua fortis* which the father used in his engraving work and had carelessly left on the table beside a bottle of wine from which Carl Maria had intended to drink. Doctors were immediately summoned, but it was with great difficulty that the youth was brought back to life. As a result of this, he was for a time unable to fulfil the duties of his office, and his enemies and opponents, headed by Schnabel, made full use of the opportunities thus unexpectedly afforded them. He later returned to find all his reforms rescinded and his orchestra undermined. But that was not the worst. Hampered as he was on every hand by the father who was now completely dependent upon him, by the load of debt which, owing to the reckless life he had lived and to his long illness, had piled up around him, and by the voice of scandal, not altogether undeserved, which jealousy, envy and enmity did everything possible to foster and extend, his further life in Breslau became unendurable, and, much to the regret of Rhode, he resigned his conductorship at the municipal theatre. A more prudent line for Weber to have taken would have been to pocket his pride, continue his labours in the theatre and gradually reintroduce his reforms as opposition died down, as it must surely have done in face of the undoubted genius by which all his professional activities were inspired. But Weber and prudence were absolutely contradictory terms. So, with nothing but his teaching connection, which at best gave him scarcely a bare living, his further prospects at Breslau were very poor indeed, and he eventually declared his intention of shaking the dust of that inhospitable city off his feet and faring forth again as 'a tramping musical pedlar.' But this was the proverbial hour before the dawn of a better condition of affairs for the poor artist, which, while it lasted, probably opened the happiest period in Weber's life. The circumstances may perhaps best be described in the words of his son, Baron Max von Weber:

In one of the few noble houses where the poor artist was admitted as teacher, he made the acquaintance of a Fräulein von Belonde, maid of honour to the Duchess Louise of Württemberg, who, with her husband, Prince Eugen Friedrich of Württemberg, dwelt in their domain of Carlsruhe in Silesia. Fräulein von Belonde was an admirable piano-forte player, and she took the liveliest interest in the pale, amiable young artist, whose wonderful powers of improvisation enchanted her by their rich fancy. She was touched by his sad position, and resolved to assist him by every means in her power.

She had not long to wait for an opportunity of fulfilling her generous and benevolent resolve. There was no greater or more sincere lover of music than Duke Eugen Friedrich. He had built a magnificent theatre in his domain, and under the direction of the Chevalier von Rohr dramatic or operatic performances were given there twice a week, and concerts of classical music frequently, admission to which, except on special occasions, was entirely free. The duke had heard Weber play and had seen him conduct at Breslau, and Fräulein von Belonde, knowing the favourable impression these performances had made upon him, urged Weber to appeal to him for patronage and protection in some form or another. He did so, in the form of a petition that the duke should give him a testimonial which might be of use to him in his wanderings, no doubt backed by the lady's personal recommendation, whereupon the duke bestowed on him the title of *Musik-Intendant*.

The Napoleonic invasion, however, was then in full flood in Austria and southern Germany and it was rapidly advancing on

Breslau, where matters were steadily going from bad to worse—for Weber, at all events. He was now in a state of absolute destitution, and matters were not improved by the arrival of Aunt Adelheid, whom the war had driven from Munich back to the family fold. Hearing of his desperate plight, again doubtless through Fräulein von Belonde, the duke and his excellent spouse offered Carl Maria accommodation in the palace at Carlsruhe, for as long as he cared to remain, and this generous consideration was, a little later, offered to Franz Anton and Aunt Adelheid as well. Although the offer was made freely and with no expectation of, or desire for, any return, Weber at once unreservedly placed him-self at the disposal of his benefactor for the performance of any artistic services it should be within his power to give. And, as might be expected, he found no lack of inspiration in such pleasant scenes and circumstances as now, for the all too short period of his sojourn there, encompassed him. The scenery surrounding Carlsruhe reminded him of that of his native Eutin, and the memory of it was later reflected in the lovely forest music of *Der Freischütz*. But the more immediate fruits of his happy winter in that delectable place were two Symphonies, both in C major, the only symphonies he ever wrote, and both composed within six weeks; one, according to his son, written seemingly for the purpose of displaying the talent of Dantrevaux, a famous horn player then attached to the ducal orchestra; the other, in all prob-ability, in honour of the duke himself, who was a distinguished virtuoso on the oboe. For Dantrevaux he also composed a Concertino for horn and orchestra, and for Fräulein von Belonde the song *Ich denke Dein* (Op. 66). Other works which came from his pen at this time were a *Kleiner Tusch von 20 Trompeten* and *Sechs Variationen für Alt-viola und Orchester*. Not at all a bad record for a single winter.

Germany, however, was still sadly beleaguered by the Napoleonic armies, and the duke had, before the end of 1806, been called upon to join the army of defence. His duchess kept her little court intact in the castle of Carlsruhe all through the winter, but as the spring of 1807 progressed misfortunes fell fast and furious upon the Prussian arms, till at last the country passed into such a state of social disruption and political anarchy that her position became untenable, and the happy little party had to be broken up and dispersed. But even in the midst of the disastrous strife and confusion the good Duke Eugen had not forgotten the Webers and, in the hope that something might be done for them, he communicated with his brothers, Friedrich I, King of Württemberg, and the profligate Duke Ludwig. As luck would have it, the latter's private secretary had just been promoted in the royal service, and the vacant post was at once offered to the young musician of noble birth who had been so highly recommended by his brother. For lack of any immediate opening in his own profession, Weber accepted the situation, but without enthusiasm.

On leaving Carlsruhe he first returned to Breslau in order to retrieve some papers he had left there, and, falling in with some of his old acquaintances, he spent several jovial evenings in their company. Rumours of these orgies soon came to the ears of his creditors in the town, with the result that he was compelled to leave Breslau again, more secretly and hurriedly than he had entered it. It was in the early morning of 6th March 1807 that he left Breslau, like a thief in the night.

We come upon another of these tantalizing periods during which we obtain only vague and passing glimpses of the weary and disillusioned artist, working his way westward through a war-harassed Germany, giving concerts where he could, successfully here and disastrously there. We know that Dresden, Leipzig, Bayreuth, Nuremberg and Anspach were visited during these four *Wander-Monate*, and that Stuttgart was reached at last on 17th July. One can scarcely imagine Weber making that journey at such a time and in such a manner without adventure, and if one could only penetrate the veil that now obscures what, were it known, might add still one more saga to the wealth of artistic lore of which southern Germany possesses so wonderful a legacy, how greatly our knowledge of Weber, the idealist, artist and man, might have been enlarged; for though he well knew that the prospects held out to him at the court of Napoleon's pasteboard King Friedrich I of Württemberg were less than nothing, he never once lost sight of the artistic purpose he intended sooner or later to serve. In his autobiographical sketches he devotes only four lines to this *Kunstreise* which, if he had only kept a diary, might have filled a volume. But regrets are useless and if we know too little of what befell him during the four months preceding his arrival in Stuttgart, we know probably too much of what he suffered and lived through during the two and a half years that succeeded.

In character, intellect and culture King Friedrich I of Württemberg was as far apart from his brother Duke Friedrich Eugen as the north pole is from the south. He was gross, corrupt and tyrannous; a cad and a coward. He had truckled to Napoleon, the invader of his territory, who flattered him shamelessly and made him a king. Tinged with a species of *Caesarenwahnsinn*—the madness of kings—he ground his people under the iron heel and treated the officials with whom his court swarmed like scullions. And in this respect he made scarcely an exception in regard to his own brother, Duke Ludwig, who, being a spendthrift and profligate beyond the limits even of that corrupt court, was continually pestering the king for money, when Weber, one of whose duties, as his secretary, it was to keep the ducal treasury in funds by hook or by crook, failed to raise money anywhere else, as indeed he frequently did. The pestering was generally done by proxy, Weber invariably acting as go-between, so that the king hated the musician even more heartily than he hated his own brother. The composer's other duties were to conduct the duke's private correspondence, keep his accounts and deal tactfully and diplomatically with his creditors, who were as the sands of the sea.

For the successful accomplishment of such duties Weber possessed neither the knowledge nor the experience, and the depraved and dissolute nature of the court made it an environment of the worst possible kind for a youth of his naturally wild and recklessly ardent character. So he shamelessly neglected his secretarial duties and plunged into all the dissipation and immoralities of the time and place. He was the better able to do so because of his *Freiherr* title of nobility, and of his great social gifts. Soon both he and his father were again deeply in debt, and he thus foolishly himself opened wide the doors of opportunity for his powerful enemies, with the king at their head, sooner or later to effect his downfall. On one occasion a circumstance occurred that turned the king's mere bullying dislike of him into perpetual enmity. It happened that the duke's financial embarrassments were more pressing than usual and Weber, in the customary manner, was delegated to make a personal appeal for relief to the king, who, after keeping him probably waiting for hours in an ante-room, as was his wont, covered him with bitter invective and foul abuse and turned him rudely out of the room. In the corridor the composer met an old woman who asked him if he could tell her where she could find the room of the court washerwoman. In a spirit of impishness, and perhaps still smarting from the vulgar severity of the treatment he had received, Weber pointed to the door of the apartment whence he had just been so ignominiously ejected. 'There!' he said, and went on his way. The old woman entered, and the king, who had a horror of old women, turned all the venom of his wrath upon her. In her terror she blurted out that a young gentleman who had just come out had told her that she would find the 'royal washerwoman' there. The king had no difficulty in guessing who the young gentleman had been, and immediately he issued an order for his arrest and incarceration. Weber was thereupon seized, and he must have been kept in prison several days, for his son records that, while there, he managed to procure a dilapidated old piano, which he put in tune by means of a common door-key and composed thereon his famous song, *Ein steter Kampf ist unser Leben*. But, through the intercession of Duke Ludwig, his pardon and release were presently obtained and he returned, unfortunately unrepentant, to his secretarial duties.

Here again, however, his irrepressible high spirits broke loose. He had frequently to write letters from the duke to the king, and he began to load them with expressions and innuendos that he knew would be likely to drive the irritable monarch into a frenzy of passion. The duke, too lazy or too careless to read over what was written, signed every letter that Weber placed before him, and for a time the trick had the desired effect. But King Fried- rich, with all his madness—his *folie des empereurs*—with all his bodily appetites and with all his ingrained malice, was no fool; it was not long before he detected the real author of the letters and guessed the underlying scorn and ridicule with which they were imbued. And he had both the power and will to make Weber suffer in many subtle ways for his wicked audacity before he finally wrung him out like a wet dish-cloth and threw him over the frontiers of his kingdom for any one to pick up who cared to do so.

In spite of the wild life Weber had led at the Stuttgart court, however, it cannot truthfully be said that he had altogether wasted his time or entirely neglected his opportunities during his sojourn there. While, on the one hand, his title of nobility opened for him the door into a social circle it was far above his means to enjoy without restraint, on the other hand his position as the duke's financial secretary brought him into the closest touch with people of high intellectual standing, who opened his ever- receptive mind to all the artistic and literary movements of the time. Among those who exercised a good influence upon him may be cited Dr Kellin, Duke Ludwig's physician-in-ordinary; Haug, the editor of *Das Morgenblatt*, and Reinbeck, both of them poets who supplied him with words for some of the most beautiful of his songs; Dannecker, the famous sculptor; and Louis Spohr, the great violinist and now too much neglected composer, who had the courage to put a curb upon his perhaps too exuberant self-esteem by criticizing somewhat adversely, if not a little harshly, his *Rübezahl*. Under the guidance of Hofrat Lehr, the court librarian, another poet, many of whose verses he immortalized by his musical settings, he embarked moreover upon a study of the German philosophers. But most of all did he derive benefit in his own profession from Franz Carl Hiemer, a young dramatist who, though lazy, careless and dissolute, yet kept Weber's interest in operatic composition alive by supplying him with a libretto, bad enough in all conscience, yet sufficient to enable him to keep his still prentice hand in practice, and to enable him to broaden his experience; and from Franz Danzi, the conductor of the royal opera. Danzi had been born nearly a quarter of a century earlier than Weber, yet he had retained enough freshness of outlook to realize that the latter was no ordinary musician. His interest in the youth was so obviously sincere and unaffected that very soon a strong reciprocal admiration and affection grew up between these two.

The suggestion that Hiemer should write an opera-book came from Weber himself, and he actually supplied him with the material from which the libretto was to be prepared: a story by the Chevalier Steinsberg of a dumb forest girl—*Das stumme Waldmädchen*—who recovers her speech through the power and influence of love. Hiemer made a poor enough job of it, but Weber, whose judgment in the matter of opera libretti was amazingly poor, thought it all but perfect and, encouraged by Danzi, he set to work upon the score. But it made slow progress, and although it was begun in July 1808, it was not finished until February 1810. Through the influence of Danzi it was accepted, under the title of *Sylvana*, for production in the court theatre.

Weber's association with this institution, however, brought him into touch with a giddy, coquettish young singer, Margarethe Lang, and a strong reciprocal attachment grew up between them; but her caprices and extravagances soon plunged him deeper than ever into a vortex of debt and dissipation. Danzi, whose favourite maxim was that 'to be a true artist one must be a true man,' did his best to guide him to a better state of being; but by the time Weber was beginning, partly as a result of his own efforts, and largely from a certain degree of personal surfeit, to abandon the worst of his excesses, it was too late for any one to prevent the final tragedy. The unexpected arrival of his father at Stuttgart in April 1809, with his interminable load of debt, increased his financial embarrassments a hundredfold, and his royal master, the duke, was in no better case. War was still raging on German soil, and conscription had been introduced into Württemberg in order to fill up the blanks in the decimated army. But court officials were exempt from this law, and, as might well be supposed, in so corrupt a court the sale of offices by many who were already in positions of trust about the king became prevalent. There is no direct evidence that Weber ever had any part in these corrupt practices, but about the end of 1809 he discovered that his father, whose mind was now beginning to weaken, had misappropriated certain sums which Carl Maria had, as secretary, received from the duke in order to pay off certain obligations on his estates in Silesia. The discovery drove Weber nearly distracted, and in his terror he vainly endeavoured to borrow 1,000 florins from one Höner, the landlord of an inn at Schwieberdingen, in which he had spent many hours of wild dissipation. But what he could not effect, a rascally groom named Huber—by what occult means did not immediately transpire—succeeded in accomplishing for a consideration. Weber signed an acknowledgment on behalf of Höner, received the loan and repaid the deficit. But it was not long before Höner began to importune the composer on behalf of his son, Huber having led him to believe that, in return for the loan, Weber should procure a nominal post for the son at court and thus free him from the terrors of conscription. When no such post materialized and, in January 1810, the youth was drafted into the army, Höner denounced Weber as having failed to implement the promise. The matter came to the ears of the king, who took a very serious view of such unconstitutional practices, and on the evening of 9th February 1810, while he was conducting a rehearsal of the opera Sylvana, which had been finished at last, Weber was arrested and cast into one of the loathsome German prisons of the time, where he lay for sixteen days and nights, at the end of which period he was brought up for examination, largely through the exertions of his good and faithful friend Danzi. But it was the king's turn now. The examination was largely a farce and wholly a travesty of justice. At the end of it all, father and son were declared free, but on the sole understanding of their being conducted over the frontiers of Württemburg and banished thence for life. This was clearly an act of petty revenge by the little-minded king for the many pin-pricks he had received from the impish and high-spirited youth, and that it was generally, if silently condemned, may reasonably be inferred from the fact that practically the entire population of Stuttgart believed him to be innocent.

A somewhat pathetic incident is recorded as having taken place as the two exiles were being hustled across the frontier. Between them they had only forty florins, but a certain police officer named Götz, whose duty it was to see them out of the country, pressed an additional twenty-five florins into Carl Maria's hand, as he was bidding them farewell. He also stealthily gave him several letters of introduction to people at Mannheim, which Danzi had entrusted to him for delivery at the first favourable opportunity. And so, wretched, weary and suffering in body and mind, the wanderers turned their steps towards Mannheim, where they hoped to renew some of their old friendships and secure, at least, some sort of living in the profession to which they had been trained.

A great deal of adverse criticism has been levelled against Carl Maria von Weber on account of the life he is said to have led in Stuttgart; yet he was probably the most conscientious official in either of the royal courts of Württemberg, and while the secretarial work, and especially that part of it which necessitated his having to cringe and scheme in order to keep his royal master in funds, was entirely uncongenial to his nature and abhorrent to his mind, he certainly did his best to keep the work up to date. Much of his leisure must have been given up to musical composition, for his output during the period of his sojourn there was by no means insignificant. First of all in bulk and importance was the opera *Sylvana*, and when one considers the manner of its creation, it appears almost incredible that he ever succeeded in getting it finished at all, or that the music should have become as good as it is. It was, as we have seen, composed at the special desire of his friend Danzi and with a view to its production on the stage of the royal court theatre of Stuttgart. But while Weber was engaged upon the work, he was too frequently behind the scenes of the opera house and became too closely acquainted and familiar with the singers who were to fill the various parts in the work. The result is amusingly described by his son:

In his desire to secure a successful, rather than a perfect, representation of his new opera, the young composer began to consider more and more the personal specialities of the troop and their desires to produce in-dividual effect, rather than the promptings of his own genius. When *Sylvana* was finished, its original design was gone, and it had assumed a wholly different physiognomy, more in conformity perhaps with the particular fancies of the singers, but decidedly not to its own advantage. Now it was the imperishable old tenor, Krebs—an excellent musician, by the way—who had his 'finger in the pie'; now the sweet-voiced second tenor, Deckers; now Fischer, the bass, whose talent required a good acting part; now the lively buffo-basso Weberling, whose original drollery was to have full scope; now Madame Graff, the *cantatrice à roulades*, whose speciality was to be shown off to advantage; now again, pretty Madame Gollin, who had an extraordinary talent for panto-mime action; and now, more especially, that charming, winning, coquettish little serpent, Margarethe Lang, who was to be the mocking, fluttering will-o'-the-wisp to dazzle the foolish boy during his Stuttgart life.

Nevertheless *Sylvana*, with all its minor blemishes, is a work of no mean order. 'A pretty hodge-podge had librettist, composer and artists cooked up between them!' says the baron, but he also says, and this is nearer the actual truth:

In the very inequalities of its style the opera of *Sylvana* possesses a very considerable degree of interest. A very distinct and rapid progress in the young composer's art is observable throughout the gradual composition of the work. It culminates in the last and best-written pieces— the drinking-song of Krips, the final chorus, the torch-dance and, above all, the exquisite overture, which already exhibits all his characteristic melodiousness of ideas; although in the form of its harmonies and its instrumentation it may still incline to the taste of the older masters, and reveal more especially the enduring influence of Vogler.

Another work, of even greater importance than *Sylvana*, was composed during this period. It was a melodramatic cantata entitled *Der erste Ton,* based on the poem of that name by Rochlitz. It treats of the creation of the world out of chaos and of the whole of nature receiving inspiration through the medium of sound. In the construction of this work Weber owed something to Vogler and something likewise to his friend Danzi, while the introduction to Haydn's *Creation* must have influenced the writing of his own introduction. Declamation to the accompaniment of melo-dramatic orchestral accompaniments rather than mere recitative was freely used, somewhat in the style of Tannhäuser's narrative in the third act of that opera, where Tannhäuser merely tells the story, leaving the orchestra to supply all the colour and variety that transforms a bare report into a glowing, glamorous picture. Other parts of *Der erste Ton* are sung to glorious music of the true Weber cast. In searching for his effects he makes considerable use of the diminished seventh, and not unsuccessfully. The following opening bars show a case in point:

Musically, this little work alone went far to prove the rapid and steady advance Weber was making in the grasp and command of his art. It is justly described by his son in the following well-considered terms:

The whole composition is a most successful one, as well in the colour given to the varying feelings and situations, as in the musical pictures, which never degenerate into childish imitations of the well-known sounds of nature. The modulations are admirable: the musical transitions, even when startling, are artfully combined to heighten the effect, and a character of dignity and nobleness pervades the whole. The final strophe, where the world exults in the creation of musical sound, composed for full chorus, is sublime in its effect.

But it was in something rather more than a merely successful musical composition that its full importance lay. It was to some extent an innovation and a new musical form. The church cantata was a thing of everyday use and common knowledge, while the dramatic cantata that was really a miniature opera (e.g. Bach's *Phoebus and Pan*) was scarcely less familiar; but a work of this nature that was, more or less, an oratorio in miniature was something entirely new, and it supplied a musical need that further events were soon to prove had really existed. In this work, also, we detect Weber's first use of the *Leitmotiv*, as it was to be employed to such a remarkable extent and effect by Wagner:

'Der er - ste Ton'

'This small but admirable work,' says Baron von Weber, 'was produced at various periods of Weber's career, in all the great cities of Germany, generally with the greatest applause, and contributed more than any other composition to the establishment of his fame as an artist.' Its utter neglect and complete disappearance from the musical repertory to-day is one of those apparently insoluble mysteries of which the history of music is so full.

The composition of these two major works—*Sylvana* and *Der erste Ton*—did not, however, by any means exhaust Weber's musical achievements during the Stuttgart period, for, in addition to remodelling the overture to *Peter Schmoll*, which he published as a separate work, and the *Overtura chinesa* [*sic*], which was afterwards used as the introduction to *Turandot*, for which Weber also composed some incidental music later; he also wrote the *Variations on an Original Theme* (Op. 9); the *Momento capriccioso* (Op. 12); *Six pièces pour le pianoforte à quatre mains* (Op. 10); and the *Polonaise* in E flat major, which he dedicated to Margarethe Lang, all for pianoforte; his solitary pianoforte Quartet, in B flat major; his *Variations on a Norwegian Theme*, for pianoforte and violin; an *Andante e Rondo Ongarese* for viola and orchestra; a *Potpourri* for violoncello and orchestra; and thirteen *Lieder* with accompaniment. For one who was said to have been living the life of an irresponsible libertine, and doing a job of the most uncongenial character for a bare subsistence, it must be admitted that his musical creative achievements, as recorded above, were more than remarkable; one might almost call them superhuman. And no one can assert that, unpleasant and uncongenial as they were, his Stuttgart experiences failed to prove to his ultimate advantage, for he left that city fully matured at last, both as a man and as a musician. Eight years later he himself spoke of this period: 'From this time forward I can count pretty tolerably on having settled matters with myself; and all that time has since done or can do for me is to rub off corners and add clearness and comprehensibility to the principles then firmly established.'

As a musician, likewise, he had now found his *métier* and was thoroughly established therein. The romanticism of *Sylvana* was as complete as anything he was ever to accomplish in the future, and, despite Spitta's assertion that *Der erste Ton* 'cannot be called a melodrama, because the poem is narrative and not dramatic,' I question whether there is anything more dramatic in the whole of Weber's creations than the musical treatment of this remarkable composition. Erwin Kroll shows a greater understanding of its actual place in Weber's development when he writes in effect:

So far as the melodrama form is concerned, Weber modelled the work upon those of his master Vogler (*Lampedo,* 1779), and of his friend Danzi (*Kleopatra,* 1780), although these works were certainly a little out of date. . . . But Weber transformed the text in a manner that imbued it with dramatic life. . . . We undoubtedly see in it, in embryo, the technique of the future symphonic poet, Liszt.

CHAPTER IV

MANNHEIM AND DARMSTADT

On leaving Stuttgart the Webers turned their steps towards Mannheim, which, each for a different reason, they selected as their next place of abode. Danzi's letters of introduction were a strong incentive to Carl Maria to seek a new sphere in which he might prosecute his art, unhampered by any of the uncongenial surroundings and petty irritations that had made his life far from happy at the royal court of Württemberg, and, for a time at least, he again found his true *métier* in that city of art and culture. His father, on the other hand, was not so lucky. He had returned to the city of his swashbuckling youth with the idea of renewing old friendships and linking up the roistering past with a calmer and of necessity less uproarious present. But death had been busy in the ranks of the old guard, and Franz Anton immediately fades out of the picture.

Mannheim had, before the transfer of the Elector Carl Theodor's court to Munich in 1778, enjoyed the reputation of possessing the best opera in Germany, and although it had long ago been dispersed, and the opera house battered to the ground by French artillery, the revolutionaries and Napoleon failed to exterminate the old love of art and beauty from the hearts of the Mannheimers, even at the cannon's mouth, and a handsome theatre had, like the phoenix, arisen on the very ashes of the old opera house. Supported by an annual subsidy of 20,000 florins from the elector, it made a fair attempt to emulate the musical achievements of its famous predecessor. The orchestra of this resuscitated opera was conducted by the genial but indolent Peter Ritter, who was a composer of operas and a violoncellist of considerable merit.

He had followed Danzi as conductor of the Mannheim opera and he, no doubt, was one of those to whom Weber bore Danzi's letters of introduction.

There was another musical institution at Mannheim, ostensibly amateur, but of almost equal importance in the artistic and social life of the town with the opera itself. This was a society which had adopted the curious name of 'The Museum.' It must have been a body of some wealth, for it was in possession of a handsome concert hall, and was always in a position to fill such blanks in its orchestra as the purely amateur section of the community was unable to supply with professionals from the theatre. The ruling spirit of 'The Museum' in 1810 was a civil servant—the head of the revenue department—named Gottfried Weber, then in his early thirties. He was a man of strong personality, in whom the qualities of tact, industry and dynamic energy were combined to an almost superhuman extent. He also had an exceptional talent for conducting both orchestra and chorus, and he was further remarkably fortunate in his wife who, in addition to being a social queen in respect of both charm and beauty, possessed a lovely soprano voice which she employed in accordance with the then fashionable Italian method. Other soloists who were practically always at his command were Theresa Grua, a friend of his wife's, who sang contralto with equal taste and skill, and Walther, a tenor, who was engaged at the opera. Here then was an ideal environment for Carl Maria who, when he arrived in the town on 27th February 1810, was received by all with open arms and unqualified kindness. But by none was he received more warmly than by Gottfried Weber, to whom he was in no way related, and these feelings were reciprocated by the composer with even greater warmth, if that were possible. Almost immediately a friendship sprang up between them, which became ever stronger as the years went on and, though eclipsed for a period, owing to some misunderstandings, endured to the very end. And almost the first act of friendship on the part of Gottfried was that of having the now utterly senile and barely responsible Franz Anton safely installed in the house of his own father. This was an immense relief to Carl Maria who, knowing him to be in careful keeping, was now in a position to travel on concert tours and to move about freely in the fulfilment of his vocation.

The first journey of this sort Carl Maria made was to Heidelberg, where he proposed giving the earliest of his concerts, and, following Gottfried's advice, the first person he sought out on his arrival in the beautiful old university town was Gottfried's own brother-in-law, a young student named Alexander von Dusch. The two young men were as quickly and as powerfully attracted to each other as Carl Maria and Gottfried had been. In Heidelberg, also, Weber renewed his acquaintance with old J. H. Voss, who in 1805 had been summoned to the university of Heidelberg; but, as Eichendorff said, 'he was so tangled in the dusty web of his own erudition that his unsociability seemed to carry the impression that he had a spite against old and young alike,' and soon Weber, notwithstanding his great admiration for the poet, was forced to shun his company.

Much more congenial did he find the Hout family, who dwelt in an old convent, romantically situated on the banks of the Neckar, at a place called Stift Neuburg, a short distance from Heidelberg. This was one of the families with whom he had got into touch through Danzi's letters of introduction, and Weber's association with these estimable people and contemplation of the beauties of the place, which Dusch described as an 'abode for poetic natures,' must have done much to impress the composer's already susceptible heart more deeply than ever with the spirit of romance that played so large and important a part in the creation of the music that was still to come from him.

Other friendships he formed at Heidelberg were those with Gries, the philologist; Justus Thibaut, the jurist and musical amateur; and Hoffmann, the organist, musical director and leader of Heidelberg's musical world at that time. He generously offered to further, by every means in his power, Weber's project of giving a concert in the town, and all the most influential musical amateurs rallied to his side.

Meanwhile, however, the high-spirited Dusch was introducing Weber into another circle, different from that of the staid and respectable professoriat. Cultured and esteemed by the latter as he was, Dusch was still a student, and to the student gatherings, or *Commerse*, he also haled his new acquaintance. There Weber found himself in his element. He sang the lightest of his songs, accompanying himself on his beloved guitar, and he arranged serenades to many of the most beautiful ladies in the town, which were a never-ending source of joy in the romantic climate and surroundings of the place. As the day on which his concert was to take place approached, every possible effort was made to ensure its success. Weber had already himself created a good impression by making an appearance at an important amateur concert and performing his own variations on the air 'Vien quà, Dorina bella.' But almost on the very eve of his own concert he was present at a *Commers*, when a quarrel arose which rapidly grew into so serious a riot that it became necessary to call in the military to restore order. And thus, somewhat ignominiously, ended the project of a Heidelberg concert from which poor Weber had hoped so much.

But his friends at Mannheim had not been idle in the meantime, and arrangements had been made during his absence for his giving a concert there. This took place on 9th March 1810, when he performed several of his own pianoforte compositions and heard his first Symphony performed for the first time. After paying all the expenses of this concert, he was left with only thirteen florins in hand, but, nothing daunted, he gave a second concert, which was generously supported, on 2nd April. The Symphony was repeated 'by request,' and his pianoforte Quartet, composed in 1809, was also given, Weber himself playing the piano part. But what renders this concert particularly outstanding in the composer's life and in the history of music is the fact that it was on this occasion that his epoch-making cantata,

Der erste Ton, received its first performance, the unset verses of the poem being declaimed by the great tragedian Esslair. The event is thus described by the composer's son:

The clear tones of his [Esslair's] wonderfully beautiful voice united themselves, as if by inspiration, with the music, and swelled with power and majesty over the torrent of sound; and when the storm of his marvellous declamation gave way to the full burst of the final chorus, so animated in rhythm and so rich in tone, the whole audience in-voluntarily burst forth into a tumult of applause. It was a proud moment in the young composer's life. The musician, the lover of art, the critic, were all unanimous in their delight at this remarkable con-cert. The fame of Weber's genius, it was said, was established, by this one evening, far along the banks of the Rhine, from the Black Forest to the Taunus mountains.

And he adds, doubtless not without a considerable degree of truth:

Perhaps, however, it was more to the young fellow's purpose, at that moment, that the results of the evening should have added the modest sum of three hundred and fifty florins to his miserable purse.

At this time, also, endless songs, serenades and canons were composed by Weber, and sung by the merry parties of which he was ever the soul and artistic inspiration in the homes, taverns and streets of Mannheim and Heidelberg, and, to the entrancing accompaniments of the beloved guitar, along the beautiful banks of the Neckar and Rhine. Another outcome of the association of Carl Maria Weber with his namesake Gottfried and with Alex-ander von Dusch was the formation of a Harmonic Society. For this the two first-named composed many beautiful songs, which had a far-reaching effect, in so far as they embodied the earliest idea of the German *Lied*, which was carried to such exquisite perfection in the songs of Schubert, Schumann, Brahms and Wolf. But much as Weber loved the scenery and society of Mannheim, he soon realized that it was not quite the ideal centre for the professional life he had in view, especially as the prospects of the artists' being able to live a fuller life in Germany were beginning to improve. Thus, after giving the matter careful consideration, he resolved to remove to Darmstadt, which, besides being a much better centre than Mannheim, housed his old master, the Abbé Vogler, for whom he retained a deep and sincere affection, and his old friend Gänsbacher.

Darmstadt is to-day one of those characterless provincial German towns that, in the time of their sovereign lordships, have seen better days; but even in the early decades of the nineteenth century its glory was already departing, and Weber had not been there long before he began to find it inexpressibly dull. Nevertheless, the Darmstadt period is notable to some extent in the history of the youth and in his musical growth. He arrived in the town in April 1810 and found a lodging in the Ochsenstrasse, where he slept and had dinner for the modest sum of twelve kreutzer (from sixpence to eightpence at rates current in 1938) per day. Darmstadt was the capital of the Grand Duchy of Hesse, and it was fortunate from the artistic point of view, inasmuch as nearly all the members of the ruling family for a hundred and fifty years previously had been great lovers and patrons of music. Under the reigning Grand Duke Ludwig I, who was a musician of exquisite taste and ability as a performer on the violin, piano, flute and horn, Weber had no reason to complain of its lack of importance as a centre of tonal art. The duke possessed an admirable choir and court opera house, in which operas were performed on Sundays. These were rehearsed four times weekly by the duke himself, who was inordinately proud of his forces and always on the look-out for further creative and interpretative talent. He had attached the Abbé Vogler, for whom he had a great admiration, to his artistic *entourage*, and had made him a privy councillor with a handsome pension for life. In addition to Gänsbacher the abbé had in his own household another young pupil named Jacob Liebmann

Beer,[1] the son of a rich Jewish banker of Berlin, who afterwards became world-famous, as a composer of operas, under the name of Meyerbeer. His skill as a pianist, even at this early age—he was then only eighteen—would have placed him well in the front rank of virtuosi had necessity driven him to it. It was to this little group that Weber then attached himself, and many days were spent in gaining new ideas and fresh experience. But even in dull, drowsy Darmstadt the irrepressible spirits of the youths would occasionally break forth, and the streets would ring with their laughter and serenading, much to the horror of the worthy burghers and their humourless womenkind. They also took a special joy in 'melody-hunting' in which, as Baron Max so aptly puts it, they 'snatched new inspiration from the popular ditties of the day.' This was a great game which later was to bear delicious fruit:

Out of some such common tune would afterwards grow a master melody, which bore about as much resemblance to the original as the brilliant butterfly to the dingy chrysalis. The principal idea of the famous *Invitation to the Waltz*,[2] and of the ballet music in the third act of *Oberon*, thus, it is said, sprang into existence.

Ideas for a new romantic opera were again running in Weber's head at this period. A short time before he left Mannheim, Hiemer had handed him the libretto of *Abu Hassan*, an operetta in one act based on the story of *Abu-l-Hasan the Wag, or The Sleeper awakened* in *The Arabian Nights*. It is one of the best comic stories in existence, and Weber was then perhaps just in the right mood for doing it complete justice. But his mind was torn between the spirit of romance and that of laughter, and the opera was not

[1] 'A wealthy relative made him his heir on condition that he should prefix the name Meyer to his patronymic; and Giacomo (Jakob Italianized) was later assumed as an artist-name.'—Baker's *Biographical Dictionary of Musicians* (3rd ed., 1919).

[2] The correct English title is *Invitation to the Dance*, the original being *Aufforderung zum Tanz*.

immediately composed. This is admirably illustrated by the story told by his son of how

whilst one evening at Stift Neuburg he was leaning out of the window, commanding a view of the most romantic beauty, in an apartment which he occupied with his friend Dusch, chattering, humming, dreaming in the sweet air of a bright moonlight night in spring, he burst out into a melody, which was, long years yet to come, to form the introductory fairy chorus in *Oberon*. Another melody streamed forth to the words of 'Ah, Fatima beloved!' in *Abu Hassan*, as he threw off his clothes to retire at last to bed. The next morning both were forgotten. But Dusch had treasured them. He took a sly opportunity of repeating them; when Weber flew at him, took him by the throat, and laughingly exclaimed: 'You scoundrel! You have stolen that out of my head, where I had happened to mislay it.'

It was this confused state of his artistic mind that nearly gave us *Der Freischütz* ten years before its time. But fortunately Dusch's pressing business affairs saved us from that. It was in the summer of 1810 that a newly published collection of *Gespenster-Geschichten* (*Ghost Stories*) by Apel and Laun fell into Weber's hands. The first of these, entitled *Der Freischütz*, fascinated him and Dusch, and together they devoured the contents of the book at one sitting, the result of which was that a scenario was immediately prepared, and Dusch undertook the writing of the words. But as time went on and Dusch's pressing business delayed the appearance of the 'book,' Weber gradually turned his attention to other things, one of these being the score of *Abu Hassan*.

At this time, too, Weber was again moving about a good deal, giving concerts wherever there was a chance of his making a few florins. We hear of him visiting Aschaffenburg, where he was received and entertained at supper by the Prince-Bishop Carl von Dalberg. He proceeded thence to Amorbach with letters of introduction from Count Benzel-Sternau to Prince Leiningen, and he might have settled there happily for some time had he not received tidings of a projected visit of his old friend and patron, Prince Eugen of Württemberg, to Frankfort. He hurried on to that city, urged by the opportunity of meeting his old master once again, of explaining to him the true reasons for his having had to leave Stuttgart and of exonerating himself thus in the prince's eyes. The prince received him with open arms, and they spent the whole night in happy and intimate converse. When, in the morning, Prince Eugen was at last forced to leave him, he pressed the composer to his heart, assured him that he had no doubt whatever of his innocence of all that was alleged against him at Stuttgart and took a valuable ring from his own finger, placing it upon a finger of Weber's, to be retained by him as a keepsake.

While he was at Frankfort, Weber called on the famous music publisher Simrock and succeeded in inducing him to publish his cantata *Der erste Ton*, his great Polonaise for piano in E major, a Quartet, a *Potpourri* for violoncello and six songs; but all that he was able to wring out of the miserly publisher was 150 florins (£6) for the lot. It was some remarks on this Quartet made by the publisher Hans Georg Nägeli, who had previously declined it, that drew from Weber his famous outburst against Beethoven:

You seem from my Quartet and Caprice to discover in me an imitator of Beethoven, and flattering as this might appear to many, it is far from agreeable to me. In the first place, I hate everything that bears the stamp of imitation, and, secondly, my views differ far too much from those of Beethoven ever to come into contact with him. The fiery, nay, almost incredible inventive faculty which inspires him is attended by so many complications in the arrangement of his ideas that it is only his earlier compositions that interest me; the later ones, on the contrary, appear to me only a confused chaos, an unintelligible struggle after novelty, from which occasional heavenly flashes of genius dart forth, showing how great he might be if he chose to control his luxuriant fancy. Though I certainly cannot boast of the great genius of Beethoven, still I think I can vindicate both the logic and the phraseology of my music, each individual piece causing a definite impression. For it appears to me that the aim of an artistic composition is to deduce the character of the whole from individual thoughts, and that, amidst the greatest diversity, still unity, displayed by the first principle or theme, should always shine forth.

He returned to Darmstadt through Mannheim and Heidelberg. In both places concerts were given at which new works of his were performed for the first time. He arrived to take part in the celebration of Vogler's sixty-first birthday, which the three young pupils had arranged as a surprise for the old master. Carl Maria wrote a poetical effusion for the occasion, while Gänsbacher composed two solos and Meyerbeer a trio and chorus. The occasion was secretly and well organized, and on the eventful day all was performed as it had been planned. Therese Beer, Meyerbeer's sister, and many of the most distinguished ladies and gentlemen in the town took part, but because the grand duke himself had quite forgotten the fact that his musical privy councillor had a birthday, the abbé was in one of his tantrums, and the celebration fell rather flat. But he had no grudge against his 'dear boys' and, perhaps in order to mollify any feeling of resentment that he thought might be lurking in Weber's mind, he set him the task of preparing a notice of twelve Bach chorales he was then arranging. The article duly appeared and may still be read in the composer's *Ausgewählte Schriften*. It is good but not sensational music criticism. The analyses of the chorales were very indifferently done, and not all of them by Weber.

Another important period in Weber's life now opens with an invitation from Vogler to accompany him on an artistic tour, beginning at Frankfort and Mainz. He returned to the former city, hoping to see a production of *Sylvana* there, at last. But again his hope remained unfulfilled. However, he once more met at Frankfort his old sweetheart, Margarethe Lang, and spent a little time in her company; but their old relationship was not renewed, perhaps because at a concert they attended together he first beheld a beautiful young singer, Caroline Brandt, who was afterwards to become his wife. He and Vogler proceeded from Mainz to

Hanau and Offenbach, and thence back to Darmstadt. While at Offenbach he combined business with pleasure by calling upon André, the publisher, to whom he sold his piano Concerto, his first Symphony and six unwritten Sonatas, all for the miserable sum of 150 florins (£6). On reaching Darmstadt again, he heard that the Crown Prince of Bavaria was staying at Baden-Baden, so on 19th July 1810, armed with a letter of introduction from Nägeli and accompanied by Dusch, Gottfried Weber and the latter's wife, he set out for that centre of fashion, which he found full to overflowing. The party obtained accommodation with friends only with the greatest difficulty. It soon broke up, however, leaving Carl Maria alone. He presented his letter to the Crown Prince of Bavaria and was well received. As his finances were again running low, he resolved to give a concert at Baden-Baden; but what he called his 'evil genius' was again at his heels, and the concert never came off. He tells the story amusingly, in a letter he wrote to Gänsbacher two months later:

I fixed the probable date of my concert, and anxiously awaited the arrival of Berger, and the music that Archer was to send, for an orchestra was out of the question; so I was obliged to do my best with the slender means at my command. But neither music nor Berger arrived, and to complete my annoyance, neither in Baden nor in its environs could I find a piano that it was possible to play on. I was told of one in Rastadt; so I went off there, and arrived just as the owner of the instrument had left the place. Meanwhile time passed, Princess Stephanie went on a journey, the crown prince talked of leaving; so I became provoked, and gave it up altogether. I recognized in all this my evil genius, who had too long allowed things to go on pleasantly not to play me some vile prank on this occasion.

But his stay at Baden-Baden was not altogether fruitless, for there he met several of his old Stuttgart friends: the poet Tieck, who later would have been happy to provide Weber with an opera libretto when Friedrich Kind, jealous of the musician's popularity over the success of *Der Freischütz*, dissociated himself

52

from him; and especially Cotta, the famous Tübingen bookseller, who asked him to write something about Baden for his *Morgen-blatt*, which he did, under the *nom de guerre* of 'Melos.' Weber also offered him a novel he had written under the title of *Ton-künstlers Leben* (*The Life of a Musical Artist*), which, to his great joy, was accepted. This was to have been finished by Easter 1811, but time passed and it was never completed.

Carl Maria left Baden-Baden on 2nd August 1810 and arrived at Mannheim on the 3rd, where he stayed with the Gottfried Webers. He gave a performance on 4th August in 'The Museum,' and set to work on his new opera, *Abu Hassan*. Then, on the 13th, he gave a musical *soirée* at Heidelberg, consisting only of quartets and singing, and he relates that 'in spite of the beauty of the weather and the consecration of a neighbouring church, there was a numerous and indulgent audience.' He returned to Darmstadt on the 15th, but stayed for another three days at Mannheim, on the way. He had hoped to have an opportunity of playing before the grand duke at Darmstadt, but he received no invitation to do so, and Vogler, still suffering from the birth-day slight, declined to make any move in connection with the matter. But *Sylvana* was now definitely in rehearsal at Frankfort, and the composer was kept busy between the two towns re-spectively rehearsing and composing. And on 16th September 1810 [1] *Sylvana* at last saw the light of public performance.

The difficult title-part was filled by the gifted young actress and singer Caroline Brandt, of whom mention has already been made, and who is presently to take a more important share in the history that is now being written. She was a good mimic and her voice and charm were irresistible. Spitta states positively that Margarethe Lang took the part of Mechtilde, but this is doubtful. Benedict and Kroll are both silent on the subject,

[1] The Baron von Weber gives the date as Sunday, the 17th, and he is blindly followed in this error by Sir Julius Benedict; but the composer himself, in a letter to Gänsbacher, gives the 16th as the actual date, and this is confirmed by Jähns, who quotes the actual register of the theatre.

and other writers, such as Cœuroy, who follow Spitta, give no authority for the statement. The lady was then certainly attached to the Frankfort opera and there is every reason to believe that Carl Maria requested her to undertake the part which had been 'written wholly in accordance with her own whims and fancies.' But, as his son remarks:

Mademoiselle Gretchen was tricky. She most positively refused. Weber visited her, however, went with her to rehearsal, and by the side of this being, to whom his young, warm heart had sacrificed so great a portion of his past repute, listened to the first strains of this work, from which he hoped so much for his future fame.

Yes, but that was at the rehearsal. When he comes to deal with the actual performance, he mentions how the whole orchestra, as well as the opera company of the Frankfort theatre, were animated by the truest zeal to serve the young composer and to do honour to his composition, and he particularly remarks that 'Madame Schönberger, the prima donna, who had undertaken the character of Mechtilde, was enrolled, heart and soul, on Carl Maria's side.'

But much that should have been of far greater interest has been hopelessly obscured by the emphasis placed in all reports of the event upon one of those deplorable *contretemps* it seemed to be Weber's fate to encounter all through his life. After the date of the performance had been fixed for 16th September, it was advertised that 'the celebrated Madame Blanchard' would make a balloon ascent from Frankfort on that day. That itself was bad enough, for balloon ascents were then matters of all-absorbing interest; but when the hour at which it was to take place was postponed from some time in the afternoon to half past seven in the evening, the prospects for the success of *Sylvana* were by no means bright. Nevertheless the birth of the work was, as Weber himself writes, 'propitious, and it was received with great applause; one aria was encored, and at the conclusion Silvana and I were called before the curtain.' The financial result, however, was not so good, Weber's remuneration amounting to no more than 100 florins (£4). But even this, small as it was, constituted a welcome return, and it is greatly to his credit that he sent the whole amount to Stuttgart for the liquidation of part of the debts he had left behind him there, although, as he said, it left himself again with 'nothing but a little talent in the cupboard.'

After the production of *Sylvana* Weber again made an effort to settle down at Darmstadt to solid work and serious composition, but the 'leathern old town' bored him now more than ever, as Gänsbacher had gone to Prague to enter upon a business career there, and the old Heidelberg circle was entirely broken up. On 9th October, in a letter to Gänsbacher, he gives an amusing account of his doleful state:

What would I give to be able to fly to you in my beloved Vienna! . . . when once I have left dismal Darmstadt, I trust I shall get on more briskly. . . . Our little maid-servant—the ugly creature—is actually going to be married to a chancery clerk who is said to be fond of the bottle, but otherwise, no doubt, is a very worthy fellow. Herr Reiner still makes witty remarks; Marianne snivels, and Therese sings as much out of tune as ever. The little bear [Meyerbeer] writes canzonettas and psalms; the old woman consumes enormous quantities of snuff, and Bärbel cooks. The family is increased by an abominable black poodle, which Beer's servant is always thrashing and his master continually hugging. And there you have all the news of our household.

But all the time his work was going steadily on. He was giving intermittent attention to the score of *Abu Hassan* with its famous opening chorus, 'Geld, Geld, Geld'; he completed his piano Concerto; he wrote also the six piano Sonatas he had promised to do for André, and he was likewise working hard upon his *Tonkünstlers Leben*. While all this activity was proceeding, Weber received a number of flattering letters from Frankfort, intimating that the public of that town would be greatly interested to hear a concert given by the composer of *Sylvana* in person, and that the production of a new work would be acceptable. So on 18th October he set out to fulfil these requests. On the way he visited Offenbach with the new sonatas [1] for the publisher André, who received him kindly and as a special favour placed reverently in the composer's hands a manuscript musical score. Weber, somewhat surprised, asked:

'What am I to do with this pale copy of one of Mozart's sonatas, for such it seems to be?'

'It is no copy,' replied André, 'it is one of the many scores of Mozart which I possess, written by his own hand!'

On hearing this Weber laid the score upon the table, fell on his knees, touched the pages with his lips and forehead, and said, with tears in his eyes: 'How happy is the paper that his hands have touched!'

In this state of exaltation, and full of hope, for his financial needs were again pressing, he arrived at Frankfort on 20th October, the day on which his concert was to take place; but alas! his evil genius had once more taken charge of the arrangements and countered his plans in a manner beside which Madame Blanchard's balloon ascent was a mere bagatelle. In connection with the Continental blockade of English goods Napoleon had decreed that more stringent measures had become necessary, and orders were given that the trading city of Frankfort was to be ransacked and all English merchandise found therein destroyed. So, as luck—or Fate, as Weber firmly believed—would have it, the French troops entered the city on the very day of Weber's arrival, on which his concert was to have taken place. The city was in a state of chaos, and the intending concert-giver remained there only long enough to become convinced of the futility of making the attempt before, angry, bitter and well-nigh penniless, he retraced his steps to the hated Darmstadt. But before he arrived there he was fated to experience a further and even more humiliating disappointment. He called on André again on his way back, only to learn that his sonatas had been rejected, because, as he wrote to Gänsbacher, 'they were too good.' André showed him

---

[1] *Six Sonates progressives für Klavier mit obligater Violine.*

some of Démar's,[1] etc., and said that was what they ought to be. 'I explained to him,' writes the indignant composer, 'that I neither could nor would write such miserable trash, and demanded payment, on which he only gave me one half of the sum and said it was his custom not to pay the other half till the work was published.'

He reached Darmstadt again, seething with anger, and he found the place less bearable than ever. When therefore an invitation to come over to Mannheim to help in the organizing of a concert to be given in honour of the much-beloved hereditary Grand Duchess Stephanie of Baden arrived from Gottfried Weber, he jumped at the opportunity and, early in November, he was once more the centre of the old happy company which now, under his inspiring direction, was to be bound even closer together in a secret society that was to act as a kind of critical academy, to be called the 'Harmonic Society,' which 'by mutual and energetic support may act and work for the benefit of art.' Carl Maria was to be the director and Gottfried the secretary of the union, with Mannheim as its headquarters. Rules 14 and 15 of this remarkable body read as follows:

14. The chief object of the society, and consequently the chief duty of each brother, is to promote and bring to light what is good, *wherever it may be met with*, and particular regard to be paid in this respect to youthful rising talent.

15. On the other hand, as the world is deluded by so many bad productions, which are often extolled only by patronage, and by un-principled critics, it is equally a duty to expose and to warn the public against these wherever they are to be met with. But we hope that a depreciating tone in criticism may be carefully avoided.

A number of other rules regarding the submission of works by members of the society follow, and they culminate in Rule 20, which reads as follows:

If one of the brothers should compose something really bad (an occurrence by no means probable), the director must tell him so candidly

---

[1] No doubt Jean Sébastien Démar, see Appendix C.

and persuade him to take back his composition. If the author objects to the verdict of the director, the latter must then appeal to the judgment of two brothers; and if one of the two concurs with the director, and advises the composer to withdraw his work, and yet the latter still objects to do so, then Rule 15 is to be put in force against him.

Each member of this body assumed a *nom de guerre*, to be used as a signature to his criticisms and literary appreciations. Thus Carl Maria was known as 'Melos,' Gottfried as 'Giusto,' Dusch as 'The Unknown,' Meyerbeer as 'Philodikaios,' and Gänsbacher as 'Triole.'

The concert given in honour of the Grand Duchess Stephanie was, so far as the performances and its immediate effects were concerned, a great success. Carl Maria played his piano Concerto for the first time in its entirety, and what succeeded may best be described in the words of his son:

The princess was enchanted; and, contrary to all usual etiquette, on the termination of the concert she advanced, accompanied by her *Oberhofmeisterin*, Countess Walsch, to greet the young man, and said that she had heard so much from her cousin, Ludwig of Bavaria, of his beautiful singing to the guitar, that she should feel personally obliged if he would allow her also the chance of enjoying so great a pleasure. A guitar was fetched, and, standing in the midst of a small circle of the court party, Carl Maria sang some of his most pathetic and some of his sprightliest songs. The princess, now with tears in her eyes, now with laughter on her lips, forgot all, to linger on, and hear more, and yet still more. When at last, after a long conversation with Carl Maria, she retired, all flocked round him with congratulations; and when the chamberlain of the princess returned to ask, by her command, upon what conditions young Weber could be induced to remain in Mannheim, Gottfried fell upon his friend's neck with tears of joy, and exclaimed: 'Now you are won to us for ever!' But Carl Maria stood alone un‑moved. 'No,' he said, shaking his head with a bitter smile, 'I know the influence of my evil star. It will come to nothing. Such happiness were won too lightly.'

And he was right. For some days his hopes ran high.

The affair was now daily spoken of [he wrote to Gänsbacher], the *Oberhofmeisterin* of the princess arranged the whole, and I was offered at once 1,000 florins, lodging and firewood, and the thing was considered settled, when one day (after I had been repeatedly with the duchess, singing and playing) the *Oberhofmeisterin* informed me the princess had spoken to her treasurer, and she regretted much that the state of her finances would not admit of her engaging me at present. I was not told this till after I had been paraded about for a fortnight, having lost much precious time, and not even received a present.

This was the last straw, and it was the deciding factor which led to his giving effect to a resolve that had been simmering in his mind for some time: to throw himself once more upon the world and take whatever fate might bring him. He finished his opera, *Abu Hassan*, composed a beautiful farewell song, *Des Künstlers Abschied*, and, early in the new year (1811), he bade good-bye to his friends at Mannheim, writing in his diary: 'Shall I ever again find in this world friends so dear, and men so true?';[1] and to his dear old master Vogler at Darmstadt; and started 'in God's name, for Munich, Berlin, Hamburg and Copenhagen,'[2] with many letters of introduction from the grand-ducal couple, but otherwise entirely alone, a strolling artist-pedlar, offering his wares to whoever might choose to buy—and these were few and stingy enough in all conscience.

[1] Fifteen years later, shortly before his death, he wrote opposite this entry: 'No!'
[2] 1810. Letter to Gänsbacher of 7th December.

CHAPTER V

MORE WANDER-YEARS

BEFORE the year 1810 had ended Carl Maria von Weber must have touched almost the lowest depths of misery, as may be judged from his becoming, at that time, rather morbidly introspective. His diary for the year closes with these remarks:

God has sent me many vexations and disappointments, but He has also thrown me with many good kind people, who have made life worth living. I can say honestly and in all quietness, that within the last ten months I have become a *better* man.

And one can scarcely regard a man who writes in such a strain as he did, on 12th January 1811, as being in the best state of physical and mental health:

My path in life was cast from my birth in different lines from that of any other human being; *I* have no happy childish days to look back upon, no free boyhood; though still a youth, I am an old man in experience, learning everything through my own feelings and by myself, *nothing* by means of others.

Weber was the last man on earth one should have expected to express such sorrow for himself, and it was obviously high time that he had a decided change of scene and environment.

Carl Maria left Darmstadt, therefore, on 14th February 1811 and turned his steps northward to Frankfort, and thence to the little university town of Giessen, where he had a little trouble with the police. 'When I went for permission to give my concert,' he wrote to Gottfried Weber, 'I was treated and examined like a vagabond. But I let out in good style, utterly confounded them, and then went and got a permission from General Wittgenstein.'

And, as usual, he was received by the students with open arms. He left Giessen on 24th February, richer by eighty-one florins as a result of his concert, and this time he returned southwards to Aschaffenburg, chiefly for the purpose of visiting the Abbé Johann Franz Xaver Sterkel, who had been chaplain and pianist to the Elector of Mainz there. Sterkel was a composer and pianist of considerable distinction, and was much admired by Vogler, who had strongly recommended Weber to make his acquaintance. He was something of a character, and Weber records that 'he received me in the most absurdly sentimental fashion, and preached to me by the hour in the same tone.'

The next stopping-place was Würzburg, to which Carl Maria had been attracted by another great musician—indeed, one of the greatest musical professors of his time—Joseph Fröhlich. He received Carl Maria with kindness and affection. The latter had hoped to give a concert at Würzburg before the Archduke Ferdinand, Grand Duke of Tuscany and brother of the Emperor of Austria, whose court was then established there; but it was bristling with intrigue and, in spite of considerable influence exerted on his behalf, he did not succeed. The grand duke, however, accepted the scores of *Sylvana* and *Abu Hassan* from the composer and suitably rewarded him. He lingered at Würzburg, where he had a small affair of the heart with a woman who crossed his path at a masked ball, but whose name does not emerge. From Würzburg he passed through Bamberg, Nuremberg and Augsburg, and eventually reached Munich on 14th March. At Bamberg he renewed his acquaintance with the well-known poet and dramatist, Franz von Holbein, who was then manager of the theatre of that town, where also he met and admired the principal actress, Madame Renner. But most important of all, while sitting one evening in the Rose tavern, leisurely sipping his 'cool Franconian wine,' he fell into conversation with two men who were seated at a neighbouring table. One of them, he learned in time, was the famous Ernst Theodor Amadeus Hoff-mann, who was then serving as musical director at the theatre, under Holbein's management; the other was a youth named Bader, who was then beginning to make a name for himself as a tenor, also at the theatre. The composer's son writes of this encounter: 'Weber knew not then that he saw before him the man who, eleven years later, was to embody his own character of Max in *Der Freischütz*, with unsurpassable life, spirit and grace.'

From Bamberg, Weber passed through Erlangen, Nuremberg and Augsburg, where he visited the music publisher Gombart and sold him an Italian canzonetta entitled *Momento capriccioso*, composed at Bamberg, and he promised to write for him six sonatas and some smaller pieces. And so at last he arrived at Munich on 14th March, where he was immediately and cordially received by King Max Joseph I of Bavaria, his charming queen and indeed by the whole of the court party. He put up in a modest apartment in the Neuhäuser-Gasse, but it was in the house of Wieberking, the court director of public works, that he found his real home during the five months he remained in the Bavarian capital. Wieberking also was something of a character, and his original ideas on architecture delighted Weber. His daughter, Fanny, possessed an admirable talent for the piano, and Weber repaid a great deal of kindness he received from the family by giving her lessons.

In this house he first made the acquaintance of the celebrated clarinet player, Heinrich Bärmann, whom he describes in a letter to Gänsbacher as 'a truly great artist and admirable man.' A warm friendship and close comradeship immediately sprang up between these two artists, which only death was to sever. It was not long before the composer had laid his first offering—the fore-runner of many that were to appear during the next few years—at the feet of this executant, the popular Concertino for clarinet and orchestra (Op. 26). In the hospitable and scintillating *salon* of the Russian minister, Prince Bariatinsky, to which he had ready access, he also met the great philosopher Schelling, regarding whom he afterwards wrote, with delightful ingenuousness: 'Schelling and I are such good friends.'

There was one man in Munich, however, and one alone, with whom Weber could never succeed in getting on friendly terms. This was Johann Peter Winter, a noted composer of operas and church music in his day, and the court *Kapellmeister* there. He had a sour, envious and malicious disposition, and he seemed to make it ever a point of honour to keep youthful talent and rising genius in its place. But he had, under his own admirable con- ductorship, a body of instrumentalists which, at that time, were unexcelled, even in Germany. At its full strength the orchestra amounted to eighty-seven performers, many of whom were, in point of ability, well on the first-rate solo plane, and his body of singers at the opera were of equal artistic standing, and capable of doing complete justice to operas of both Italian and German origin and style. Writing to Gottfried Weber, Carl Maria said of the orchestra and its conductor:

The members of the orchestra are mighty grand fellows, and as arrogant as you please; but they have taken into their heads to pet me amazingly. The envious old Winter had been uncommonly divert- ing. When I first paid him a visit, he took me for a dilettante, and overwhelmed me with politeness; but when, after a day or two, he discovered how matters stood, he was so abominably rude that all the musicians called him a beast. How can a man who has already earned his laurels so tarnish them, by letting himself down in this manner?

Weber gave his first concert in Munich on 5th April 1811, when his Symphony was indifferently and *Der erste Ton* badly performed, a fact the composer took very much to heart. But he had no reason to complain of the success which crowned the rendering of his piano Concerto with himself as soloist, and of the new clarinet Concertino which Bärmann played with marvellous charm. The court party had taken fifty tickets for this event, and the king, who was present, was so delighted with the Con- certino and Bärmann's rendering of it, that immediately after the concert he gave Weber an order for the composition of two more works for the same instrument. The concert left Weber with a net profit of 448 florins and established his fame as a composer and pianist in Munich. The king's request pleased him greatly, and it proved to be a stimulating influence towards the creation of fresh work, as well as a powerful inducement for others to employ the artist whom the king himself had so signally honoured. In a letter to Gottfried Weber he writes as exultingly and hopefully as he ever before or afterwards allowed himself to do, with that 'evil star' of his ever hovering in the background:

The whole orchestra seems possessed by the devil, every man of them wants me to compose a concert piece for his especial instrument. You see that I have tolerably hard work on hand; and, consequently, I shall probably remain here the whole summer. My earnings are pretty considerable; and another concert, given before my departure, will doubtless prove remunerative. There seems a very general feeling here that I ought to receive the appointment of *Kapellmeister*; but you know what my feelings on that subject are. At all events I have some hopes that my operas may be given here.

Nor were his hopes in vain, for all of a sudden, probably acting upon a hint from royalty, Winter turned a complete somersault in his favour and informed him that he intended putting *Abu Hassan* into immediate rehearsal. He was as good as his word, and the first representation of that opera took place on 10th June. An untoward incident nearly ruined the opera on this occasion, when a false alarm of fire was raised in the theatre. It was admirably performed, however, and received with great applause.

At this time Weber was busily engaged in literary work, some of his best critical notices of opera performances having been written while he was at Munich. Towards the end of the summer he resolved upon the continuance of his wanderings, but abandoning his former plan of covering the North German cities, and possibly Copenhagen, he now set his face southwards upon what he called an 'art and nature pothouse journey' (*Kunst* und *Naturkneipreise*), with Switzerland as his objective. Before leaving

Journey to Switzerland

Munich, however, he received from Gottfried Weber, who had been commissioned to find a suitable *Kapellmeister* for Wiesbaden, an offer of the post, which, however, he declined, as neither the proposed arrangements nor the salary were sufficiently advantageous to entice him to settle there.

A similar bit of trouble to that which arose on his arrival at Giessen, after Weber's departure from Darmstadt, met him at Ravensburg, shortly after his leaving Munich. The most direct route to Constance necessitated his journeying over about thirty miles of territory which formed part of the kingdom of Württemberg, from which, eighteen months previously, he had been so ignominiously expelled; but Weber was the last man in the world to worry about a trifle of that sort. Without giving the matter a single thought, he crossed the border, submitted his passport for inspection and was allowed to proceed. But at Ravensburg he was again interrogated, placed under arrest and lodged, under police surveillance, in a room of the 'Lamb,' the only inn of which the town could boast, until the king's decision as to his ultimate disposal should be obtained. Five days elapsed before this came to hand. To his relief it was to the effect that his passport should be restored to him, and that he should be passed on immediately to the next frontier. While he was awaiting news of his fate at Ravensburg, he had one of his frequently recurring attacks of fever, and the postmaster of the town, Paur by name, took pity on him and brought him a doctor. And so, while the vindictive monarch allowed the chief delinquent to get off scot-free, he meted out a very different verdict to the kindly but unfortunate Paur, who was, for his charitable action, dismissed from the royal service for ever.

Carl Maria, still suffering from fever, was conveyed to Mörsburg on the Lake of Constance, hustled on to a boat and sent across the lake to the town of Constance, which was the very place to which he wished most of all to go. There he stayed for some days with an old friend of his Munich days, Baron Hoggner, at Schloss Wolfsberg, and there, in the heart of the baron's family, he soon

F   65

recovered his health. On his departure for Schaffhausen he left them a canzonetta to the words 'D' ogni amator' la fede è sempre mal sicura,' which he had composed during his stay. At this time he seems to have taken a fancy to the Italian canzonetta for, under the opus numbers 29 and 31, there are several which were composed during this journey. At Schaffhausen he attended a festival of the Helvetian Musical Society, which, he writes, 'gave me an agreeable surprise by politely appointing me an honorary member.' Here, also, he met Nägeli the publisher, and, purely by accident, Meyerbeer, who was on his way to Italy. The latter was in the company of his parents, with whom Weber was soon on excellent terms, and a friendship grew up between them that was later to prove very greatly to his advantage. They travelled together from Schaffhausen to Winterthur, where Weber gave a concert, under the usual difficulties—the orchestra, composed of amateurs, was quite incapable of accompanying his great piano Concerto, and he spent a whole day and night reducing the score to a quartet. After this had been accomplished, he found that there was not a decent piano in the town. The concert brought him a great deal of applause and—sixteen florins.

On 29th August, the day after this concert, the composer proceeded to Zürich, where again he met Nägeli and tried vainly to interest him in a musical journal which the 'Harmonic Society' was anxious to publish. On 3rd September he gave a concert at Zürich, this time to a crowded and again enthusiastic audience, but his greatest delight lay in the fact that, for the first time, he played on a piano by Erard, which must have consoled him for the meagreness of his profits—eight florins. On 6th September, he set out on a walking tour to the Oberland, with 'an accomplished musician and excellent man,' Anton Liste[1] of Zürich.

[1] There seems to have been some confusion in the minds of various translators regarding the name and identity of this Zürich acquaintance of Weber's. Palgrave Simpson, in his translation of Baron von Weber's biography, gives the name as Siste, while the French translator of the letters describes him as the 'pianiste List.' But Lady Wallace

One of the objects Weber had in view in going to Zürich was the desire to study at first hand the Pestalozzi system in Nägeli's celebrated singing academy, but the result was a failure. To Gottfried Weber he wrote: 'It was altogether a curious affair, the fellows sang well—but how? Just like people in a Lutheran church. The compositions I could in no wise make up my mind to; they appeared to me so dreadfully commonplace and vulgar! Perhaps, however, I could not understand them. I suppose it is national singing.'

The excursion to the Oberland lasted till 21st September, after which he turned his steps northwards again, visiting Berne, Solothurn, where he stayed with the Bavarian minister, Herr d'Ollory, and composed several songs including *Künstlers Liebes-forderung*, Jegisdorf and Basle. In the last-named town he gave a concert and thereby augmented his now sadly depleted funds to the extent of 130 florins. He then returned to Munich where, to his great joy, he learned that Bärmann had arranged to accompany him on another artistic tour through North Germany. On 11th November he gave a concert in conjunction with Bärmann in Munich. The king and queen, and the cream of Munich society, were present, and the outstanding feature of the concert was the performance of his reconstructed overture to *Rübezahl*, now entitled *Der Beherrscher der Geister* (*The Ruler of the Spirits*). Eventually a good, serviceable travelling-carriage for two was procured and the two drove out of Munich on 1st December on their art-pilgrimage, bubbling over with joy and hope.

Only one thing preyed upon Carl Maria's mind at this time: an unfortunate misunderstanding that had arisen between him and Gottfried Weber. The latter, immersed in mundane affairs, had become jealous and suspicious, and he conceived the idea

---

goes the whole hog, translating the passage in which the name appears thus: 'Early on the morning of the 6th I went accompanied by the pianist Liszt . . .' which, of course, is pure nonsense.

that Carl Maria was using the 'Harmonic Society' largely for his own interests and advantage. This was quite erroneous, but it cast a cloud over their friendship that was only dispersed long afterwards, when they met again face to face.

By travelling at what was then express rate, the two friends arrived at Prague on 4th December, where they were received with open arms by Gänsbacher, who had already been apprised of their coming and made arrangements, at Weber's request, in connection with their concert. But he had gone much farther than that, and soon, by his diplomatic skill, the two artists were moving freely in the very inmost circles of the royal and aristocratic society of the city. But even more important than that was his meeting with Liebich, the director of the theatre, who, when they first met, greeted him heartily in the following terms: 'So you are *the* Weber! a capital fellow, I hear, and a very devil on the piano. Of course, you want me to buy your operas. Very well! I hear they are good. One fills up an evening; the other doesn't. I 'll give you 1,500 florins for the two. Is it a bargain?'

It was a bargain, subject to Weber's returning to Prague in the following spring to conduct the rehearsals. Meanwhile, the concert took place on an evening of snow, sleet and fog, which did not, however, debar the good citizens and tradespeople of Prague, any more than the aristocracy of the place, from filling the hall. *The Ruler of the Spirits* Overture was again a prominent item in the programme; Bärmann played one of the clarinet Concertos and Weber the piano Concerto in E flat major, both to enthusiastic applause. *Der erste Ton* was also performed, but not too well. To each the concert brought a clear profit of 1,240 florins, Viennese currency. Next day, they departed for Dresden where, armed with letters of introduction from the King and Queen of Bavaria, they hoped to have an opportunity of playing before the royal family of Saxony; but the court was absent, and after Carl Maria had 'heard the celebrated soprano Sassaroli sing vespers like a demi-god to Rastrelli's execrable music,' they turned their steps towards Leipzig, where they arrived on the 27th.

In Leipzig he met Rochlitz, the famous critic and editor of the *Musik-Zeitung*, with what might have been disastrous results for music in Germany; the brothers Seconda, who directed the Leipzig and Dresden theatres, but were entirely on the side of Italian opera and, if not antagonistic, utterly indifferent to the opera of Germany; and Härtel and Kühnel, the music publishers, from whom he received warm hospitality and kindness. His relations with Rochlitz turned his mind again towards literary pursuits and he began to work feverishly at his novel, *The Life of an Artist*, and small pieces of musical criticism, and he actually began to think of giving up music, for the time being at least, and devoting himself entirely to literature. But an invitation from the Duke of Saxe-Gotha for him and Bärmann to visit his court and to spend some time there, made him change his mind. He sent the following characteristic new year's greetings to Gänsbacher:

> Zounds! Jörgl, I had almost forgotten,
> *A happy New Year!!!!!!*
> Canone à 4 voci.

> Canone in infinitum sempre dacapo.
> No change in us !!
> And here is a hearty kiss, O.

The friends then gave a hasty concert, again successful, including *The Ruler of the Spirits* Overture and *Der erste Ton*; and on 17th January 1812 they departed for Gotha.

Duke Emil Leopold August of Saxe-Gotha was an eccentric,

but he was a great patron and genuine lover of art. The great composer Ludwig Spohr resided permanently at his court, and he would fain have had Weber do so also. Yet, in spite of the pressing invitation, when the musicians arrived at Gotha he was not there to receive them, and after many days had passed, and they had given a public concert on 25th January in order to restore their depleted funds, they received a polite and flowery letter from the absent duke, in which he expressed his regrets that, as unforeseen business demanded his almost immediate departure for Erfurt, he would not be able to enjoy Weber's society at Gotha as much as he had expected; but that he hoped in the autumn to allure him to a more protracted stay, and, meanwhile, trusted to see him as soon as possible in the palace, in order to have the pleasure of making his acquaintance. Weber was furious and drove to the palace with something akin to murder in his soul, but his rancour completely melted under the sunshine of the duke's smile and enchanting manners whenever they met, and thereafter the duke would scarcely allow him out of his sight for a single moment. Melodies had to be improvised on the guitar or piano and sung to the duke's poetry, impromptu performances were given with Spohr and Bärmann, and the duke's own compositions scrutinized and discussed. It began at last to get on Weber's nerves, but Spohr only laughed and said: 'Had I wanted to do all this intellectual business with the duke, I should long since have held no fiddlestick here.' But the artistic debauch came to an end at last, and the travellers set out again, armed with letters of introduction and 'thirty ducats and a couple of handsome antique rings,' this time for Weimar.

At Weimar the wanderers were received with the greatest kindness by the Grand Duchess Maria Pavlovna, daughter of the Emperor Paul of Russia and wife of Carl Friedrich, the hereditary prince of Weimar, to whom especially they had letters of introduction. They were practically given *carte blanche* in the palace, and many happy musical evenings were spent there. It was on one of these occasions that Weber met Weimar's Grand

Panjandrum, Goethe, who received him coldly, indeed almost rudely, and Wieland, who was not so great a poet, but a man of infinitely greater humanity and sensibility. Here he also met Vertuch, the editor of the *Allgemeine Literatur-Zeitung*, and Pius Alexander Wolff, whose dramatic arrangement of *Preciosa* he afterwards set to music. An attempt was made to have *Sylvana* produced in Weimar, but it was frustrated by the intrigues of *Kapellmeister* Müller. So, in due course, they left Weimar and arrived in Dresden again on 5th February, Weber miserably ill with a cold and rheumatism in his chest. After a few days in bed, however, he was busy trying to arrange a concert, which was eventually given on the 14th after 'thousands and millions of obstacles,' as he wrote to Gänsbacher. 'The people here,' he said, are far too poor and sordid,' and Bärmann, when he saw the subscription list, burst out laughing and exclaimed: 'They won't catch us in Dresden again in a hurry.' Their total receipts came to only twenty-eight thaler each. The audience, such as it was, was appreciative, however, although a critic described Weber's style as 'a mere imitation of Spohr, and his music strange and false in modulation and harmony when new.' But, as Weber was to find later, much to his cost, the Dresdeners of that time could see nothing good in any music that was not Italian. One bright spot stands out, however, in the Dresden sojourn of this year. He mentions it thus in a letter to Gänsbacher: 'On the 18th we were promoted to the high honour of playing before the king in his private apartments, a thing quite unexampled, and in return we were treated to a couple of pretty little gold boxes.' On the 19th they left Dresden, and arrived in Berlin on the 20th.

Immediately on his arrival in the Prussian capital, the composer was welcomed with open arms by Meyerbeer's parents, and urged to make the princely and luxurious dwelling of the wealthy banker his home for as long as he cared to stay in the city. But he was not happy, as what truly artistic soul ever could be in such a stronghold of crude Prussianism? 'On the whole,' he wrote, 'I do not like this place. The people are cold, full of talk, but devoid of heart, regular reviewer souls, carping at everything.' Still, it was his great desire to see *Sylvana* produced on the Berlin stage, and here the greatest of his struggles began.

The musical directors of the Berlin Opera, Bernhard Anselm Weber and Righini, 'received him with repelling coldness, shrugged their shoulders, and told him, after a hearing of the music, that, although his opera gave evidences of musical talent, it presented too many difficulties for representation on the stage.' The former even went so far as to declare 'that it was a very crude work, requiring considerable revision.' But the Crown Prince of Bavaria had written to King Friedrich Wilhelm III, who was a monarch of a particularly unamiable and unapproachable disposition, of Weber in the most flattering terms, and the king, quite contrary to his usual custom and disposition, accorded the composer a very warm and friendly reception, on hearing which, the two old diehards of the opera began to change their tactics, and the work was put into rehearsal. Then, suddenly, the chamberlain Friedrich von Drieberg, who at that time exercised a profound influence upon the musical life of Berlin, declared that the music was overladen with unnecessary effects, obscure in intention, the vocal parts sacrificed to the instrumental, and the whole composition wearisome and monotonous. Weber had met Drieberg at the Singakademie, to which, and its component *Liedertafel*, he had been introduced by the director, Zelter. The *Liedertafel* was a body which had originated and burst into patriotic flame from the smouldering fires that underlay the oppression by the French invader, and the far from extinct national spirit was there, swiftly finding expression in songs whose general themes were the fatherland, hearth and home, freedom and honour. The highly impressionable Weber soon became completely imbued with this spirit, and the result became apparent before long in a new cantata entitled *Turnierbankett*, composed to words by Bornemann and produced with conspicuous success in June; *Kriegs-Eid*, a chorus, with an accompaniment for wind instruments, which was performed by the soldiers of the Brandenburg brigade; and a number of patriotic songs. The fact of their being so closely associated together in this work caused Weber a good deal of heart-burning when Drieberg thus adversely criticized his *Sylvana*. But it also aroused the composer's spirit of self-criticism. 'There is much that is true in his remarks,' he wrote in his diary, 'but while duly acknowledging my faults, I will not in future lose confidence in myself, but bravely, prudently and watchfully march onwards in the path I have chosen.' His first act in fulfilment of this resolve was to undertake a complete revision of the opera, in the course of which he deleted two of the principal airs and composed two new ones in their stead, which afterwards gave him the satisfaction of being able to write:

My opera has won by these two new airs: and I have gained new notions about the true form of such pieces. I have remarked also that I must watch strictly over my manner of treatment. In the forms of my melodies the suspensions are too frequent and too prominent. I must also seek more variety in my tempos and my rhythms.

Still, the difficulties that lay in the way of the production of *Sylvana* increased. Righini died and the whole matter fell into the hands of Bernhard Anselm Weber, who seems to have had no insurmountable objection to the opera, but a deeply rooted prejudice against his young namesake. But Carl Maria calmly bided his time, making music while and where he could—he gave a second concert on 25th March with Bärmann, who, much to his regret, departed for Munich on the 28th—and forming new friendships with, to name but a few, Prince and Princess Radziwill, Tiedge the poet and novelist, and Heinrich Lichtenstein the zoologist. And at last, on 10th July, chiefly under the pressure of public opinion, the opera was performed. For once, all went well. The work was well cast, and after a bitter struggle for what was his undoubted right the composer was allowed to conduct.

During this period of struggle and intrigue in Berlin, Carl Maria received a letter from Gottfried Weber, conveying the sad news that on 16th April 1812 his father, old Franz Anton, had died suddenly at the age of seventy-eight. It is almost sacrilege to pry into a man's soul at such a time, but the few words he wrote in his diary must be quoted, if we are to obtain even the smallest conception of the true nobility of character that constituted the life's inspiration of Carl Maria von Weber:

He fell asleep at last, they say. May heaven grant him, in another world, the rest he knew not here! It is almost intolerable pain to me to think that I have not been able to bestow on him happier days. May God, in His mercy, bless him for all the love he bore me—all the love I so little deserved—and for the education he bestowed on me.

And to Rochlitz he wrote:

I am now indeed, alone, the consolation that I may still have a home in a friend's heart is my only support. You are right, I know; this perpetual wandering cannot be good for me. But how can I do otherwise than seek a fitting arena for the true exercise of my art? With time comes counsel. Meanwhile, I must go on my weary way, doing my best.

Weber left Berlin on 31st August 1812, somewhat sadly at having to part from several kind friends, the Beers in particular. 'This parting has been very painful,' he wrote. 'Where can I find such good loving souls again? God bless the dear ones! They tended me as their child!' His immediate destination was Gotha, but he made, by the way, a short stay at Leipzig, where he sold his overture, *The Ruler of the Spirits*, and some other pieces, and received from Rochlitz the words of a hymn, *In seiner Ordnung schafft der Herr*, which he set to music during the following two months at Gotha. He arrived in this town on 6th September, at the court of which he was received by the duke, 'with affection as well as friendliness.' But he was not happy there. The duke, like so many of these small German potentates, was an amiable tyrant, and artists like Weber were required to be at his beck and call at all hours of the day and night. Weber gave several concerts while he was there both of a public and semi-private character, and at one of the latter an incident occurred which marked him out as the consummate executive artist he was. The story may best be told in the words of his son:

The duchess had given him the minuet out of *Don Juan* as a subject [for improvisation] to which the duke had added two other motives as heterogeneous as possible in character, in order to increase his difficulties, laughingly saying: 'I think I have tamed the young lion now.' But Weber's spirits were high that evening. Difficulties were feathers to him in his brilliant state of mind; and he dashed into his task as if borne upon an irresistible torrent of artistic power. Now varying each theme severally, now weaving all the three together, until they formed a new and enchanting melody apart, now bursting into a rapturous jubilee of harmonies, he carried all hearers away on the powerful wings of his own inspiration. He was implored to write down this marvellous performance; but he resisted every entreaty, as he always did on such occasions. The spirit of improvisation had soared to the heavens and could be recalled no more.

When, in the early hours of the morning after that soul-stirring performance, Weber and Spohr were wending their way through the streets of Gotha, to their respective lodgings, they passed a military barracks, in which a body of Spanish soldiers, who were in garrison there during the war, were singing some of their national songs. The two composers were so profoundly struck by the originality of these melodies that they stood by the barrack-walls for two hours, drinking them in, and it is said that Weber found inspiration in these melodies, which he afterwards used extensively in *Preciosa*.

While sojourning at Gotha Weber paid another flying visit to Weimar, where he gave the Duchess Maria Pavlovna a few lessons in piano-playing, and he played over to her his piano Sonata No. 1 (Op. 24), which was dedicated to her. He also met Goethe once more, this time with more friendly results, and Wieland, to whom he played with his usual brilliance and charm. While at Gotha he composed the cantata already referred to, his piano Concerto in E flat major and a number of smaller pieces. But the need for money was again pressing. Franz Anton had left many debts behind him, which Carl Maria resolved to liqui-date as soon as possible. So, on 19th December 1812, he turned his face towards Leipzig, where he arrived on the 26th. He gave a concert there, sold the *Rübezahl* Overture and other pieces to Kühnel, the publisher, and early in January 1813 he set forth upon what he had planned to be a two years' journey to include Italy, Switzerland and France, but with Prague as his first place of call.

CHAPTER VI

PRAGUE

LITTLE did Weber imagine, when he set out from Gotha on his projected two years' tour of Europe, that his wandering days were really at an end and that the year 1813 was destined to be the first of a new era for him. He arrived in Prague on 12th January, highly elated with the success which had attended the first production of his hymn, *In seiner Ordnung schafft der Herr*, and his own performance of the E flat major Concerto. It was a success, he wrote, 'such as was perhaps scarcely ever known in Leipzig before. It is pronounced to be the first of concertos for effect and novelty. Truly these people, once so cold, have quite adopted me.' It was always a joyful occasion for him, too, when he was able to have a reunion with his old friend Gänsbacher; but the news the latter had to impart this time came as a surprise to him, appeared to shatter his cherished desire for further travel and loaded his mind with doubts. Wenzel Müller, the prolific Moravian composer, had just resigned the musical directorship of the Prague theatre, and the news Gänsbacher conveyed to Weber was to the effect that the manager, Liebich, was anxious that Carl Maria should accept the vacant appointment. At first Weber was disposed to decline the honour so unexpectedly thrust upon him, and even the arguments of the board of patrons, consisting of some of the most distinguished members of the Bohemian aristocracy, still left him undecided. But Gänsbacher himself haled him before the manager, affectionately called by his company 'Papa' Liebich, whose persuasive arguments not even Carl Maria could resist. The terms offered were most generous: a salary of 2,000 gulden (about £200), an annual benefit guaranteed at 1,000 gulden, a yearly leave of absence of three months' dura, tion and an absolutely free hand in the matter of organization and opera production. But what influenced him most in arriving at a final decision was the fact that the appointment would afford him 'the delight of paying all my debts, as an honourable fellow.' And although the opera company was to be disbanded at Easter, and to be reorganized by the new musical director only during the summer, Liebich insisted upon paying his salary from that very day.

Weber was thus immediately placed in an independent position, and he was still allowed a certain amount of scope in travelling, as fresh artists had to be sought for the reorganized opera. During the first three months of his sojourn in Prague he devoted himself to gaining a general understanding of the attitude of the inhabitants of the city towards his art, and to consolidating such friendships as, by the assistance of Gänsbacher, he succeeded in forming. The chief of these were with the Jung and Kleinwächter families, and with the music, loving Bohemian noble, Count Pachta, who will always be revered as the founder of the Prague Con, servatorium. On 6th March he made his first formal appearance before his new constituents with a concert that was conspicuously successful. Then, on 27th March, in his quest for singers, he set out for Vienna, but, just before leaving, he received a letter from Caroline Brandt, informing him that she was without an engagement and seeking employment. He had not forgotten the fine performance of the title, part this talented young singer and accomplished artist had given in his opera *Sylvana*, when it was first produced at Frankfort on 17th September 1810, and, little dreaming of what the ultimate outcome of it would be, he engaged her there and then.

Arriving in Vienna, he found himself at once in the midst of a circle of friends: Vogler, Bärmann, Spohr and Meyerbeer. He seems, at this time, to have had some difference with Meyerbeer, who was enjoying the most brilliant success as a pianist in Vienna, for he writes to Gänsbacher:

78

With Beer the matter stands thus: I met him with all the old love and cordiality, and made no allusion to what had passed, and he too has not as yet taken any notice of our difference; on the surface we appear to be just as we were, but my implicit trust in him is at an end. Bär, mann, and still more Vogler, complain of him, amazed by his pride and insatiable vanity and his touchiness, all equally great, and which must repel every one.

And, a fortnight later, he again refers to the matter: 'I am appar, ently on the old footing with Beer, but pure and entire trust can never return; to this a thousand other causes also contribute, too numerous to write about,' so that the dispute must have been more serious than transpires in any of the preceding letters.

While in Vienna he also made many new friends, including Salieri, Mosel, Castelli, Moscheles, Hummel and the Counts Palffy and Dietrichstein. His reactions towards some of these are interesting. Vogler was most anxious that he should court the friendship of Salieri, but the latter was known to have hated Mozart, and Weber remained obdurate to all Vogler's efforts to cement a friendship between them. His invariable answer was: 'No; I will have nothing to do with him.' He thought Hummel's pianistic style 'correct and hard,' and he wrote to Gänsbacher that he had found everything beneath his expectations. 'The great lights appear so little when seen closely,' he continued, 'Moscheles, Hummel, Kruft, etc., are all only stars of good but common magnitude.' The critics, on the other hand, took an entirely different view when they heard Weber himself at a matinée concert which, for once, was scarcely a success. 'His perform, ance,' they declared, 'wanted neatness and precision, and was inferior to that of such pianists as Moscheles and Hummel,' a declaration which amused him exceedingly. 'The criticism of my concert made me laugh heartily,' he wrote to Gänsbacher, but there was probably more in it than appeared even to Weber him, self, for he was again suffering from his old bilious disorder. Indeed in hardly any sense at all, apart from his having made close and intimate acquaintance with several new operas, was his visit to Vienna a success. As his indisposition grew upon him, he hurried back to Prague and arrived there in a more or less delirious condition which, but for the tender care that was taken of him by Count Pachta, who discovered the state he was in purely by accident, might well have proved fatal.

By the end of the summer of 1813, however, Carl Maria had sufficiently recovered to enable him to plunge into the task of reorganizing and stabilizing the Prague opera. His entire com/ pany, which included Caroline Brandt, was, with the exception of three members, new. As Spitta truly remarks: 'He entirely reorganized the whole system and developed a marvellous capacity for that kind of work. It now became evident that it was not in vain that he had passed his childhood behind the scenes, and been a *Kapellmeister* at eighteen.'

He displayed untiring energy in disciplining and bringing to heel his vocal and instrumental forces—an unruly band at best. And that was probably the least of his troubles. The following letter to Gottfried Weber is illuminating to an extent that only a personal testimony of that nature could be:

The orchestra is in complete rebellion, and, in the midst of all this worry, I have to correspond with all the new members to be engaged; to draw up their contracts; to bring the confused library into order, and write a catalogue; to correct scores; to prepare the scenarii of the operas first to be produced; to describe scenery to the painters, costumes to the costumiers. And then, one is never left a moment in peace from the influx of people. I ought to go to Eger for the restoration of my health; but the press of business is so great that any thought of the kind is impossible. I get up at six o'clock, and am often at work until mid/ night. How happy shall I be when the great machine is at last put in movement!—then I shall feel that the victory is more than half won.

It is a remarkable fact that wherever Weber went he was con/ stantly sought after by the most intellectually eminent personalities of the place. On his return to Prague he was soon the centre of a glowing circle comprising such celebrities as Niebuhr, Hum/ boldt, Stein, Schwartzenberg, Ludwig Tieck, Ludwig Robert

THE NATIONAL THEATRE, PRAGUE

and Clemens Brentano.[1]   He was seldom so fortunate in respect
of his female acquaintances, however, and Prague was destined,
before long, to be the scene of one of the most devastating of
Weber's love affairs, and that under the very eyes of Caroline
Brandt, his future wife.   On 12th August he began the rehearsals
of Spontini's *Fernand Cortez*, with which he proposed to inaugu-
rate his first season with the now practically completed company.
But soon he began to have further trouble with officials of the opera
themselves, and with members of his orchestra, who for some
months had been openly rebellious and had aired their grievances
to each other in his presence, but in the Czech language, of which
Weber was ignorant.   Nothing daunted, however, in the midst
of all his duties the composer had plunged into a study of the
language, of which he soon acquired a working knowledge, and
about the end of July we find him writing to Gänsbacher:
'The members of my orchestra are gradually submitting to the
iron sceptre, and knuckling under to me.' Yet 'the iron sceptre'
notwithstanding, there seems to have been a great deal of laxity in
connection with those who were allowed to attend the rehearsals
that were now in full swing.   Among the company that was
constantly in attendance was a dancer named Brunetti, whose wife,
then a woman of thirty-one and the mother of five children, was
also frequently to be found there.   She had originally been a
member of the ballet, but had risen to the rank of a vocal artist,
and she had occasionally sung some of the lighter parts with
conspicuous success.   She had an attractive appearance and
considerable charm, which she employed in the exercise of all the
arts of coquetry, of which she was complete mistress.   Weber
was thrown much into her company, and very soon she had him

[1] It is interesting to note that Brentano was then engaged in the
preparation of an opera libretto on the subject of Tannhäuser which later
he pressed upon Weber, but apparently the subject did not interest the
composer, or time and opportunity was then lacking for the necessary
concentration to enable him to embark upon the composition of a new
opera on such a subject, for nothing came of it.

dangling at her 'apron string' and completely in her power. She
was utterly unprincipled, and her sole motive in captivating the
young conductor was, apparently, the feeling of satisfaction she
acquired by having him in her toils. She first induced him to
give up his present lodgings and take up his abode in Brunetti's
house. Then she took a delight in flaunting him in the face of
the horrified and scornful society of Prague. And, worst of all,
she used all her arts to keep him in a state of maddening jealousy
and doubt as to her feelings for him. The following extracts
from his diary can give no more than a partial idea of the agonizing
feelings she kept constantly surging through him:

November 8th. Terrible scene [with Therese]! It is really a hard fate
that the first woman whom I love truly and with all my heart should
believe me faithless; and, before God, that is false. The enchanting
dream is over. Confidence cannot return. Calina[1] came; painful
situation! The chain broke!

November 9th. Seen Therese: unspeakably painful explanation.
Flow of tears caused by the pressure of sorrow; feverish agitation.

November 14th. Again seen Therese. Long estrangement: at last
reconciliation; indescribably affecting, our sufferings vanishing as if by
enchantment. So powerfully does the mind affect the body.

November 23rd.—She loves me not; if she did, would it be possible
for her to speak with such warmth of her first love, to dwell with delight
on each small incident of its commencement, to relate her own peculiar
feelings of that time? For me she never experienced them; and could
she be so pitiless if she loved me? No. This dream has also fled;
I must never know this bliss, but always stand alone. Here I love
for the first time. And this woman possesses every quality which could
make me happy. She fancies sometimes that she loves me—but it is
not true. The necessity of a confidant, on whose rectitude she could
implicitly rely, drew her to me. She can sit by the hour quietly beside
me; but if by chance the conversation turns upon Hans, then she glows
with rapture. I will now again shut myself up in myself, and she,

---

[1] A wealthy lover with whom she afterwards lived.

Caroline, on her part, was not a 'pink and white,' trusting simpleton either. She had not been blind to the Brunetti liaison, and being herself of a somewhat temperamental character, she was not disposed to accept Weber merely on his face value. She was constantly assailed by doubts, fears, uncertainties and jealousies, and the course of their love did not always run smooth. But he was now entirely freed from the trammels of Therese Brunetti, who still, however, did all in her power to make trouble between them.

Weber remained for three weeks, as he had intended, at Liebwerda, resting, taking the baths and the waters, and dreaming of his beloved Lina. On 31st July 1814 he set out for Berlin and arrived there on 3rd August. Here he found himself in a very different place from that of his previous visit, and he was immediately immersed in an atmosphere of glowing enthusiasm and tense excitement. The battle of Leipzig, fought on 18th October 1813, had left its mark. As Benedict succinctly puts it, there was

the French invader driven over the Rhine; France itself conquered by the allied powers after the most stubborn resistance; Paris taken [30th March 1814]; the mighty Napoleon, from an empire larger than that of Augustus, exiled to a puny island, Elba; Louis XVIII reigning as king in France, a congress in Vienna, where all the nations of Europe were represented, regulating its destinies.

Germany was free. But it was a freedom gained by the might of the sword, and it was hardly surprising that the whole body of the people should therefore unite in glorification of the sword. Weber, whose whole being was a packet of romance, and whose second passion was a super-ardent love for the German fatherland, was immediately infected by the patriotic furore and, under this inspiration, he was soon adding to the myriads of war songs that were pouring from the pens of poets and composers like water from a fountain. The favourite poet of the day was Theodor Körner, who had died for his country on the field of Gadebusch, and his song-cycle, *Leier und Schwert*, soon appealed to Carl Maria with a force that was presently to bear fruit in the creation of some of the most beautiful and distinctive of all the *Lieder* that were born at that time.

It was then that Brentano and Weber discussed the proposal of an opera on the subject of Tannhäuser, and for a short time the composer's heart glowed with the idea; but the time for the romantic opera was not yet, and he soon cooled off. While in Berlin he gave a concert and effected another representation of *Sylvana*, but, although he himself was satisfied with the results, neither was particularly successful. He benefited greatly, however, both in health and spirits, from his renewed association with his many old friends, who on their part did everything possible to keep him in the city, but without success. He left Berlin, there-fore, on his return journey to Prague, on 7th September, and paid flying visits to Leipzig and Weimar as well as one of rather longer duration to Gotha, where he met his old friend Duke Emil August and spent some happy days with him in his old feudal castle of Gräfentonna. Regarding this visit he writes to Caro-line: 'I drove here with the kind of anxious feeling I always entertain when I have not seen a friend for some time, and fear to be received with less warmth than I anticipated or consider myself entitled to. My fears, however, were this time groundless, for the duke welcomed me as cordially as one could wish.'

Two days later his patriotic fervour at last found definite musical expression in the composition of two of the greatest of Germany's national melodies, *Lützows wilde Jagd* and the *Schwertlied*, both written to poems by Körner. In another letter to Caroline, he relates how he was inspired to the creation of great things by the stimulating ideas and sentiments enunciated by the duke:

There are few who would find themselves satisfied in the midst of this solitude in which the duke rejoices so much. Here, far removed from the turmoil of the court, he is surrounded only by those he really likes. Generally he is content everywhere with his boundlessly fertile imagination. What he most delights in is to sit near me at the piano, to dictate as it were sentiments and images which I have to embody in my performances, so that he invents and relates whole romances while I illustrate them with my music, and, through tones, amplify them still further. So passes day after day, and I may rely on returning to my room every evening enriched by some new idea or impression.

But Liebich was getting anxious about the fixing of contracts for the approaching opera season, and, yielding to his frenzied entreaties, Weber reached Prague again on 25th September, a full fortnight earlier than his leave stipulated. On the road between Gotha and Prague he composed a third of the patriotic Körner songs, *Männer und Buben*, which was no less masterly than the two that had preceded it, or than the remaining songs from *Leier und Schwert*, which, as Benedict asserts, 'at once raised his popularity to an almost unprecedented degree, wherever the German tongue was spoken, and wherever a German heart beat.'

He found that things had not been going on too well in Prague during his absence. Franz Clement, who had been acting as his deputy, although a very good violinist, was a very bad director, and Weber had to begin a certain amount of reorganization all over again. He returned also to the backbiting and scandal-mongering of Therese Brunetti, and the petty jealousies and recriminations of Caroline Brandt, which were a perpetual source of worry and distress to him.

The rest of the year was a period of unremitting labour. By the end of the year he had finished the composition of all the songs in *Leier und Schwert*. His great achievement at the opera was the production of Beethoven's *Fidelio*, which took place on 21st November. He had studied and rehearsed it with the greatest possible care, and it was admirably performed, but very indifferently received. Weber was furious. 'On the 21st,' he wrote to Gänsbacher, 'I gave Beethoven's *Fidelio*, which went to perfection; what magnificent things are in that music, but they don't understand it. It is enough to drive one mad ! Kasperl [Punch and Judy] ¹ is their level !'

The work again began to tell upon his health, and towards the end of the year he once more became a victim of depression. He therefore clung more than ever to Caroline, and early in the new year he asked her to become his wife, but only on condition that she should renounce the stage for ever. Caroline, probably influenced by her worldly-wise mother, hesitated and asked for time to consider. Scandal had been busy with their names, however, and Weber resolved to leave Prague in order to save her reputation. But not even to this would she agree. Their differ-ences on these matters grew wider as time went on, and they nearly came to a fatal conclusion when his new work *Leier und Schwert* was received with enthusiastic applause and rapturous praise. Caroline had always regarded Napoleon as 'the greatest hero of his age,' and she considered that Weber had committed a gross outrage upon her feelings by the implied attacks on him which she considered were embodied in the work. Political disputes, added to lovers' quarrels, led to a bitterness that seemed to be carrying them steadily on to a final disaster. In order to distract his mind from these cares and worries, he plunged more recklessly than ever into work and composition. Many operas were rehearsed and produced in a manner that brought back much of its ancient glory to the Prague opera, and for his own benefit he gave a fine performance of Mozart's *Così fan tutte*, with fresh words and under the title of *The Magic Test*. This brought him the sum of 1,204 florins. He composed several works, including an *Adagio* for piano, flute and cello that was afterwards extended to become his Trio for these instruments (Op. 63). Two other works he wrote at this time have disappeared.

Matters between the lovers did not improve and a crisis at last

¹ Guy de Charnacé, the translator of Weber's letters into French, confuses the German Punch with Kaspar, one of the foresters in *Der Freischütz*, and explains it in a note as 'Personnage du Freyschütz,' which, of course, is meaningless and ridiculous.

occurred when he engaged an actress named Christine Böhler for the opera. This roused in the heart of Caroline Brandt an unreasoning and causeless fit of jealousy, and she now became as insistent on Weber's leaving Prague as she had formerly been against it. He had been offered posts in Berlin and Königsberg towards the end of the preceding year, but had declined both. But, until he had finally decided upon his future course of action, he anticipated his leave of absence for 1815 by a month, and, with letters of introduction from some of the royalties there, 'left Prague in deep sorrow on 7th June, and went to solitary Hradec, where I was received with cordial and considerate friendliness.' He stayed there for ten days and then proceeded to Munich, where he was received and lodged with welcoming joy by his old friend, colleague and former fellow-traveller, Bärmann.

Shortly after Weber's arrival in Munich the news of the Allies' victory over the French at the battle of Waterloo came to remove, once again, the nightmare of another French invasion from the minds of the German people, and the city went half mad with joy. On that very day the composer had made the acquaintance of Wohlbrück, the renowned actor and poet, and after the former had attended the thanksgiving service in the church of St Michael, where, listening to the rendering of the *Te Deum*, he had felt an irresistible urge to compose something to celebrate the event himself, he, by chance, again encountered the author, and told him of his idea. Wohlbrück was immediately fired by Weber's enthusiasm and promised to supply the words which, under the title of *Kampf und Sieg*, he submitted early in August.

Meanwhile Weber gave successful concerts in Munich and Augsburg, but melancholy had apparently 'marked him for her own' as a consequence of the unhappy correspondence that continued between him and Caroline. After receiving the completed poem from Wohlbrück, he began at once to work out his musical ideas, as was his custom, in his head, and it was the 17th August before he first put pen to paper. Even then he only completed two choruses. At last he informed Caroline that he must soon return to Prague and she replied that in the circumstances [1] connected with their engagement, their union was impossible and it were better that the engagement should end. Weber's despair, on receiving that letter, was heart-rending in its intensity, and he returned to Prague on 7th September to meet his old friend Gäns-bacher, who helped to console him and to distract his mind to some extent from dwelling too much upon his loss. He gradually induced him also to go further into society, and one day the two friends set out together to the new house which Liebich had acquired on the outskirts of the city, in response to an invitation from the manager himself. What happened thereafter, may best be told in the baron's own words:

The two friends found a large party assembled, in which artists of the theatre mingled, in the pleasantest sociability, with members of the highest society in Prague. Caroline Brandt was present, of course; she was the favourite, the darling, the spoiled child of all. Here at last the lovers met face to face. After a moment's trembling hesitation, they looked into each other's eyes. Somehow their hands were clasped together; and thus the tie was once more bound, never to be sundered more. After all the storms, there was a sudden burst of sunshine. Weber's happiness was restored.

The composer now entered upon the new season's work with a fresh zest and vigour. As usual, his first task, on his return, was the tightening up of discipline which had lapsed somewhat, and he then proceeded to put into rehearsal Meyerbeer's third

[1] The actual reasons for this temporary estrangement between the lovers are a little obscure, but Weber's son may not have been very far from the truth when he wrote: 'The real affection she cherished for her lover . . . had been crushed, in fancy only, by the cold prudential counsels [of her mother], the detractions, the backbitings and the female tittle-tattle which had never ceased to assail her during his absence. . . . Her feminine vanity may have been piqued also by his apparent well-studied calm.'

opera, *Alimelek or The Two Caliphs*, and in order to counteract adverse criticism which had attended the work elsewhere, and to forestall it in Prague, he wrote and published in a local paper a detailed critical article on the opera, an action of very doubtful taste, but one that he afterwards repeated on several occasions and of which he set a fashion that has continued down to our own times, not always with the happiest results. The opera was given on 22nd October, and in spite of all the *Kapellmeister's* efforts, it fell flat, although later representations were more favourably received.

His reconciliation with Caroline had now given the composer a serener state of mind, and his work on the cantata *Kampf und Sieg* progressed with such rapidity that he had it completed by 11th December, and, with only four rehearsals, produced on the 22nd. A more unpropitious time could scarcely have been chosen for the production of a new work. The Christmas festivities, if they had not actually begun, were absorbing everybody's thoughts and, to make matters worse, the weather on the night was almost as bad as it could possibly be. The first part of the concert was an utter fiasco, but when the cantata came on all was changed, and such a scene of enthusiasm ensued as few composers ever witness in connection with their own works in a lifetime. Even financially it had proved a success, and the year closed with Weber's being 10,000 Viennese florins (£400) in pocket. This enabled him to pay off the bulk of his still outstanding Stuttgart debts, which were completely liquidated by February in the following year.

As time advanced towards the spring of 1816 Weber became more and more dissatisfied with his position in Prague. He made up his mind either to continue his professional tour, or to find a post more worthy of his abilities and achievements. When this became known Liebich and other friends in the city did all in their power to dissuade him. Caroline was particularly distressed and induced her mother to lodge him in her own home. He was just on the point of succumbing to these many inducements to remain, when a new president of the theatre forwarded a memorial to Liebich expressing dissatisfaction with the conduct of the opera since 1812, and this irrevocably fixed Weber's determination to resign.

In the spring he sent handsomely bound copies of *Kampf und Sieg* through influential channels to the Emperor of Austria, the Prince Regent of England, the Kings of Prussia, Holland, Saxony, Bavaria and Denmark and to other sovereign princes.[1] Along with the copy he forwarded to the King of Prussia he had begged for permission to give a performance of the work at the Berlin opera house on the anniversary of the battle of Waterloo for the benefit of invalided soldiers, and the request was granted; but at the same time an application he had made for the then vacant second *Kapellmeister's* appointment in the capital was declined in favour of Bernhard Romberg, the famous violoncellist. Count Brühl, who had been pressing for Weber's election to the post, apologized to him for having allowed Romberg to be thus forced upon him, and the orchestra, on the occasion of the cantata's performance, gave him the strongest proofs of attachment and esteem. In Berlin, although he was once more staying with the kindly Beers, and although, with perhaps the single exception of Bernhard Anselm Weber, whose ancient hostility to his great namesake was as virulent as ever, he was received everywhere with the greatest possible degree of friendly warmth, his 'evil star' was again in the ascendent, for such a downpour of rain came down on the evening of the first performance of the cantata that the theatre was only half filled. But his part of the concert, as on other occasions, was an outstanding success. He wrote to Caroline:

I must tell you of the brilliant success of last night. Bernhard Anselm's overture was played in solemn silence. Then came my

---

[1] Fourteen copies in all were thus sent abroad, but by 4th August 1816 they had 'brought very little; a medal from Prussia and a gold box from Saxony and the Netherlands; so eleven crowned heads are still in arrear.' (Letter to Gänsbacher.)

patriotic songs, which created so much uproar that *Lützows wilde Jagd* had to be repeated—an unheard-of event in the Berlin opera house. Then came my cantata, which was admirably executed both by orchestra and singers, and excited the wildest enthusiasm. I thought that at the point where *God save the King* is introduced after the battle, the applause would never end. The king dispatched Count Brühl to me directly, to tell me how deeply moved he had been, and that he desired to hear it once more. So, *nolens volens,* I must remain here a few days longer and repeat the work next week.

While in Berlin, although more material honours were refused to the composer himself, notwithstanding Brühl's very persistent endeavours to obtain them for him, Weber was more successful in representations he personally made on behalf of his beloved Lina, thereby procuring a starring engagement of six appearances for her at the opera house. He left Berlin, in the company of Meyerbeer's father, on 9th July, *en route* for Leipzig where he received an offer to conduct the German Opera there at a salary of 1,500 thaler. But, continuing his journey to Carlsbad, he met, probably by an arrangement made on his behalf by Count Vitz-thum of Eckstädt, the equerry to the King of Saxony, this count's brother, Court-Marshal Count Heinrich Vitzthum, who was the director of the royal opera at Dresden. The last-named had conceived the idea of establishing a German opera in the Saxon capital, where hitherto only Italian opera had been the vogue, and he forthwith offered Weber the post of *Kapellmeister,* which, after some hesitation on the question of terms, was accepted.

He then hurried back to Prague and, as usual after an absence, found the affairs of the theatre in a state bordering on chaos. Liebich, who had long suffered from a painful disease, was at last on his deathbed, and his wife had endeavoured to keep the theatre alive; but, as Baron von Weber remarks, she 'was little loved; her temper was bad—her manner intolerably imperious,' and the natural consequences were only too apparent. But Carl Maria again worked with the power and determination of a Trojan, in spite of much discouragement and many false accusations of his having neglected his duties, to bring it up to its former standards before handing over the reins of office to his successor. He once more worked up several of the old operas and gave a performance of Meyerbeer's *Alimelek* on the occasion of the visit of that com-poser's parents, who were intensely delighted with the opera. He also revived Spohr's *Faust*. But his chief tasks lay in classifying and arranging all the books, contracts and general archives of the Opera and in putting in order the scenery, dresses and properties, so that any opera in the repertory could be staged at once, with the minimum of trouble and toil. He also wrote out full details of the plans he had had in view and suggestions for operas that might be produced in the future; of the chief characteristics and abilities of each member of the company; of the nature and idiosyncrasies of the Prague public; and of the system of organization he had instituted. All this trouble he took entirely in the interests of the art he loved. It was no part of his duties, least of all on the eve of his departure. He left for Berlin on 7th October, accompanied by Caroline Brandt and her mother. Whatever feelings of bitterness against the directorate of the Prague Opera he may have entertained on leaving, he certainly could have none against his former fellow-workers, for we are told that 'the whole body of the com-pany, from orchestra and stage, from high to low, from leading singers and first tragedians to carpenters, thronged round his carriage with broken voices and tears in their eyes to sob to him a farewell.'

The reception Weber received on his arrival in Berlin was again overwhelming, and Caroline and her mother were struck dumb with astonishment on beholding the marks of respect, admiration and attachment that were showered upon him. From that moment the relations between the lovers changed, and happi-ness, so far as these relations went, became their future lot. Caro-line's natural charm soon captivated the Berliners almost as much as did the fact that she was the chosen of their much-loved idol. On 19th November Lichtenstein, with whom Weber was lodging on this occasion, gave an oyster party, to which the composer was so partial, and there Caroline at last consented to become engaged to him. He immediately announced the fact to the assembled company, who hailed the news with unrestrained joy and the wildest acclamations. Next day she preceded her lover to Dresden, where he had procured an engagement for her through Count Vitzthum. In Berlin, Weber renewed his acquaintance with E. T. A. Hoffmann, at whose house he met Ludwig Devrient, the greatest actor of his day. He was greatly interested in Hoffmann's romantic opera, *Undine*, and was present at its first performance. Meanwhile negotiations regarding the terms of his appointment at Dresden were still proceeding, but at last all was more or less satisfactorily arranged. It was a joyful Christmas morning of 1816, when he received a letter containing full confirmation of the appointment.

Long did I look on Count Vitzthum's letter without daring to open it [he wrote to Caroline]. Was it joy? Was it sorrow? At length I took courage. It was joy! So round I went to all my friends, who laughed and made the new royal *Kapellmeister* the most reverential bows. I must rig myself out now in true court style. Perhaps I ought to wear a pigtail to please the Dresdeners! What do you think? I ought to have an extra kiss from you for this good news.

CHAPTER VII

DRESDEN

IN going from Prague to Dresden Weber jumped out of the frying-pan into the fire. Yet never before had his prospects seemed rosier. The reconciliation with Caroline Brandt and the almost certainty of his marriage in the following autumn, added to the idea of a royal *Kapellmeister's* post, and what he believed was to be a happy change of scenes and faces, seemed to have given him an entirely new lease of life, for while he was putting everything in order for his successor in Prague, and filling engagements, social and professional, in Berlin, the creative urge, doubtless stimulated by the happy turn events had taken, must have been strong upon him. During these few weeks he wrote two beautiful songs, *Die Gefangenen* and *Die freien Sänger*, a Divertimento for piano and guitar and a great *Scena and Aria* which he did at the special request of Count Brühl, who wished to have them for insertion in Cherubini's *Lodoiska*, to be sung by the *prima donna* Anna Milder, a favourite at that time. Weber also completed his fine pianoforte Sonata in A flat major and wrote the greater part of that in D minor as well as of the *Duo concertante* for clarinet and piano. He took over his new duties on 13th January 1817. The appointment, according to the usual custom, was only for one year, but there had never been an instance of its not having been transformed into a life engagement. The town, situated in a broad, smiling valley, was an ideal place for a man of Weber's uncertain state of health. But King Friedrich August of Saxony, having been the recipient of numerous dignities from the late Emperor Napoleon, had become a devoted ally and admirer of that ruler. Weber came into Saxony, therefore, with an evil political reputation which, with *Leier und*

Schwert as a standing testimony against him, could neither be slurred over nor denied. The chief minister of state at this time was a certain Count Einsiedel, a man of considerable refinement, who was not without ability himself; but he was a bureaucrat and formalist of the worst possible type, who immediately quelled every ambition on the part of his understrappers and would allow only a level standard of mediocrity to exist within his jurisdiction. Until the advent of Weber the only productions that were allowed to have a representation in the Dresden opera house were those of Italian origin. Dresden, indeed, was the last stronghold of Italian music in Germany. This was largely the result of the royal family's having changed their religion to Roman Catholicism and of their having adopted Italy as their spiritual home. As might have been expected of such a man as Count Einsiedel, he was one of the staunchest props of the Italianized opera and had the loyal support of practically the whole of the local aristocracy. When, therefore, Count Heinrich von Vitzthum, who was the chief director of the theatre, began to suggest the establishment of a national German opera in the town, the opposition of the aristocratic party was absolutely solid. The general public being entirely in favour of it, however, the king, with not too good a grace, gave his consent, and a new arrangement was effected whereby a second *Kapellmeister* was to be appointed to act as colleague to the reigning Italian conductor, Francesco Morlacchi. Morlacchi, who had originally made a name for himself as a violinist, was a sound musician and a talented and industrious composer of operas, but an indifferent conductor. He had been educated by the Jesuits and was sly, servile and a master of the art of intrigue—the perfect state servant in Count Einsiedel's eyes. Weber, on the other hand, had no time for such unworthy methods. Music, to him, was the one thing that mattered and, so far as that alone was concerned it made no difference to him who, or of what nationality, the composer might be so long as the music was good. But he himself was the composer of the songs in *Leier und Schwert*, and that constituted a weapon in the hands of

Einsiedel, which he used against the new *Kapellmeister* with deadly effect, never losing an opportunity of reminding the king of Weber's joint authorship of this paean of triumph over the defeated Napoleon. The count, on his first interview with the composer, had conceived a deep-rooted antipathy to him, and this prevailed to the end.

On the evening of Weber's arrival at Dresden he stumbled upon an old musical acquaintance named Schmiedel, who held a small musical post at the court. He greeted the composer kindly, gave him some insight into the state of affairs in Saxon court circles, and straightway found him a dwelling-place in what was known as the 'Italian Village,' an ideal spot close to the city walls, so named from the fact that the Italians who had been brought to Dresden to build the Roman Catholic church had been the first occupants of the beautiful little cottages there. His first visitor, after Schmiedel, was Morlacchi who, having heard of his colleague's arrival, hastened to 'pay his respects.' One aspect of Morlacchi's cunning had been his refusal to learn or to recognize the German language, and he knew very little French, so that the awkwardness which arose at their first meeting acted as a stimulant upon the indefatigable Weber, who there and then resolved to master the Italian language, as he had previously, in Prague, made up his mind to learn Czech. In a phenomenally short time he was able to speak the favourite language of the Saxon court almost as well as Morlacchi himself. This proved to be a great advantage in his dealings with the material out of which he was expected to mould a German opera. This material was of good quality both musically and histrionically, but natur-ally it was mixed and, owing to a laxity that had crept in through indolence or through some underhand intention on the part of Morlacchi, sadly lacking in discipline.

Weber detected this at the very first moment of his meeting with the company. After having been introduced by Count Vitz-thum, who presented him as the new *Kapellmeister* and remarked that 'great value had evidently been laid in the highest quarters on the establishment of the German opera, since so distinguished a man had been selected to be placed at its head,' Weber greeted his forces in a few pleasant and friendly words, assuring them of his hearty goodwill and of his intention to interest himself in all of them equally. He then proceeded on a sterner note. 'In return,' he said, 'I expect implicit obedience. I shall be just, but pitilessly severe with all who need severity, myself among the number.'

This was no idle threat, as was soon to appear. The vice that prevailed among the Italian singers of that period—the habit of altering the written music in performance, of interpolating runs, turns and even cadenzas and of generally pandering to whatever vitiated taste might be in fashion with the public for the time being —was rampant in Dresden, and it was not confined to the Italian singers. The first opera to be given under Weber's direction was Méhul's *Joseph in Egypt*, and on the opening night, 30th January, a young bass, Genast, who was musician enough to know better, burst into a cadenza in the duet between Jacob and Benjamin, which ruptured the severe simplicity of the music and went far to spoil the scene altogether. To Weber this was an unpardonable offence; it was, indeed, in his opinion, sinning against the light, and a glance from his eyes was sufficient to upset the young singer, who, to avoid Weber, attempted to leave the theatre with only a cloak thrown over his costume. But the conductor was too quick for him: 'What stupid sort of trick was that you played?' he exclaimed. 'Do you think that Méhul, if he had wanted any such crinkumcrankum, could not have done it better than you? I will have no more of it in future! Now, goodnight. Go home and sleep off your drunken freaks!'

This sort of thing aroused a considerable amount of opposition and resentment at first, but the company was on the whole sound enough fundamentally. Apart from the few sycophants and timeservers who are seldom absent from any body of workers, it soon settled down to work contentedly and in good order. Of Weber, at this time, his pupil Benedict remarks: 'Respected and feared at first, beloved and almost worshipped afterwards, Weber exerted a magic influence on all his subordinates.'

Before this had come to pass, however, the new *Kapellmeister* had had his first bitter experience of the petty double-dealing and sordid intrigue of the small German courts of that age. Strange as it may seem, two men who proved to be his best friends in Dresden were of Italian origin: Franz Seconda, who had been the director of the theatre for many years previous to the Russian occupation and the theatre's becoming an appendage of the Saxon court; and the baritone singer Luigi Bassi, for whom Mozart had written the part of Don Giovanni in 1787. Weber had known the latter in Prague [1] and they had met again as old friends who mutually respected each other; but the singer expressed angry surprise at the fact that his 'dear young *Kapellmeister*' should have so far condescended as to accept a subordinate position under 'that abominable Morlacchi.' Weber was at first at a loss to understand what his friend was driving at and explained that he had been engaged by Count Vitzthum as joint *Kapellmeister* with Morlacchi. 'Nothing of the kind,' replied Bassi. 'It makes no difference what may have been the terms of your engagement with the count; that will doubtless be disowned in higher quarters. Your diploma, which I have seen, designates you a director of the German opera, not *Kapellmeister* at all!' Weber's surprise and indignation at such duplicity may better be imagined than described. He had noticed, on his arrival, a certain degree of constraint on the part of Count Vitzthum, but had thought little of it. But now all was clear to him. He stopped all preparations for his investiture and resolved to leave Dresden at once should Bassi's information prove to be accurate, and he rushed to the theatre to demand an explanation from the count. That wretched man confirmed all Weber had been told, but he entreated the composer, 'for both

---

[1] In a letter to Gänsbacher, written from Prague on 1st December 1814, Weber remarks: 'That old Don Juan, Bassi, is here just now, and boards with the Liebichs.'

their sakes, and for the sake of the art they both loved, to remain at least for a time and see whether amends could not, after all, be made.' Weber, however, would give no such undertaking, and he left the count in a towering rage. The next morning he again declared that he neither would nor could work in a position subordinate to Morlacchi; but, on the count's renewed supplications, he at last agreed to assist in the furtherance of the German opera scheme until a new director could be found, though he declared that on no consideration whatever would he remain longer unless he were placed in a position exactly equal to that of Morlacchi. These terms the count could only accept unconditionally.

In giving an account of what had occurred to Caroline the composer wrote: 'The determination I have displayed cannot fail, I trust, in producing a good result. I have shown that I am not a man to be lightly dealt with, that under any circumstances I am prepared to act as firmly as honourably, and that I shall never be put to it to find an existence elsewhere.'

Two months later, in recounting the matter to Gänsbacher, he wrote in a somewhat similar strain:

I was obliged to begin my career here with much annoyance, and many struggles against cabals; and in fact I was several times on the point of setting off again; but all this seems eventually to have done good, in so far as it is now evident to them that they have to do with a man who will not permit himself to be trifled with, and who has sufficient independence not to submit to any kind of neglect or want of respect.

Count Vitzthum assured Weber, and Weber accepted his assurances, that he would do everything he could to redress the wrong that had been done to him, but Weber drew up a complete and formal statement of all the circumstances of the case, for submission to the king. This, added to the pleadings which the count honestly made on his behalf, was successful in finally counteracting the machinations of Count Einsiedel, Morlacchi and the other Italians who were working against him, for, within a fortnight, Vitzthum was able to inform him that the king had signed the diploma appointing him *Kapellmeister* and given orders that the fact should be communicated to all personages connected either with the Italian or the German opera, or with the music of the church. Weber, afterwards, had many similar troubles to contend with at this somewhat ridiculous court, but he had established his position, and in later tussles he generally required, so long, at all events, as his health was good, only to 'show his teeth,' in order to quell unjustified opposition. To Lichtenstein he thus summed up the situation:

The Italians have naturally moved heaven, earth and hell to swallow up the whole German opera. But they have found a precious hard morsel to digest in me. I am not to be swallowed so easily. I can maintain my rights and defend a just position. . . . I have positively no materials here to work upon, from the humblest copyist to the *prima donna*, and a thousand difficulties are thrown in my way at every step. But courage!

When Weber made his first appearance at the Saxon court he was coldly received by the king, but the queen was more friendly towards him and inquired after Caroline Brandt, whose singing she had greatly enjoyed when she appeared at Dresden. The princes, Anton and Max, also received him in a more friendly spirit later on. He did not make friends at Dresden as rapidly as he had done elsewhere. The general atmosphere was one of suspicion and snobbery, and much of the vaunted culture was purely superficial. He renewed an old acquaintance with Ludwig Tieck, and he met here, for the first time, Böttiger, the celebrated archaeologist, as well as Friedrich Kind, the well-known poet, to whom he was attracted on account of his wide theatrical experience and to whom he broached the idea of a libretto for the next opera. Various subjects were discussed and, looking around for ideas, Weber again came upon Apel's *Gespenster-Geschichten* with the legend of *Der Freischütz* which had caught his fancy before. Kind was equally struck by the dramatic quality of the story, and in three weeks the complete libretto was in the composer's hands.

Another friend he made was Count Bombelles, the Austrian ambassador, at whose house he was an ever-welcome guest, while the English minister, Morier, a giant in stature, almost worshipped him. Count Nostitz, who, in literary circles, had some reputation under the pseudonym of Arthur von Nordstern, also received him with much cordiality. With such distinguished supporters he soon, in spite of many adversaries, had the entrée to the Casino, the Ressource and the Harmonie, then the principal clubs in Dresden. But his enemies were no less active for evil than his friends were for good, and the most virulent of these was a woman named Therese aus dem Winkel, a blue-stocking who painted and played the harp, after a fashion. Weber met her at her own house where a kind of social club, called the 'Poets' Tea,' was held. In some respects, of course, Weber was himself not without blame in calling down enmity on his head. Although he was well aware of the limitations that were tacitly imposed upon the servants of a small German court, he constantly set these at defiance. To write articles on his artistic aims and objects in connection with his duties at the court to a local evening newspaper was bad enough, but to sign them with his own name and designation was the unpardonable sin on the part of one in his position. The lady referred to replied to one of these articles by another in which she made some sneering aspersions upon the German opera and contrasted it unfavourably with the Italian. Weber, in the worst possible taste, instead of pocketing the insult, retorted with a biting witticism which reflected upon the quality both of her harp-playing and of her poetical effusions, whereupon the two became implacable enemies for life. And, as time was to show, her ability to do him harm was not small. Another offence he committed, no doubt unwittingly and perhaps out of a sense of general friendliness, was his invitation to the chiefs of the opera, Morlacchi, Schubert and Polledro, to meet some of the singers and actors of the theatre at a banquet in the 'Goldener Engel'; and, a few days later, the ball he gave to the entire operatic company at the Hôtel de Pologne, where he mixed up Germans and Italians in the most unheard-of manner. These things were 'not done' at Dresden in those days.

Meanwhile Weber's labours at the opera went on apace, and in spite of keen opposition to every reform, such as the rearrangement of the orchestra, in connection with which much of the old Breslau history repeated itself, were steadily bearing excellent fruit. The king had declared himself satisfied with the first production of Méhul's *Joseph*. Other works appeared in rapid succession, and the new *Kapellmeister*, in a friendly endeavour to gain Mor-lacchi's favour, even produced the outrageous oratorio, *Isacco*, by that snake-like colleague of his.

All this time there generated and simmered in his brain the exquisite themes that were later to become the very breath and life of his great masterpiece, *Der Freischütz*. Weber's first action, after receiving the 'book' from Kind, was to submit it to Caroline Brandt for her opinion. This was a somewhat bold and drastic gesture which eventually involved the elimination of certain scenes. Weber was at first annoyed at Caroline's suggestions, but soon came to recognize their value. Kind, however, would hear of no change and, after some argument, threatened to with-draw the work, but after a time even he began to see reason. Weber then tentatively suggested to Kind the idea of his buying the book outright. Again the poet demurred; he candidly ex-pressed a desire to share in the profits; but Weber demonstrated, from his past experience, how unsatisfactory such arrangements were, and to what unhappy complications they frequently led, so that at last Kind agreed to cede all his property in the libretto for thirty ducats, and within a few hours the work was Weber's own. Its first title, fixed by Weber and Kind together, was *Der Probe-schuss* (*The Trial Shot*), but this was altered a few days later to *Die Jägersbraut* (*The Hunter's Bride*), and it was not till 1820 that it finally, on the suggestion of Brühl, came to be known as *Der Freischütz* (*The Free-shooter*). As already recorded, the complete book was in the composer's possession by 1st March 1817, but it was not till 2nd July that he first put pen to paper for its musical setting. Under that date the following entry appears in his diary: 'The first note of the *Jägersbraut* has been written to-day'; but of course much of the music had already been composed and clearly fixed in his mind.

Early in March Weber paid a flying visit to Prague in order to engage a famous singer, Madame Grünbaum, who had become available owing to the collapse of the opera in that city. As he was leaving Dresden he learned that the firm with which all his and Caroline's savings were deposited had gone bankrupt—yet another dispensation of his 'evil star'; but 'Courage!' he wrote in his diary. 'Heaven has helped me thus far and it will do so again in my need. I trust to its mercy!' He said nothing about this to Caroline, for he was able to save from the wreck just enough to make good the amount she would otherwise have lost.

In Prague he was received with enthusiastic greetings of affection and regard. On 20th March *Sylvana* was given in his honour, with Caroline in the part she had herself created and the composer conducting. 'I had only shown the top of my head in the orchestra,' he wrote of this performance to Gänsbacher, 'when the most uproarious applause burst out and seemed as if it would never end. Every piece was applauded and at the end of each act 'Bravo, Weber!' was shouted out. Everything went well, and the orchestra and chorus were inspired with the old spirit once more, for they played and sang as if electrified and intoxicated with joy. Ah, yes! they now realize what they have lost!'

He left Prague again on 1st April, with Madame Grünbaum practically 'in his pocket.' He spent two days at Dresden arranging matters for the coming season, and on the 4th he set out for Leipzig, where on the 8th he played a concerto and conducted *Kampf und Sieg*, which, strange to say, fell flat; returning to Dresden the same night. The season was an extremely busy one, and many operas, the very titles of which are completely unknown to-day, but which were then highly regarded, were performed. And through it all Weber was fighting enemies who worked against him in the dark; he was organizing, reorganizing and striving towards the dissociation of the German opera from the Italian; and he was composing immortal music, some of it on paper, but the bulk still in his head. In the face of great opposition he introduced the conductor's baton into the Dresden orchestra, arguing that whatever the requirements of the Italian opera might or might not be, German music called for a more direct influence to be exercised by the conductor. But the outcry that was made against the baton was nothing compared with the uproar that arose when he rearranged the orchestra in the opera house, a controversy in which even the king himself took sides against his own *Kapellmeister*. But Weber refused to give way.

Then came the summer season of 1817, which was not without significance in the life of Weber. The Saxon court, in its cus-tomary fashion, removed to the castle of Pillnitz, a beautiful little village situated on the Elbe, about eight miles above Dresden. There was a little theatre there attached to the Linkesches Bad, so called from the name of a former proprietor. It was essentially a home of German opera and drama, and Weber was instructed to restore its prestige, which had fallen somewhat, with a performance of Weigl's opera *Das Waisenhaus*. At the same time he was in-structed to be ready to give performances, when required, at the little private court theatre in the castle. This was too much for the peace of mind of the Italians, as the first company to be summoned to give performances there, before the king, was re-garded as taking precedence over the other. Cabals were imme-diately set afoot and the famous battle of the operas began. With Count Einsiedel on the side of the Italians there was little hope of Weber's carrying the day, but for once his 'evil star' was defeated by Einsiedel's succumbing to an attack of influenza at the psycho-logical moment. Illustrious guests were due to arrive at the castle, so that the matter was urgent. Count Vitzthum was called to a royal interview and the German opera was victorious. Morlacchi had just committed a breach of tact and for the time being was out of favour. The first opera to be performed was Isouard's *Le Billet de loterie*, translated into German as *Das Lotterieloos*, with

Madame Grünbaum as prima donna, and Weber's own comment on the performance was 'That was a triumph!'

On 27th June Augustin Gürlich, the *Kapellmeister* of the Berlin opera, died, and on the same day a letter was dispatched by Count von Brühl to Weber, offering him the vacant post. He immediately consulted Vitzthum, who, however, threw cold water on his strong urge towards accepting, and argued that his honour was involved in the establishment of a German opera at Dresden, to which the composer replied that, whereas the Berlin appointment would be a permanency, his tenure in Dresden was only for a year. This, as the event was to prove later, was carefully noted by Vitzthum. Still undecided, however, Weber kept the impatient Brühl waiting for an answer. Meanwhile, on 27th June, he had conducted a performance of Naumann's *Vater Unser* in the Roman Catholic church of Our Lady at Dresden, for the benefit of the peasantry of the Harz Mountains who had become destitute through the late wars, much to the annoyance of Morlacchi, who had looked forward to having his own *Isacco* performed on that occasion. Weber had also composed a cantata to words by Kind, now apparently lost,[1] in honour of the fête-day

---

[1] There seems to be some mystery about this cantata, which I have been quite unable to trace. In a letter written to Caroline Brandt, quoted by Baron von Weber, the composer states: 'After breakfast I drove out with our good singers to Pillnitz. The princes were at breakfast when we arrived. Schmiedel laid the words upon the table. The doors were opened; and our music began. The joy, the emotion, the surprise of the royal party were something indescribable. We were obliged to repeat the cantata; and I thought that all my singers were going to cry too.' He wrote to Gänsbacher on 18th July 1817, but never even mentioned this work. He did not write to his friend again for over a year, when he stated: 'I had hoped to have wed my beloved Lina by Michaelmas, but I did not find this so easy. The nuptial festivities of Princess Marianne and the Grand Duke of Tuscany intervened, for which I had to write a grand cantata; but the preliminaries were greatly protracted, and I was in the most painful position.' The grand cantata was *L'accoglienza*, which was not finished till October, and the libretto

of the Princess Marianne who had recently been betrothed to the hereditary Grand Duke of Tuscany, and had had it performed before the royal family. Even if he had been blind to the intrigues of the Italians which these proceedings occasioned, he could not help feeling the results of them. He was again somewhat tactless in his dealings with the higher court officials, and he committed the unpardonable offence of letting it be known that he had another post in reserve, which was his for the taking. But that was settled for him in a way he little expected. On 31st July 1817 the Berlin theatre was burned to the ground, and the King of Prussia decided, in the circumstances, to postpone making an appointment to fill the vacancy.

Weber now began to turn his attention seriously to the composition of *Der Freischütz*, the musical ideas of which had been steadily growing in his head ever since he had received the book from Kind. How naturally this growth took place was later on involuntarily expressed by the librettist in these words: 'I cannot see what there is to make such a mighty fuss about in "The Bridesmaids' Chorus." Why, from the very words, it could not have been otherwise. Any man would have hit upon the same idea!' But just as he was beginning to enter wholly into the spirit of it, the work was once more interrupted by Morlacchi's receiving an offer to compose an opera for the San Carlo theatre at Naples, and his demanding leave of absence for eight months. Count Vitzthum definitely refused the request, but the cunning Italian, by a series of intrigues and underhand means, eventually succeeded in gaining his point. This, of course, threw the whole

---

was not by Kind, but by the Abbé Celani, who had written it specially for Morlacchi. The work stated to have been composed to Kind's libretto is not mentioned by Jähns, who to-day still remains the outstanding authority on Weber's works and is not likely ever to be superseded now, nor by Benedict, Spitta, Kroll and other writers on the composer who simply follow Jähns in all that concerns Weber's compositions.

of the musical direction at court upon Weber's shoulders. The details of this sordid and petty trickery, which was all engineered for the glorification of Morlacchi and the discredit of Weber, need not be entered into here, but the man who suffered most from it was the composer's loyal friend and constant supporter, Count Vitzthum, who even in the hour of his own humiliation seized the opportunity to have Weber's appointment as *Kapellmeister* confirmed and fixed for life, using the fact of his being able to obtain more remunerative situations elsewhere, as had been proved by the Berlin offer, and of his having had, by Morlacchi's long leave of absence, so much additional work and responsibility thrust upon him.

This summer, indeed, was one of incessant work and worry. The interruption of his work on *Der Freischütz* applied only to the manual labour of getting the music on to paper, for the actual composition of the music was now feverishly proceeding in the inner recesses of his mind. At the theatre he was conducting and directing both the German and Italian operas, and on Sundays he conducted two services, while he had always to be in attendance for musical performances at the court of Pillnitz, when required. And, as if all that were not enough, he was compelled to compose a festival cantata, this time for the wedding of the daughter of Prince Max with the hereditary Grand Duke of Tuscany, which had to be done to an Italian libretto, and at the same time make all arrangements for his own wedding and the proper reception of his bride. The cantata, entitled *L'accoglienza*, to hopelessly uninspired words by the Abbé Celani, was finished by 8th October. The royal marriage took place, by proxy, on 29th October; the cantata received its first performance on the same evening and was enthusiastically acclaimed, and the king sent Weber a diamond ring in recognition of his august satisfaction.

Weber's own marriage took place six days later, on 4th November 1817. He had gone to Prague for the purpose, and the ceremony took place in the church of St Henry there. Nothing shows more clearly than the manner in which he entered upon this new state that the old reckless Weber was no more and that high seriousness was to be his guiding rule for the remainder of his life. On the early morning of his wedding day he went to confession and took the sacrament with his bride, and thereafter retired for an hour of religious communion by himself. The service was highly choral, the whole operatic company, which now had cause enough to bewail his departure from Prague, taking part. When it was all over, he wrote in his diary: 'May God bless our union and grant me power and strength to make my beloved Lina as happy and contented as my inmost heart would desire! May His mercy lead me in all my doings.'

On the day after the wedding the happy couple set out on their honeymoon, accompanied by Caroline's mother. They proceeded by Eger, Bayreuth, Bamberg, Würzburg and Heidelberg to Mannheim, where Caroline met her father in whose charge they left her mother. Weber allowed her a pension of 100 thaler, which was regularly paid up to her death. Proceeding to Mainz, the composer visited his old friend Gottfried Weber, an event to which he had been looking forward with great eagerness. But he found him vastly changed; self-centred, dogmatical and dictatorial, and the happy impetuous bridegroom could only sum up the situation in the philosophical reflection: 'Well, all joys cannot be realized!'

Even on this tour Carl Maria was under a certain degree of compulsion to combine at least a little business with a great deal of pleasure. He was ever on the watch for new talent, both vocal and instrumental, for the opera at Dresden, and he had no compunction about giving concerts by the way in order to help to pay the expenses of the journey. Such concerts were given at Darmstadt, Giessen and Gotha, where once again he was kindly received by the duke, to whom, as well as to the Grand Duchess of Weimar, he had the privilege of presenting his bride. He also made special halts at Weissenfels and Leipzig in order to meet the

CAROLINE WEBER, NÉE BRANDT

then famous dramatist Müllner, and his old friend Rochlitz, respectively. At last, on 20th December, Dresden was reached, and Caroline installed in her new home. On the night of 31st December 1817, when a new year was about to be ushered in, Weber again wrote in his diary: 'The great important year has closed. May God still grant me the blessing which He has hitherto so graciously accorded me; that I may have the power to make the dear one happy and, as a brave artist, bring honour and advantage to my fatherland! Amen!'

In Dresden society the Webers were a conspicuous success, 'their simple, graceful and unaffected manners,' as Benedict remarks, 'winning all hearts, while their artistic accomplishments enhanced the pleasure of their company.' But in the musician's own sphere there was a different tale to tell. He himself informed Gänsbacher of his arrival at Dresden, 'where I found plenty of secret intrigues and cabals.' His first tussle was with no less a personage than the king, on the old and ever-recurring problem of the proper distribution of the orchestra. The Italians, as usual, supported by the ignorant interference of Fräulein aus dem Winkel, augmented the trouble which otherwise might have died a natural death, and kept it very much alive. Weber's own vigorous defence of his innovations also roused the ire of his opponents and stimulated, even to a greater degree than ever, their venom and spleen, with the result that such influence was brought to bear on the king by Einsiedel, who still retained the royal favour, that Weber was commanded to abandon his reforms entirely; but against this command he indignantly raised his voice in no uncertain manner and, for once, he had public opinion on his side. The rest of the story may best be told in the words of his son:

With all his contempt for those beneath him, Count Einsiedel could never bear the idea that he was regarded in public as having done 'the wrong thing'; and it was evident that in this case the contemptible public had dared to hold this opinion. So, without compromising himself with the monarch, he now took the opportunity of assuring Weber of the king's complete satisfaction with his conductor-ship; and he coupled with this assurance the remark that, if the German *Kapellmeister* would carry out only just some little portion of his in-novation, the fact might be overlooked. This suggestion Weber at first rejected with indignation; by Count Vitzthum's advice, however, and for the sake of the good cause, he ultimately adopted it, without eliciting any further remark. It may here be recorded that, in con-sequence of this counsel, and of the express desire of the queen in the year 1820, the whole of Weber's orchestral arrangements were ulti-mately carried out, and even adopted for the greater part by Morlacchi for the Italian opera.

It was at this time that Vitzthum put forward the composer's name as a worthy subject for the receipt of a royal order or decoration, but the request was refused. Perhaps the time was not well chosen, or the backstairs influence was again at work. To soften the refusal, however, the king 'deigned to present Herr von Weber with a ring in token of the value he placed on his services.'

Although Carl Maria had again, through stress of official duties, been compelled to lay aside *Der Freischütz*, the year 1818 saw the composition of the majority of his *pièces d'occasion*. The first two months of the year were devoted to the creation of his Grand Mass in E flat major, a work of great beauty, much of it written under considerable mental stress. It was completed on 1st March and performed in the Roman Catholic church a week later. The court stayed away, but the reverential beauty of the work created quite a sensation. Prince Anton requested a further performance, which was given on 24th March, this time in the presence of the entire court and of a congregation that filled the church to overflowing. The Mass was followed by a large number of songs and of smaller compositions of all sorts. Of greater note were the *Jubel-Cantate* written for the king's golden wedding celebrations, but through jealous intriguing on the part of Morlacchi not performed; the *Jubel-Ouvertüre*; a cantata entitled *Natur und Liebe*; and incidental music for Gehe's *Heinrich IV* and

Grillparzer's *Sappho*. Yet it was about such works that Weber
wrote to Gänsbacher:

These compositions for special occasions, which are mere ephemera
in the artistic world, belong to the dark side of an official position, and
from their transitory nature are always dreary work, however devoted
and loving and loyal one may feel towards the person for whom they
are written.

It was after Morlacchi's return from his leave of absence that
Weber began to experience the full effects of the hostility evinced
on every possible occasion by the disgruntled Italian, and we have
it on the authority of Benedict that 'these constant attacks and
mosquito-bites exerted a fatal influence on Weber's delicate con-
stitution, and hastened the development of the dreadful disease
to which he fell a victim.'

The bright spot of this year, however, was the domestic felicity
which, with the coming of Caroline Brandt, had for the first time
in the composer's life entered into a heart that had so long cried
in vain for true love and affection. Caroline, after the usual
failures and tears which every newly married girl experiences to a
greater or lesser degree, quickly developed into the real German
Hausfrau, careful, efficient and economical; an admirable cook
and an ideal hostess. 'In every sense as *Hausfrau*,' her son declares,
'Caroline von Weber was perfection.' She still had a little
tendency towards jealousy of the many other women Weber's
calling compelled him to meet and, during the first year of their
married life at least, this engendered a good deal of unhappiness
in the home.

The couple was lavish in hospitality, and to such a home the
Dresden society people were never loath to go. Not infrequently
the composer himself was to be found in the little back-shop of
the Italian warehouseman Chiapone, sampling his Hochheimer
and Burgundy, his oysters and caviare, in the Olympian company
of the founder of the ironical school of poetry, Ludwig Tieck,
the scientist Böttiger, the 'German Petrarch' Carl Förster, the

disgruntled and supercilious Friedrich Kind, always standing on his pinchbeck dignity, that complete man of the theatre Theodor Hell and the old exponent of Don Juan, Luigi Bassi, always roaring with the laughter of the gods. There Weber was always at his best. Nevertheless, the Webers were never inconspicuous in society. Baron von Weber has recorded how

Persons . . . who had an opportunity of meeting the gifted pair in the 'Liederkreis,' or in the hospitable house of the minister Nostitz, or in other social circles,

forty years after the events still retained

the impression which the Webers made when they sang together the composer's sprightliest songs, or Caroline declaimed a poem, to which her husband improvised on the piano; and when Weber's joyous humour electrified all hearts, and inspired the most serious of the statesmen of the day to gaiety. In his own house, when friends were assembled around him, he was the most joyous, whilst the most unaffected of hosts.

And a particularly typical aspect of his character is shadowed forth in the record that

To the young talented members of his operatic company he showed his most pleasant attentions; and would call to them at times, when dancing took place, and he himself set all going by the inspiriting dances which seemed to flow spontaneously from his fingers, 'Come, look alive! When the father plays, the children must dance their best.'

In their charming little flat under the shadow of the castle at Pillnitz, the couple found, for a time at least, an almost Elysian bliss, and the five miles' walk to Dresden and five miles back when his day's work was done, were as nothing to the happy singing-bird who had at last found so comfortable and beautiful a nest. And the surrounding country was as beautiful as the house itself.

From his window the composer commanded a view over the garden and the neighbouring corn-fields and orchards, to the woods and chestnut alleys of the park of Pillnitz, and the vine-clad hills of the valley of the Elbe. Close by the house was a narrow, shady, sweetly green valley, through which a path led to hills commanding views of almost unsurpassable loveliness. At the entrance stood a small country inn, with an excellent bowling-green, where he loved to have a game with other zealous players; and higher up, on a rocky platform, the most picturesque of water-mills. On every side the most romantic forms and loveliest colours from nature's palette offered inspiration to the composer on his walks. Woods whispered to him in soft murmurs, and falling streams plashed melodiously over rocks and gravel.

Can one wonder that it was from this dwelling, and those scenes, that the greater parts of *Der Freischütz*, *Euryanthe* and *Oberon* were to emanate?

While for a time these scenes and the life at Pillnitz had a beneficial effect upon his health, the cares of office and the ever-lasting intrigues and insults of the Italian faction continued, and, when the new season opened, counteracted all the good that had accrued to him. His first rebuff was the refusal of the court officials to allow his *Jubel-Cantate* to be rendered on the special occasion for which it had been composed. This was all the more mortifying to Weber in view of the enthusiastic reception his *Natur und Liebe* had been given in the queen's apartments at Pillnitz in presence of the assembled court, but on that occasion Morlacchi was engrossed in the composition of an opera, otherwise not even that performance might have taken place.

In November, again, Weber resolved to produce his own *Sylvana* at Dresden, and when his intention became known, Morlacchi and his sycophantic satellites threw every obstacle in the way, until the composer abandoned the project in utter disgust. To the eternal disgrace of the Dresdeners for allowing such a state of affairs to prevail, it was many years after Weber's death before the opera was given there at all. But the greatest insult to the now thoroughly disheartened and suffering composer was yet to come. On 22nd December 1818 his first child, a girl who received the names of Marie Caroline Friederike Auguste, was born, after the mother had undergone a long and harrowing period of suffering, which itself had added greatly to Weber's distress. He solicited the honour of having the king and queen as sponsors to the child. The baptismal ceremony took place on 26th December, and while he did not hope that their majesties would appear in person, as a noble by birth, a high official of the court and a celebrated artist he had a right to expect that at least a chamberlain and one of the queen's ladies of honour would appear as proxies. Many foreign ambassadors and members of the aristocracy and of the literary and musical world honoured the composer by their presence, but the representatives of royalty, to the surprise of all the guests and the indignation of most, appeared in the persons of Herr Schmiedel, the king's valet, and one of the queen's *femmes de chambre*. In justice to the rulers it must be said that Weber was aware that they had had no hand in the matter and, knowing this, he thanked them personally for the honour they had done him. He knew who had dealt the blow, but never had he felt any insult so keenly as he did this. A week after the child's birth Caroline learned of the death of her father, and there can be little doubt that the ensuing illness of herself and of her husband, and the death of the child itself, can all be attributed to the worry and anxiety that arose from these events.

Although suffering acutely, the composer resumed his work in the new year—1819. He produced several operas that received only lukewarm receptions and finished his second Grand Mass, in G major, to be performed in the Roman Catholic church on 17th February. But it was much mutilated in performance, and largely overshadowed by music made to order by Morlacchi and Polledro and by an Italian tenor, Giovanni Cantù, who had been brought by Morlacchi from Milan. One of Weber's long illnesses followed, and during his convalescence he composed the famous *Rondo brillante* (Op. 62); the *Aufforderung zum Tanz* (Op. 65); *Polacca brillante* (Op. 72) and other works for pianoforte solo and duet, the Trio for piano, flute and cello (Op. 63) and a considerable number of songs, all in his best and purest vein.

A brighter day seemed to dawn for him, however, when he unexpectedly received a commission to compose an opera for the approaching wedding of Prince Friedrich August and the Archduchess Caroline of Austria, the subject of which was to be of his own choice. He fixed upon a fairy libretto by Kind, *Alcindor*, derived from one of the tales in the *Arabian Nights*, and at once began to sketch out the music. Seldom or never before had he thrown himself so completely into the creation of any work as he did into this, and the degree of cruelty that characterized the cancellation of the commission, two months later, could then scarcely have been exceeded, nor even be equalled in these coldly materialistic days in which we are ourselves living. In place of Weber's opera, a tenth-rate work entitled *Amore e destino* by Morlacchi, which has long ago sunk into a merciful oblivion, was given on the wedding-day, 9th October.

Meanwhile the Weber infant died, and mother and father both lay prostrate for weeks on their beds of sickness, hovering on the very border-line that separates life from death. As a consequence of the cancellation of Weber's opera-commission, Vitzthum had resigned from the directorship of the theatre, a fact that was not calculated to lessen the composer's troubles there. But he found much pleasure and gratification in meeting, during the autumn of this year, the young composer, Heinrich Marschner, whose opera, *Heinrich IV und Aubigné*, he accepted for representation on the Dresden stage; and the old composer, Ludwig Spohr, who had come for the purpose of giving a concert at court, previously to paying a visit to England. Weber, with a disinterestedness that contrasted remarkably with the narrow outlook and petty jealousies of his fellow-*Kapellmeister*, did everything in his power to ensure the happiness and success of these noted musicians during their sojourn at Dresden. It is interesting also to learn that the celebrated Berlin banker, Abraham Mendelssohn, who was a great admirer of Weber, visited him in his flat at Hosterwitz and that he was probably accompanied by his son, Felix, then a curly-haired boy of ten.

This year of much sickness and trouble ended on a brighter note. In August Weber had sent a copy of the libretto of *Der Freischütz* to Count von Brühl of Berlin, who proposed to open the new theatre, then in course of erection, with a performance of the opera. This was the incentive necessary to drive Weber on to the completion of the work. He now concentrated all his energies towards that end, and he informed Brühl that the work would positively be finished in March 1820. Although Brühl informed him on 21st December that the theatre would be opened with the performance of a play by Goethe, he tempered the announcement with the remark that the first opera to be given there would, he trusted, be *The Hunter's Bride*, so that the composer regained some of his old spirits and celebrated the occasion by attending a masked ball on New Year's Eve and, at the end of it, penning in his diary these words: 'And thus the year which has brought me so many sorrows has ended gaily. May God give us His blessing, and grateful hearts for the strength He has given us to bear all the trials He has imposed.'

We now enter with Weber the year 1820, which Benedict, with justice, states 'may be recorded as the culminating point of his musical career.' Although there appeared to be a marked improvement in his health, that was only on the surface, the dire seeds of the fell disease which was so soon to end his too brief life had already taken root in his poor tortured body and were working steadily and insidiously towards their deadly end.

The year opened with another wordy tussle between Weber and the Italians, consequent upon the production of Meyerbeer's *Emma di Resburgo*, which the former gave in Italian out of loyalty to his erstwhile friend and fellow-student, but criticized, not too advantageously, in the *Abendzeitung,* a fact to which the Italian faction chose to take exception. As usual, owing to its treachery, Weber came off unvictorious in the battle. To make matters worse, another child was prematurely still-born, and Caroline was long in recovering her strength. But fortunately more visitors of note helped to keep Weber's mind from brooding too much upon his own misfortunes. Amongst these were the celebrated flute player Anton Bernhard Fürstenau, Chladni a well-known professor of acoustics, Nepomuk Hummel the world-renowned pianist, and the younger son of Mozart. Early in the year also, Weber had the immense gratification of learning from Geheimrat von Könneritz, who had succeeded Count Vitzthum as general director of the theatre, that at the request of the queen his majesty had at last consented to Weber's complete rearrangement of the orchestra, which previously he had so harshly declined to do. This was a source of great joy to the composer.

But all his energies were now turned to the work of getting *Der Freischütz* off the stocks. That the whole of it lay already completed in Weber's brain is proved by the state of the original manuscript of the opera which, after his death, was presented by Caroline to the Royal Library at Berlin. In the whole of this manuscript there does not appear one single correction or erasure. The last note was written on 13th May, and the score was dispatched to Brühl. In acknowledging its receipt Brühl complained that the title, *The Hunter's Bride*, was weak and colourless, and suggested that of *Der Freischütz*, which the legend originally bore, as a name more in keeping with the wild romantic spirit of the subject. To this Weber at once agreed, and so the opera, as we know it to-day, was launched.

At this time also Brühl asked him for new incidental music to a play which had long before been written by Weber's old acquaintance Pius Alexander Wolff. It was a play entitled *Preciosa*, adapted from the novel by Cervantes entitled *La Gitanilla* (*The Little Gipsy*). Wolff's play was poor enough and the incidental music originally written for it by the Weimar *Konzertmeister*, Eberwein, was worse; but Brühl liked the play and thought it worthy of better treatment, musically, so that he advised Wolff to offer it to Weber, who readily undertook the task. The play brought back to his memory the national melodies he had heard eight years before, sung by the Spanish soldiers at Gotha, and soon after the completion of *Der Freischütz* we find him over head and ears in the new work. He described it as 'a heavy piece of work and an important one, more than half an opera,' yet from the date on which he began his labours to that on which he finished and sent the score to Brühl there elapsed only seven weeks.

Even then he was already working on the score of yet another opera, the comic one entitled *Die drei Pintos*, the libretto of which had been sent to him by Theodor Hell, whose real name, by the way, was Karl Winkler, and purchased by Weber for twenty ducats. This work was never finished by Carl Maria himself. His son states that 'the score of the first act . . . which Weber took with him to England, was never recovered after his death,' but Spitta, in a footnote, says that 'the autograph sketches were in the possession of Weber's grandson, Capt. Freiherr von Weber, at Leipzig,' and he calls it 'a work full of promise.' Lichtenstein goes further and asserts that the work was almost complete when, in 1825, it disappeared in England. Of what has survived, there are altogether seven pieces, and from these attempts have since been made, notably by Meyerbeer and Gustav Mahler, to reconstruct the whole opera. Weber certainly worked at the opera, off and on, from May 1820 till November 1821. The intelligentsia of Dresden showed a decided taste for all things Spanish at this time, and it was more than the mere memory of the Spanish national songs, sung by the soldiers at Gotha, that turned Weber's genius, for the time being, into such a channel. The Spanish dramatic poets were then all the rage, and Tieck was giving periodical readings on Calderón and the other great dramatic authors. It is not surprising, therefore, to find the composer, while still engrossed by the music of *Die drei Pintos*, seriously contemplating the idea of producing a grand tragic opera on the story of the Cid, a plan for which was actually drawn up by Kind. But the appearance of Aiblinger's *Rodrigo und Ximene* in Munich entirely banished the idea from his mind and turned him to a new trend of thought, which eventually gave us *Euryanthe*.

Meanwhile, the completion of the new theatre in Berlin having been still further delayed, and Spontini having been engaged as

Kapellmeister there and being likely, for some time to come, to overshadow all composers of operas less pompous than his own, Weber resolved to utilize his leave of absence during the summer of 1820 in carrying through his long-anticipated artistic tour. So, on 25th July, accompanied by Caroline, he left his quiet and peaceful home on the banks of the Elbe; he had found a new dwelling named Kosel's Garden in the Anton suburb near the Linkesches Bad a few months earlier, having found Pillnitz inconveniently far removed from Dresden; and set his course, in the first place, for Leipzig, where once again he visited Rochlitz and his wife and met, for the first time, the composer Gottlieb Reissiger, who afterwards became his successor as German *Kapellmeister* at Dresden. Then on to Halle, where he gave his first concert and was received with tumultuous enthusiasm by the entire personnel of the university, professors and students alike. In the evening he was serenaded by about four hundred students recruited from the various *Singvereine*, who 'after a "vivat," which seemed almost interminable,' sang in full chorus several of the composer's own songs, which highly delighted him and 'sounded like a blessing on his journey—a happy omen for his future course.' Nor was his reception at Göttingen, the next university town he visited, one whit less warm. 'If I am everywhere to be warmed by such fire as this,' he wrote to his friend Roth, 'I can console myself for the cold chill thrown on me in Dresden.'

But such excitements soon proved to be too much for the weak constitutions of both Weber and his wife, and when they arrived at Hanover they were both too ill to give a concert there. At Oldenburg, however, they had sufficiently recovered to appear before the court, and Caroline's singing was such as almost to eclipse the marvellous playing of her husband. Bremen and Hamburg were next visited, but in the latter city Caroline, soon again to become a mother, was once more too ill to appear, and she had to be left there for the time being. At Hamburg Weber found his elder brother Fritz, who was musical director of the town, and on 10th August they set out together for Lübeck, where they were joined by another brother, Edmund. The three drove over to Eutin, Carl Maria's birthplace, where he gave an impromptu concert to the good townspeople, who would not be denied and heaped such honours upon him as almost to over-whelm him. Then, by sea from Kiel, the composer proceeded to Copenhagen, and had his first taste of sea-sickness. In the Danish capital, where on 27th September he was presented to King Frederick VI and his queen, at Frederiksborg Castle, the same tremendous enthusiasm as had accompanied him all the way from Dresden was encountered. His success there exceeded all his hopes; but no sooner was his concert over than, all impatience to be back with Caroline again, he was southward bound and in Hamburg once more on 14th October. He found his wife much better, her confinement having prematurely taken place in the interval, and they rested together at Hamburg till the 25th, when they turned their steps homeward.

Weber had an inordinate love of animals and kept quite a little menagerie at Dresden. While in the northern seaport, he was one day attracted by a comical little monkey which looked 'so like a not-much-esteemed acquaintance' that he could not resist him and purchased him on the spot. He was christened Schnuff and was 'a little devil, but worth his weight in gold,' and as an addition to the Weber family he accompanied them to Dresden, and was later one of the prime favourites of the household there. Dresden was reached on 4th November and five days later the *Kapellmeister* resumed his duties when he conducted a performance of Mozart's *Entführung aus dem Serail*. Apart from a visit from his old friend Bärmann, when the first public performance [1] of the

---

[1] Weber's son states in the *Life* of his father that 'Weber resolved that on this occasion the overture to his *Der Freischütz* should be given for the first time.' But Cœuroy, without any reference to the above, states, regarding the tour, from which the composer had just returned: 'Au cours de cette tournée, il joua deux fois son ouverture du *Freischütz* (le 8 octobre à Copenhague en première audition, et le 13 à Brunswick; il la donna une troisième fois à Dresde le 18 décembre à un concert de

overture to *Der Freischütz* was given, a visit from Meyerbeer, and the fact that the pianoforte arrangement of the opera had been sold to Schlesinger for 220 thaler, after much haggling on the part of the publisher, the rest of the year passed without any outstanding incident.

In the beginning of February 1821 Weber acquired a new interest in life by the arrival of Julius Benedict, the son of a wealthy banker at Stuttgart, who came as a pupil—Weber's 'only real pupil,' according to Spitta—on 'Hummel's strong recommendation' asserts the baron, although Benedict himself never mentions Hummel, but, on the other hand, declares that he was accepted 'on the special recommendation of his [Weber's] old friend, Herr von Gerstenberg of Weimar.'

I shall never forget the impression of my first meeting with him [writes Benedict]. Ascending the by no means easy staircase which led to his modest home on the third story of a house in the old market-place, I found him sitting at his desk, and occupied with the pianoforte arrangement of his *Freischütz*. The dire disease which but too soon was to carry him off had made its mark on his noble features: the projecting cheek-bones, the general emaciation, told their sad tale; but in his clear blue eyes, too often concealed by spectacles, in his mighty forehead, fringed by a few straggling locks, in the sweet expression of his mouth, in the very tone of his weak but melodious voice, there was a magic power which attracted irresistibly all who approached him. He received me with the utmost kindness, and, though overwhelmed with double duties during the temporary absence of Morlacchi, he found time to give me daily lessons for a considerable period.

This charming picture of Weber's appearance and gentle manners, surely a masterpiece of descriptive writing, is amplified

---

son vieil ami Baermann)'; and Kroll has it that 'Meyerbeer und Bärmann kamen gleichzeitig zum Besuch. Bei einem Konzert des letzteren erklang die *Freischütz*-Ouvertüre. Weber hatte schon einmal in Kopenhagen dirigiert.' Neither quotes any authority for his statement.

by an equally alluring account of his achievements as an executive musician:

> I could not have arrived at a more propitious moment. The two works [*Preciosa* and *Freischütz*] which were so soon to make the tour of the world were then closed letters to all except a privileged few. To hear them interpreted by the composer, who, with the mere shadow of a voice, knew how to give so much variety of expression to his singing, and who imparted so much strength and delicacy combined to his accompaniments, was a treat, the recollection of which could not be effaced, even by the fine performances, with all the scenic prestige, at Berlin and Dresden. His playing his own pianoforte music had also a peculiar fascination; but what impressed me even more was his rendering of Beethoven's sonatas, with a fire and precision, and a thorough entering into the spirit of the composer which would have given the mighty Ludwig the best proof of Weber's reverence and admiration for his genius.

On 14th March 1821 Wolff's *Preciosa* was performed, for the first time with Weber's music, in Berlin, and although the music made a powerful impression upon the general public, the press was decidedly lukewarm. But in the preparations he was then making for a greater and more sensational *première*, the composer seems to have treated the latter fact with more or less indifference. It was not until 2nd May that Weber and his wife left Dresden for what was to be, perhaps, the greatest event in his greatly chequered career, the first performance of *Der Freischütz*, which was also to be the first operatic performance in the new Berlin Schauspielhaus. But much had to be arranged in the interval. He had left the casting arrangements entirely in the hands of Brühl, as many of the singers were unknown to him. This was no doubt a mistake on his part, and rather like asking for trouble. It came! Johanna Eunicke, to whom the part of Aennchen had been allotted, in the true manner of all prima donnas immediately raised objections to the falling-off of the vocal prominence, which she considered her part ought to have, towards the end of the opera, and begged for at least one other aria that might place her to better advantage in the third act. Had she been dealing directly with Weber, who had strong opinions on the futility— not infrequently fatality—of interpolations, it is almost certain that her request would have been summarily declined, but it was made through Brühl, who recommended the addition. The composer reluctantly agreed, and after consulting Kind he obtained from him the so-called romance, 'Einst träumte meiner sel'gen Base,' which, notwithstanding some fine moments, is an irrelevant parody of the supernatural elements fundamental to the opera as a whole, and a little ridiculous. It was a mistake on Weber's part to have allowed himself to be talked over, and the result only serves to prove how sound was his judgment on all artistic matters.

At last the great day of the opening of the Berlin Schauspielhaus came within the bounds of realization, and Weber was instructed to be in attendance for the production of his opera towards the end of May. Leave of absence from Dresden was more easily obtained because the theatre there was undergoing alterations at that particular moment, and Weber, in the highest of spirits, set out with his wife and an enormous dog in a roomy travelling-carriage. He arrived in Berlin on 4th May, and was joyfully and affectionately received by the kind-hearted and hospitable Beers. But in Berlin, as in Dresden, he found the same opposing forces in operatic affairs, with the scales weighted by royal favour predominantly on the side of the Italians. The pompous, arrogant Spontini, contemptuous of all German art, and taking an unholy pride in the appellation of 'the Napoleon of music,' had recently taken up his residence in Berlin as *Kapellmeister*, and was about to produce his gorgeously spectacular opera *Olympia*, in a version which had been entirely remodelled by the composer after its original production in Paris. Immense sums of money had been spent on this production and the music had unquestionable merit, so that there was no lack of good reasons why Weber's friends in particular, and the German party at large, should feel an extreme degree of nervousness about the comparisons that were sure to be drawn between the two works and the support that the German opera was likely to receive. But Weber himself had no such fears and remained in the best of spirits during the entire period of waiting and suspense. *Olympia* was given, for the first time, in the Royal Opera House, on 14th May, before an audience that filled the vast theatre to suffocation, and this was repeated during a period of twelve succeeding nights. The Berlin public was at first mightily pleased with the spectacular effects, but these soon began to pall, and not once was the public moved to any degree of enthusiasm by the music, which deserved a better fate, but must have been overborne by the too lavish scenic splendours.

Weber began his rehearsals on 21st May. The chief members of the cast were Caroline Seidler (Agathe), who possessed a beautiful and highly cultivated voice and a fine figure; Johanna Eunicke (Aennchen), of whom we have already heard; Stümer (Max); Blume (Caspar); and Hillebrand (Samiel); all capable singers and the second a notable actor as well, chosen for their respective parts with sound judgment and discrimination. The chorus was equally good and entered into the spirit of the work with a zeal and enthusiasm that was as remarkable as it was unusual. So far as one can gather the rehearsals ran without a hitch until the day preceding the first performance, which had been fixed for 18th June, the anniversary of the battle of Waterloo. What happened on that day of the dress rehearsal can only be told adequately in the words of Benedict. The general rehearsal,

though very long, had realized the most sanguine expectations. The composer was received with acclamation by all the principals, chorus and orchestra, who looked forward with the utmost confidence to the next day; but the accessories, machinery, etc., were still woefully deficient, principally in one of the most important scenes—the Wolf's Glen. The celebrated painter, Gropius, had furnished splendid decorations for the limited stage of the Berlin theatre. The main object in the construction of the new house, however, had been to establish a permanent home for the German drama, and for light operas such as Boïeldieu's *Jean de*

STAGE SETTING FOR THE BERLIN PRODUCTION OF
'DER FREISCHÜTZ'

Paris, Le Petit Chaperon rouge, etc., and scanty accommodation was therefore given to the machinists for sensational effects.

Thus the gigantic owl, intended to flap its wings, and whose glowing eyes were supplied by two little oil lamps, met with an accident disabling one of the wings, *et ne battait que d'une aile*, whilst the threatening eyes of the night-bird resembled small street lanterns. The fiery carriage was so badly contrived that the fireworks never went off at all, and a common empty wheel, garnished with inoffensive crackers and rockets, ludicrously crossed the stage. The wild hunt, painted on canvas, could not be distinctly seen from the front; Caspar, in his eagerness, had given the cue 'Seven! the wild hunt: Zamiel, help!' too soon, thus destroying the effect of the infernal chorus, and upsetting all the arrangemens of the stage-manager.

All except Weber himself ominously shook their heads at this lamentable display, and Caroline went home in despair. Rumour was busy with tales of a conspiracy organized by Spontini to wreck the performance, but Weber, with his customary philosophical 'Be it as God will,' already had his mind full of other things, and on the very morning of that fateful 18th June 1821 he actually devoted two tranquil hours to putting the finishing touches to a new composition for pianoforte and orchestra, the now world-famous *Concertstück* in F minor (Op. 79), and immediately thereafter he played it over to Benedict and Caroline. For once Weber seemed to have forgotten his 'evil star,' and when he took his place on the conductor's stand in the packed Schauspielhaus, and was received with such thunderous applause as seemed to threaten to bring the roof down, he must have felt that here at last the victory was achieved. And so, indeed, it was, for the performance went through without a hitch, and the applause and enthusiasm when, after the final curtain, he appeared on the stage leading Frau Seidler and Fräulein Eunicke by the hands, seemed to exceed all bounds. 'The success of *Der Freischütz*,' wrote his son years later, 'had been immense—unparalleled! Critics, artists and dilettanti appeared intoxicated; and all with one accord—for that night at least—had no word but of delight and joy and praise.' The composer was entertained to a supper after the performance at Jagors in Unter den Linden, by a select company of the eminent literary men in Berlin and a number of his personal friends, including the Beers, Lichtensteins and Wolffs. All the operatic artists who had taken part in the work also were there, and E. T. A. Hoffmann crowned Weber with a wreath of laurels.

In the cold light of the following morning, however, some at least of the glory seems to have faded. The music critics of the press were by no means unanimous on the merits of the opera, and many were decidedly hostile. Even some of Weber's friends were considerably less than lukewarm in their appreciation or lack of appreciation. Zelter wrote to Goethe in a derisive vein, and wound up his remarks by saying that out of a *small* nothing the composer had created a *colossal* nothing. Tieck, anticipating the critical methods of the Wagnerian critics half a century later, described the work as the most unmusical row that ever roared upon a stage, while Spohr, some months later wrote: 'As I never had any great opinion of Weber's talent as a composer, I wanted to hear this opera, in order to discover upon what its wonderful success is founded; but the riddle was by no means solved; and I can only explain it by the gift possessed by Weber to write for the general masses,' which, considering the opinion held by Weber himself on the artistic insincerity of the Italians, was surely 'the unkindest cut of all.' Yet, as has so often happened in the history of the arts, and is still happening to-day, when dealing with works of a novel character they do not yet sufficiently understand,

the critics admitted . . . the great musical importance of the work, the heart-stirring qualities of its melodies, the ability with which Weber jested at all the rules of art without offending them, the originality of the instrumental effects, the breath of genius that breathed over the whole. They accepted the fact that the opera commenced a new era in dramatic musical composition, at the same time that it placed the master in the rank of the first operatic composers of all time. . . . But they never could quite forgive the audacious novelty, and complained that classical repose was sacrificed to effect, that the originality was often monstrous, that the characterization bordered on caricature, that musical impossibilities were 'music no more.'

But Weber, usually hypersensitive in the face of adverse criticism, was not insensitive to the humour of this, for he wrote to Lichtenstein:'Had not I the testimony of so many good and honourable judges, I myself might have been led to think that I owed all my success to Monsieur Zamiel.' But he was deeply affected by an unkind and bitter article which his erstwhile friend Hoffmann contributed to the *Vossische Zeitung*. A suggestion made therein that he had plagiarized some passages in Spontini cut him to the quick. Yet, the critics notwithstanding, his popularity in the theatre and in the homes of princes and people alike continued with undiminished warmth.

Before leaving Berlin, Weber, on 25th June, gave a farewell concert in the concert-room of the Schauspielhaus, which was, probably on account of the fine weather, not well patronized and only brought him the sum of 115 thaler (£17 10s.), and inspired the remark which he inserted in his diary: 'Molto onore, poco contante.' Nevertheless, the event was historic, in so far as it marked the occasion on which his newly finished *Concertstück* received its first public performance, the composer himself rendering the solo part to perfection. Taking part in the programme of this concert, also, there was a French violinist, an eccentric named Alexandre Boucher, who claimed the distinction of having been exiled from his native country because of a *malheureuse ressemblance* to the Emperor Napoleon, which indeed was real enough. Boucher was billed, probably by an act of kindness on Weber's part, to play the composer's *Variations on a Norwegian National Air*. He had stipulated to be allowed to contribute a short cadenza of his own near the end of the work, and Weber, who accompanied him, good-naturedly consented; but his astonishment and that of the small audience knew no bounds when the performer,

after various gambols, arpeggios, shakes and mysterious chords, brought in a regular *pot-pourri* of motives from *Der Freischütz* dished up *à la*

Boucher. In vain the tortured composer tried to cut short the fancy-flights of his would-be interpreter; on he went, regardless of Carl Maria's supplicating glances, till at last, after an attempt to represent 'The Wolf's Glen' on the fourth string, he laid down his violin, rushed to the piano and, clasping Weber in his arms, exclaimed: 'Ah! grand maître! que je t'aime! que je t'admire!'[1]

The composer's son informs us that 'the public accepted the eccentricity with favour; and a storm of applause, with cries of "Long live Weber!" ended the extraordinary scene.'

The composer left Berlin on 30th June and reached Dresden on the evening of the following day. There he found again the same petty intrigue and studied insult that had become so typical of that wretched capital. While practically the whole of Europe was ringing with his name and fame, the court and inhabitants of Dresden treated him with complete indifference. Caroline's health also began to cause him more uneasiness, and he was compelled to get her away for a course of treatment at the mineral springs of Spandau. An unfortunate break with Friedrich Kind further pressed heavily upon his mind. So great had been the success of *Der Freischütz* and the pecuniary returns he was deriving therefrom that Weber, although under no obligation to do so, offered, with delicacy, tact and kindly feeling, a share of the proceeds to the author of the libretto; but Kind, whose vanity had been wounded by the widespread praises that had been showered upon the composer, with seldom or never a word about the author of the words, indignantly refused, and fulminated against 'composers who bought their libretti in the cheapest market, and then thought they had nothing more to do.' Weber did everything it was humanly possible to accomplish with a view to healing the breach, but all in vain, and the only truly successful collaboration that he ever achieved with any of his librettists came to an end. Some months later, poor Weber, in one of his miser-able spasms, wrote to Gänsbacher: 'Every day one becomes more

[1] *Weber*, by Julius Benedict, p. 72.

lonely in the world; I have met with ingratitude without end. Some do not approve of my being more esteemed than themselves, and so I live here quite deserted, from an artistic point of view, and in other respects happy only with my wife.'

Yet he must have found some consolation in the old adage that 'a prophet is not without honour save in his own country,' exemplified in an offer that was made to him at this time.

The old elector of Hesse-Cassel, Wilhelm I, having died, his son and successor, Wilhelm II, in the manner of omniscient youth decided that the royal theatre of Cassel required reorganization, and he gave orders to the director, Feige, that he should at once engage the best *Kapellmeister* and operatic organizer to be found in Germany. There were no doubts in Feige's mind as to where this person dwelt, and he wrote at once to Weber, offering him the post at a salary of 2,500 thaler, a life appointment and a pension. But Carl Maria hesitated.

Just a thousand thaler more than I have here [he wrote to his wife]. I have passed a sleepless night; but the more I reflect upon leaving Dresden, the heavier falls the weight upon my heart. I handed over Feige's letter to Herr von Könneritz. He read it without a word. I dined with him yesterday and drove over to Pillnitz with him: but he still held his peace; and I was too shy to speak on the matter myself. I cannot thrust such an offer aside as though it were nothing . . . but in truth you cannot be more attached to Dresden than I am.

Time passed, and nothing more was said, so that Weber was at last driven to set aside his shyness and revert to the matter himself. He did so with a considerable degree of tact, expressing warm appreciation of the honour he regarded as his in being attached, in his present position, to the Saxon court, and assuring his chief that he was really unwilling to leave Dresden, but he could not overlook the fact that his achievements, the fame of which the whole of Germany had acclaimed, had been completely ignored at Dresden, and all the zeal and endeavours he had expended upon the duties of his office had gone unrecognized.

He spoke feelingly also of the duties he owed to his wife and family and asked that his case might be laid before the king. Könneritz thereupon drew up a report, placing the composer's claims in the most favourable light, but it had little or no effect upon the stiff officialdom of Weber's old enemy, Count Einsiedel, who, however, considering it still advisable to retain him at Dresden, obtained an advance of salary of 300 thaler for him, but at the same time arranged that Morlacchi should likewise receive a similar addition. Weber, weary of all this underhand antagonism and desperately longing for rest and peace, accepted the matter as it was presented to him, and wrote to Feige declining his offer. The latter thereupon submitted a request to Weber for assistance in obtaining the ablest man available, and he replied immediately recommending Ludwig Spohr in the warmest possible terms. Spohr was thereupon offered the post, which he accepted and filled, with credit and repute, to the end of his life.

Meanwhile, at Dresden, the old antagonism to the poor, suffering *Kapellmeister*, aggravated almost beyond endurance by the subtle, scheming Italians, continued with more venom and greater virulence than ever. The royal theatre had been thoroughly renovated during Weber's sojourn in Berlin, and it was his great desire to have it reopened with a performance of Mozart's *Don Giovanni*, which had never yet been sung at Dresden in German, and his friend Bassi, who, under Mozart's own eyes, had been the first to sing the title-part of that stupendous work, was there, with Weber, to see the work worthily produced. But, only a week before the date of the theatre's reopening, a royal edict went forth that the event was to take place with the production of an Italian opera, while Mozart's masterpiece was to be relegated to the miniature stage of the hole-and-corner Linkesches Bad.[1]

---

[1] It did not, of course, occur to Weber, obsessed as he was with the idea of German opera and the notion that a German master should not be a cosmopolitan, as Handel and Mozart were, to disarm the authorities with the observation that *Don Giovanni* actually was an Italian opera.

This insult to Weber was bad enough, but such a slight to the greatest work of one who, to the master, ranked little short of a god, nearly broke his heart.

It was, again, only after many troubles and mortifications that he obtained a command from the king to produce *Der Freischütz* at Dresden in the new year, but once more cabals did everything they could to wreck the opera while it was in rehearsal. They affected him so much that for many days he could neither eat nor sleep, and the symptoms of his already deeply rooted disease increased to such an extent that his cough became more frequent and painful, his fever more constant, and blood-spitting appeared for the first time, to the terror of poor Caroline. And thus, dismally, ended the year 1821, yet not altogether without a ray of hope for the year that was about to dawn.

CHAPTER VIII

THE LAST YEARS

AFTER the successful *première* of *Der Freischütz* in Berlin the opera
went round practically all the great European operatic centres.
Its success in such places as Breslau, Carlsruhe, Königsberg,
Hanover, Pesth and Copenhagen surpassed even that of Berlin,
and at last it reached Vienna, where it was given in celebration
of the fête-day of the empress, 3rd October 1821, but in a terribly
garbled version, owing to an idiotic idea of censorship then prevailing in the Austrian capital. Weber was furious and wrote
to Privy-Councillor von Moser, one of the joint directors of the
imperial opera there, vigorously protesting against the senseless
mutilation of his work. In face of the censor Moser was, of
course, powerless, but it is a curious coincidence that, very
shortly afterwards, Weber should have received a request from
Domenico Barbaja, who then rented the Kärnthnerthor Theatre
in Vienna, to compose an opera for performance in his theatre
during the 1822–23 season. Does one see in this the influence
of the kindly Moser acting on Weber's behalf? It is not, I think,
outside the bounds of probability. The mercurial composer was
overjoyed, and he immediately wrote to Barbaja inquiring into
the conditions upon which the work was to be undertaken,
both as regards librettist and composer. Barbaja at once replied
inviting Weber to come to Vienna to settle terms and study the
capabilities of the singers, all expenses to be paid by the management of the theatre.

He was already searching feverishly for a book. Several ideas
were considered, including the *Cid* which Kind had already

begun; but unfortunately the breach between the composer and poet had not been healed, and that was rejected. Then one day Weber heard a reading given at the 'Liederkreis' by that amazing female, Helmina von Chezy, who is described by Benedict as 'a stout, elderly lady, with all the qualities of a real blue-stocking, careless and slovenly in her appearance, not blessed with any earthly goods, but with a great deal of self-sufficiency.' She had a certain facility in versification, but she was absolutely ignorant as regards the framing of an operatic scenario or as to what constituted a libretto. She had, however, somewhere come across an old legend entitled *Histoire de Gérard de Nevers et de la belle et vertueuse Euryanthe sa mie*, which she showed to Weber, who, allured by the romantic character of the story and the opportunities it contained for large scenic effects, accepted the two first acts of the work as adapted by Madame von Chezy, with the right to make such alterations as he should deem advisable. But when he came to adapt it for stage purposes, he found it no easy matter, and the strange fatality that seemed to attach to the libretti of practically all of Weber's operas applied here to the greatest extent of all.

Having decided upon the subject of his new opera, Weber then obtained the necessary leave of absence, and set out at once for Vienna with a view to judging the artists who were likely to be available for its performance and the musical conditions prevailing in that city. Caroline, whose health was still unsatisfactory, did not accompany him, and how fully he realized the precarious state of his own health is shown by the fact of his leaving with her a sealed document which gave full information relating to his will and contained 'a touching declaration of his undying love and of his gratitude for all her affection.' On the journey he stayed for a few days at Prague, where, yielding to a universal desire, he conducted one performance of *Der Freischütz*, and heard, for the first time, the great prima donna, Henriette Sontag, then, although only in her eighteenth year, already the idol of the Prague public. Weber himself, however, was not greatly impressed by her singing. He was received in Vienna with open arms and warm enthusiasm and hospitality, and very soon he was completely cognizant of all the material that was likely to be available for the adequate representation of the opera. Another young singer he heard, Wilhelmine Schröder, then also a mere slip of a girl of eighteen, but later to become world-famous as the great Madame Schröder-Devrient, made a much greater impression on him than Sontag had done, and only her extreme youth and the danger of completely alienating some of the older pillars of the Viennese opera probably prevented his writing one of the principal parts in *Euryanthe* for her.

The new opera was wanted for the beginning of July 1822, but to this Weber declined to bind himself. He had his duties at Dresden to consider, and he still had in view the completion of his opera *Die drei Pintos* for the Dresden stage. He intended to dedicate this work to the king and he had actually sent in a petition for permission to do so, a request which the king himself probably never saw, for a few days later the composer received, from the minister Count Einsiedel, a definite refusal, on the ground that permission to produce *Der Freischütz* had already been given, and it was out of the question for two expensive operas by the same composer to be staged so soon after each other. This came to Weber as one of the crowning mortifications of his life and probably constituted the suffering musician's actual death-blow. Steady and consistent work on *Die drei Pintos* was therefore, from this moment, abandoned, for although he kept the fragmentary score by him to the end, even taking it with him on his last fatal journey to London, his work on it must have been very desultory and any real interest he had had in it had long waned. On 17th May 1824, indeed, he wrote to Lichtenstein: 'I think as little of the Pintos now as of music in general. I am quite tired of it, and am not likely to undertake any more elaborate works in a hurry.'

A third reason for his inability to commit himself to an early completion of *Euryanthe* was Caroline's condition and the uncertain state of her health. About 28th April 1822 [1] she gave birth to a son who, two days later, was christened Max Maria Christian Philipp, the 'Max' having been given in honour of the hero of *Der Freischütz*. Yet, in spite of all these factors, Carl Maria undoubtedly made extraordinary progress with the composition of the opera, especially when one considers the apparently endless trouble, uncertainty and anxiety that was entailed upon both the librettist and composer before they succeeded in getting the utterly hopeless book into even the amazingly inadequate creation that stands before us to-day. That an opera with such a book has lived and exercised such a universal influence upon the evolution of grand opera as *Euryanthe* has done, can only be accounted for by the soaring genius and unique originality of Weber himself. He had received the first act in what was almost its final form as early as 15th December 1821, and the remainder was in his hands during the Vienna visit in the spring of 1822. There can be little doubt that, while savouring the sparkling gaiety of the Austrian capital and tasting the joys and intellectual pleasures of Viennese society, he was steadily gathering up impressions and working out many a theme and episode that later appeared in concrete form in his mighty score. It may be mentioned in passing that, on this visit, he renewed many former

---

[1] The actual date of the birth is very much in doubt. In a letter to Gänsbacher, dated 28th April 1822, Weber wrote:

'On 25th March, at eleven o'clock in the forenoon, my Lina gave birth to a healthy boy.' This is more likely to be right than the date given in the text, which is derived from the *Life* written by the baron himself. It is scarcely likely that Weber would be writing to Gänsbacher on the very day on which the child was born and date the event more than a month earlier. On the other hand, the composer only arrived in Dresden, on his return from Vienna, on 26th March, the day following that on which, in accordance with his own statement, the child was born, while Benedict tells us that he 'returned to his yearned-for home, where his wife *soon afterwards* gave birth to his eldest son.' Kroll gives the date as 25th April, but, as usual, without quoting his authority.

and established several new acquaintances, including those with the humorist Castelli, the poet Grillparzer, Caroline Pichler the novelist, the critics Kanne and Steiner and the musicians Schubert and Salieri. It is characteristic of Weber that he could never forget the treatment that the last-named was supposed to have meted out to his hero Mozart, and although Salieri was then exactly double his age, Weber refused to unbend in his presence, so that the two parted, as they had met, coldly and distantly.

After attending a performance of *Der Freischütz*, mutilated beyond recognition by the censor, Carl Maria in an access of disgust nearly changed the whole course of his final development when he was offered an attractive commission to write a grand opera for the Parisian music publisher, Maurice Schlesinger; but saner views prevailed when the censor withdrew many of his objections to *Der Freischütz* and its creator was allowed to conduct it with 'my devil and my rifle-balls' restored, and Wilhelmine Schröder in her original part. So great was its success that the composer wrote in his diary: 'It is impossible I can ever expect to witness greater enthusiasm. I have reached my climax, and I tremble for the future.' To his friends he remarked laughingly: 'It is all over with me. That young rascal, *Der Freischütz*, has shot his poor sister *Euryanthe* dead!'

On 15th May Weber, Caroline and the infant Max took up their residence in the comfortable little cottage at Hosterwitz, adjoining the royal summer palace of Pillnitz. Here all was beauty and charm amid river, forest and mountain scenery in which the composer's love of nature must have found a veritable nest of inspiration. It is little wonder, therefore, that the work of composition proceeded with lightning rapidity. Distinguished visitors, who by coming to him honoured themselves as much as the composer, were not lacking at the smiling farm-cottage at Hosterwitz. Among the most distinguished were Tieck, Jean Paul Richter, Wilhelm Müller the poet and Wilhelmine Schröder. Spontini also, of all impossible people, appeared, and while Weber doubtless received him with hospitality that was equal in warmth and sincerity to that accorded to his other guests, the stately Italian was not a cordial personality, and the Weber household could scarcely be sorry when he took his departure. The place and its surroundings were ideal for the work of composition, especially to one of Weber's temperament, and the congenial company was scarcely less inspiring. Thus the opera soon came well within sight of completion.

All this time his duties at Dresden were three times more than normal. *Preciosa* was given there on 27th June, with little success, which rather added to the depression under which the composer was then labouring; but this lack of enthusiasm on the part of the Dresden people for a work that was being greeted with unreserved applause all over Germany only proved to his mind how hopeless it was to continue the attempt to win over a court and people that were so completely influenced by Italian intrigues. In spite of the happy times he had and the progress he made with *Euryanthe*, Weber himself, however, considered that the summer had been bad as well as good—

bad [he wrote to Gänsbacher] because I could scarcely work at all, for owing to the illness of the church composer Schubert, the whole weight of the official service was laid on me alone, and as we lived in the country near Pillnitz, one German mile from this, I was constantly on the high road, thus wasting both money and time. Morlacchi being ill at present, the Italian duties also devolve on me, and likewise all the festivities in honour of the nuptials of Prince Johann; indeed, I was obliged to conduct Morlacchi's new cantata.

The baron very amusingly tells thus of some of the composer's adventures on the high road:

Weber, in his state of chronic weakness, found it impossible to be ever going from country to town and back, and conceived the unlucky idea that it would be better to have a carriage and horses for his own driving. Vainly did Caroline protest—vainly did friends joke at the idea of Weber as a dashing Phaëton. A handsome open carriage was procured. For a day or two all went well. At last came an upset, to prove that the composer had no talent as a coachman; and his illness was increased by the shock, as well as by the unwonted exertion of returning home on foot. Spite of this accident, however, the passion for horses and carriages remained with Weber to his death and cost him endless annoyances and countless expense. The desire for being renowned as driving the handsomest equipages in Dresden was one of his little vanities.

The end of September saw the family back at Dresden, the composer, in the midst of interminable bickerings with the ridiculous Helmine von Chezy over the incorrigible libretto of *Euryanthe*, bubbling over with irrepressible wonder and delight at the remarkable achievements of the young eight- or nine-months-old Max—cutting his first tooth, devouring his first biscuit, and even getting his face swollen, 'poor innocent.' Early in the year his old friend Heinrich Bärmann married for the second time, and we get a glimpse of the old happy Weber in some humorous verses fitted by him to fragments from Mozart's *Magic Flute*, which he sent on 26th December to the new Frau Bärmann, with the following covering letter:

DRESDEN,
Dec. 26th 1822.

I thank you sincerely for the kind description of me, in your letter, as the faithful friend of your Heinrich. As such, I am certainly entitled to your sympathy and I would not have hesitated to claim it, if your kind letter had not so agreeably forestalled me. But thereby you furnish matter for reproach on my part, for is it right that you should thus overwhelm your husband's intimate friend with so much flattery as completely to shut his mouth? Do not allow yourself to be dazzled, nor look upon me through the spectacles of my friend Bärmann, who apparently has not hesitated to conjure me up before your eyes in a manner that only his love for me should inspire. It will end in my fearing to make your acquaintance, a thing, indeed, which I particularly desire, for should it come to pass, you will see in me only a very ordinary individual, only good enough not to be considered bad, a little gloomier than is necessary, but filled with good sentiments towards

his friends, and with everlasting gratitude for your warm regards. I
am fully convinced that, one day, I shall become deeply in your debt for
the happiness you will bring to my good Heinrich. That is a debt
which I beg of you to heap, without measure, upon my shoulders, for
thus you will render me for ever,

Your entirely devoted,
C. M. von WEBER.

One of Weber's greatest deprivations during long years of labour
at Dresden was his separation from his old student friend Gänsbacher, for whom he had an affection that almost surpassed the
love of women, and towards the end of 1822 he began an active
movement towards obtaining for him a post at the Saxon court.
Johann Gänsbacher was a composer of church music which,
although of little originality, was yet sincere and characterized by
solid workmanship. His suitability for the office then held by
the Schubert whose illness, destined to prove fatal a year later, and
already necessitating Weber's having an assistant, seems to have
been established beyond cavil, and Weber moved heaven and
earth to get him appointed as one of the directors it was proposed
to engage for carrying on the work. But the Italians were again
employing all their underground methods of obstruction, and
matters moved with a degree of slowness that drove Carl Maria
almost to distraction. Gänsbacher sent Weber composition after
composition for submission to the king or performance at court,
but frustration of one sort or another was the fate of every attempt
on Weber's part to achieve his purpose.

Meanwhile, the work on *Euryanthe* steadily advanced. From his
sketches he had scored the work in sixty days, but that signified
only the beginning of his troubles. He was still wrestling with
the impossible libretto. An example of what this implies may be
gathered from the fact that the finale of the second act was remodelled three times before he considered it to be even tolerably
effective. He discussed the question of alterations with Tieck
and Carl Förster, and quarrelled with them over it, and at one

time he conceived the idea of raising the curtain in the middle of the overture in order to exhibit a *tableau vivant* to explain certain points that were left in obscurity in the actual book. Fortunately, he was dissuaded from that, but by this time he must have recognized the complete absurdity of the literary aspect of the work, though no doubt it was then too late to consider its abandonment, and there was no alternative to his plodding on with it to the bitter end. Perhaps, also, he was glad of a little interruption at this stage. This was occasioned by a request that he should compose a *Festspiel*.[1] With Wilhelmine Schröder in Dresden, he also conceived the idea of producing Beethoven's *Fidelio*, and he entered into correspondence with the great master on the subject. Many letters were exchanged, all of which have completely vanished, except one in which Beethoven, acknowledging the receipt of forty ducats 'for the performance of *Fidelio* at Dresden,' speaks of Weber as 'my dear friend.' The opera was produced on 29th April 1823, with Wilhelmine Schröder as Leonore, and conducted by Weber from a score that had been sent to him by Beethoven himself. About this time, too, *Abu Hassan* was given at Dresden, and by a lucky chance a visit paid to Dresden by

[1] Baron Max von Weber states 'in honour of the birthday of the Princess Theresa,' and he is followed by Kroll, who identifies the work as the small Cantata, *Wo nehm' ich Blumen her*. But the baron goes on to say that 'Of this little work nothing remains but the vocal parts. The pianoforte score only shows a few dotted indications. Probably Weber, in the press of business, never wrote it down, and played from memory.' Kroll describes this work as being 'for three solo voices with piano accompaniment. It was only for high voices that Weber set the charming, popular, singable music of this work. It begins with an instrumental and recitatival introduction, a highly representative soprano feature, "Ach, die Blumen sind dahin," with an interchange of singing of all sorts, following.' The words of this composition were written by Theodor Hell. But Benedict has quite another story to tell: 'A *Festspiel*,' he says, 'the words by Ludwig Robert, composed for the wedding of Prince Johann, formed the only interruption to the incessant labour at his opera.'

Ludwig of Bavaria gave Weber a welcome opportunity of giving a special performance of *Preciosa*, which so delighted the Bavarian monarch that, to the scandalized astonishment of the Dresden public, 'he leaned from his box to address the conductor in the orchestra, clapped his hands with energy, and called "Bravo!" like any common man.' Last of all came the great performance of *Der Freischütz* with Wilhelmine Schröder as Agathe and her future brother-in-law, Emil Devrient, who later made a great name for himself as an actor, as Caspar. In his diary Weber wrote of him, somewhat prophetically: 'He sang abominably, but he may one day become a very great actor.'

On 10th May Weber returned to Hosterwitz and every spare minute he had was now consecrated to work on *Euryanthe*. 'By 8th August,' we are informed,

the whole opera was designed and sketched out. Composition and instrumentation were carried on together. With such persistent labour was the whole put on paper that by the 20th of the same month the entire score, with the exception of the overture, was completed. The develop-ment of the already conceived ideas for this last task was commenced on 1st September, and was ready on his desk on the 8th. The pre-paration of the pianoforte score of the first act had been carried on simultaneously.

And his son adds:

Never was a greater proof given of the clear perspicuity of Weber's genius, which enabled him to build up the entire edifice of his work before his pen was put to paper, to note it down without correction.

On 16th September 1823 the composer, accompanied by his young and beloved pupil Julius Benedict, and with the score of *Euryanthe* in his portfolio, set out for Vienna. Again, to his regret, he was compelled to leave Caroline, whose health was still very uncertain, with her child at Dresden. On his way through Prague he sold the right of representation of the opera in that city to the manager of the theatre there, Herr Holbein, who sent him in payment ten ducats more than he had asked for.

He arrived in Vienna on 21st September. By that time an apparent relapse into his trouble had caused his high spirits to evaporate, and a depression had come over him which brought back to his mind, more poignantly than ever, the idea that his 'evil star' was again very much in the ascendant. Undoubtedly, his arrival was ill-timed. His imitators, Weigl and Kreutzer, had carried to such excess the magico-romantic effects that the musical public of Vienna was already turning away from the German opera in disgust. And, as in Dresden, so in Vienna, the Italian opera was very much in vogue. An admirable company under the superintendence of no less eminent a musician than Rossini, and conducted by Carafa, was carrying all before it. Weber himself instantly realized the futility of entering into any sort of competition with a company that included in its ranks such singers as the great cantatrice and actress, Fodor, the tenors David and Donzelli, the baritone Ambrogi and that most ponderous of basses, Lablache; all of them then at the very height of their powers. In a letter to Caroline, he wrote:

I heard the *Matrimonio segreto*.[1] Oh, my beloved mousie! Such a pair of artists as Fodor and Lablache have never come before me. It was perfection—the highest, purest, grandest, most delighting that nature could bestow or art create for the delectation of the musician. Oh! could but the Fodor sing my Euryanthe! People would go mad, I think—I should.

And again:

I heard the *Semiramide*[2] last night. In song and acting everything was admirable; the Fodor and Lablache inimitable. Such Italian opera could excite nothing but enthusiasm. I grow more angry with my Germans than with these Italians.

One night, at a performance of Rossini's *Cenerentola,* he suddenly left his box in a rage, and, on the following morning, when asked why he had done so, he replied: 'When it comes to such a pass that these confounded Italians please even me with their trumpery

[1] By Cimarosa.   [2] By Rossini.

stuff, the devil must be in it. I could stand it no longer.' And then he laughed at his own comical wrath. As the baron remarks: 'He laughed, but he still suffered inwardly.' So, with a sigh and his favourite consolatory ejaculation, 'Well, as God may will it!', *Euryanthe* was put into rehearsal without delay, and they started not at all badly. With Henriette Sontag to set against Fodor, and with a chorus that sang admirably and an orchestra that was almost perfect, he should have had little to worry about. But there were underground influences still at work, and in quarters where they were least to be expected. Many of his professed friends denounced the work. His own stage manager, Gottdank, declared that 'it was hard to understand, and harder to sing such music.' And the great Franz Schubert, who evidently had a grudge against Weber, made no attempt whatever to dissemble his antagonism.

The outstanding event of Weber's sojourn in Vienna, on this occasion—perhaps, in his eyes, even greater in importance than the production of *Euryanthe* itself—was his visit to, and reception by, Beethoven. Benedict tells how he happened to be in the music shop of Steiner-Haslinger, when Beethoven appeared and passed some remarks in commendation of Weber's new work, and of the care, devotion and energy he had displayed in the production of *Fidelio* at Dresden, of which he had been informed by Wilhelmine Schröder. Someone must have then directed his attention towards young Benedict, and what then happened may best be told in Benedict's own words:

He approached me with his inseparable tablet in his hand, and in his usual brusque manner addressed me: 'You are Weber's pupil?' I gave an affirmative nod. 'Why doesn't he come to see me? Tell him to come to Baden with friend Haslinger,' pointing to Steiner's partner. Asking for his tablet, I wrote in it: 'May I come, too?' He smiled, replying, '*Ja, kleiner Naseweis*' (Yes, you saucy little fellow).

This conversation was duly reported to Weber, and a meeting was arranged. On 5th October, therefore, Weber, Haslinger and

Benedict drove out to Baden, where Beethoven was staying until the late autumn. They were received by the master with boisterous cordiality. He recognized Weber at once and greeted him with a shout: 'There you are, you little devil!' (*du Teufels Kerl* [1]). *Der Freischütz* had opened the eyes of 'the old bear' to Weber's real genius. Examining the score one day in the 'musical emporium,' he suddenly banged it with his fist and cried: 'I never could have believed it of the poor weak little manikin. Weber must write operas now; nothing but operas, one after another!' And of the finale of the second act he said: 'I see what he means, but he has put such devilish queer stuff in here! When I read the wild hunt, I can't help laughing, but for all that I feel that it is the real thing. This is music that must be heard—heard only.' Poor Beethoven! He was able to hear it only with his eyes. Nevertheless he was able to hear more with his eyes than most listeners could with their ears and he easily detected in Weber the pioneer of real nationality in German music. The visitors found his place in the most appalling disorder—'music, money, clothing on the floor, the bed unmade, broken coffee-cups upon the table, the open pianoforte with scarcely any strings left and thickly covered with dust, while he [Beethoven] himself was wrapped in a shabby old dressing-gown.' In order to find Weber a seat, a pile of music had to be pushed from an old sofa on to the floor. Beethoven, as usual, was full of complaints, but in his own rough way he treated Weber kindly. They dined together in the Sauerhof, as the guest afterwards wrote in his diary, 'in the happiest mood,' and many questions of art were discussed. At one point the question of *Euryanthe* was raised. 'How is the book?' asked Beethoven. 'Full of good situations!' replied Weber. But the master suddenly caught a glimpse of Haslinger's countenance and burst out laughing: 'Ah!' he roared, 'the old story! These

---

[1] This is an expression not easy to translate. I give it in what is perhaps the form most in keeping with our English idiom, but 'you devil's spawn' is probably a more accurate rendering.

German authors have not the least idea as to how a good opera-book should be written!' But Weber was not to be downed in this fashion. 'What about *Fidelio*?' he inquired. 'Ah, that is different altogether,' said Beethoven, 'it was derived from the French and translated into German from the Italian!' At last the time of parting arrived and Benedict tells how loath the elder master was to let the younger one go. 'Again and again Beethoven embraced Weber, and it was long before he would loose the thin delicate hand from the grasp of his mighty fist.' But at last they tore themselves away, and Beethoven's last words were: 'Success to your new opera; if I can, I will come on the first night!' Circumstances, however, prevented the fulfilment of this promise, and the two musicians never met again.

In an obscure back-street off the Graben there was in the Vienna of that time a small inn, called the 'Blumenstöckel.' To all outward appearance it was a poor enough place, and the common-room in which beer and sour Austrian wine were consumed was in no way different from the ordinary low-class taverns of the period. But beyond this apartment there lay a long, low-ceilinged room in which were placed a large deal table and a number of common wooden chairs. It was a dark, smoky chamber lit only by oil lamps and tallow candles. This cave-like apartment was already attaining a reputation that was spreading far beyond the confines of Vienna, or even of Austria, under the name of the *Ludlams Höhle*, by reason of the famous literary, scientific and artistic personalities who habitually frequented it. To this choice company Weber and Benedict were very soon introduced, and nowhere were the merits, demerits and future of *Euryanthe* more freely and frankly discussed than here. But however adversely they might criticize each other in the privacy of their 'cave,' the Ludlamites were loyal to their fellows when it came to such an event as a public performance; and, especially in view of the preference shown by the higher aristocracy for Italian opera and their opposition to the so-called German element, and of the possibility of unfavourable demonstrations against the composer, they pledged themselves to a man to give all their support to Weber on the evening of the first performance of *Euryanthe*.

Meanwhile the rehearsals were proceeding apace, and the love and enthusiasm shown by principals and chorus alike for the music of the opera could scarcely be restrained. But there were, not far away, the usual snakes in the grass. A remark passed by Franz Schubert, who had been present at some of the rehearsals: 'How Weber will manage all his awkward masses I can't conceive; he had better have left it alone!' got abroad and exercised its deadly purpose in diminishing the public curiosity and interest in the opera. Then the absurd Helmine von Chezy must needs appear upon the scene to worry Weber's life out with interminable and unnecessary alterations of the text, and by insistent demands for higher rates of remuneration than those which had been agreed upon. Worst of all, at the last rehearsal but one, when, for the first time, the entire work, including the overture, was given, the performance, without any repetitions, lasted four hours. Soon the fatal news was universally known and consternation reigned. Even Weber himself was horrified, although he passed the matter off with his now famous *bon mot*: 'My Euryanthe should be called Ennuyante.' This was completely in the spirit of Viennese raillery and other jokes followed in the same not ill-natured manner. 'Weber writes for eternity,' ran one of these, 'so, of course, his opera must be eternally long.' But the composer did not despair, and at the very last minute we find him writing to Caroline: 'My star has had its sacrifice; and so I rely on God and my *Euryanthe*.' [1]

The degree of interest and expectation that had been aroused by Weber's presence in Vienna must, in spite of every untoward circumstance that had intervened, have been immense, and it can only partially be estimated from the solid mass of people who filled the Kärnthnerthor Theatre almost to suffocation on the

[1] A quotation from the opera: 'Ich bau' auf Gott und meine Euryanth'!' repeated by Adolar more than a dozen times in the first act, to a theme also used in the overture. (See p. 207.)

fateful evening of 25th October 1823, when *Euryanthe* was to be heard for the first time in public. Everybody who was anybody in Vienna, with perhaps one single exception—Beethoven, who sent a kindly message regretting his inability to attend[1]—was in the theatre on that occasion. The cream of the Austrian aristo/ cracy packed the boxes, and Baron Max quaintly remarks that 'in the pit and galleries was the more strictly musical portion of the Vienna world.' The *Ludlams Höhle* turned out almost to a man. As the time approached for Weber to appear, the excite/ ment in the theatre became so tense that one false word or action might have had tragic effects—or the opposite, which indeed un/ expectedly happened. The incident must be told, and only Benedict's relation can do it the justice it deserves:

Out of the surging waves of the pit, swaying too and fro, arose, on the top of the last bench, the figure of a by no means prepossessing lady, past the meridian of life, in a shabby dress, an old worn/out hat, and a shawl that had seen better days. Her attempts to gain in a rational way the front seat allotted to her having been frustrated, the gangways being im/ passable, she tried to find her way *over* the crowd, exclaiming loudly:

---

[1] 'On the day following the second representation of *Euryanthe* the Steiner Emporium was crammed to suffocation by all the litterati and musical celebrities of the Austrian capital, to discuss the great artistic event of the day. On this occasion almost all the literary men were staunch on Weber's side; the professional musicians almost all ranged against him. . . . In the midst of the noisy whirl of discussion, and the skirmishing of defence and attack, the giant Beethoven entered the shop. "How did the new opera go?" he cried as he bustled in. "A great success!" wrote Haslinger. "I am delighted," cried the great man— "delighted! Yes; the German can still hold his own above all their Italian sing/song! And little Sontag; how did she sing?" he asked again eagerly. "Exquisitely!" Beethoven positively smirked with pleasure. Then, turning to young Benedict, who was present, he said: "Tell Herr von Weber I would have come, but—for many long years, you know——" He pointed to his ears, and rushed from the shop.'— MAX VON WEBER, ii, 338.

'Make room, make room for me, I say! I tell you I am the poetess! the poetess!' This, accompanied by mocking shouts of laughter, was taken up by the whole pit and echoed by the boxes: 'Room for the poetess! room for the poetess!' and did not cease till Frau Helmine von Chezy was squeezed into her seat, after having been literally passed over the heads of the people.

This had no sooner been done than the composer appeared in the orchestra, and the incident was immediately forgotten in the thunders of applause with which he was greeted. The opera then had its first public performance which, although not a failure, could scarcely be described as a conspicuous success. The overture was badly played and its essential greatness remained unperceived. After the appearance of Sontag, the audience came to life, and again applauded loudly and vigorously, but Weber doubtfully shook his head and remarked to one of his colleagues: 'They have fired off their powder too soon!' He was right. The waits between the acts were abnormally long and this, added to the complexity and obscurity of a mutilated story that itself was bad beyond repair, soon exhausted the patience of the audience, and although, at a very late hour, the curtain fell amid much applause, there were still unmistakable signs of disapproval and hostility. The occasion was afterwards celebrated by a supper at the *Ludlams Höhle*, to which Weber and all the members of the company were invited, and praises and honours were showered upon the composer's head, so that to him all seemed well. 'So closed a day,' he wrote to Caroline, 'which must ever remain impressed upon my mind, and which, I sincerely hope, may take a place in the history of art.' Which, of course, it certainly does, and the quality of the immediately succeeding performances seemed to place the opera on a higher plane than at first appeared to be its proper rank.

But the critics were already snarling at his heels. Nor was a great fellow-composer kindly disposed towards it. 'The opera,' declared Schubert, 'is utterly unmusical, deficient in all form and order, without any solid foundation for the display of real talent and, so far as scientific treatment is concerned, giving clear evidence that the composer had studied in the school of a mere mounte-bank,' meaning Vogler, of course. 'The man abuses Rossini,' he went on, 'and yet, when he does contrive to catch a scrap of melody, he is sure to crush it to death, like a mouse in a trap, with his overwhelming orchestration.' But Weber was probably beginning to feel the approach of another of the now periodical attacks of his malady, and he certainly was already suffering most acutely the pangs of homesickness, and these remarks affected him to a lesser extent than they might otherwise have done. But the crowning honour of an audience with the emperor, who had accepted the dedication of *Euryanthe*, had been fixed for 1st November, and he must perforce stay till then. The emperor received him with great cordiality and sent him a magnificent snuff-box, studded with diamonds. On 5th November he left Vienna, and he was scarcely well on his way before the *Kapell-meister* Conradin Kreutzer began to tinker with *Euryanthe*, which he eventually reduced to a work of only two hours' duration, but at such a cost that, as Benedict records, 'some of the finest points were omitted, others were so maimed and mutilated as to make them lose their original form; the libretto, always obscure, became a perfect jumble. . . .' To such a state was it thus reduced that, after twenty more performances, the opera was withdrawn, and it was not heard upon the Vienna stage again for years.

On his way back to Dresden Weber passed through Prague and had the joy of conducting *Der Freischütz* once more at his old theatre there, the management having postponed the fiftieth performance of that opera until he was able to come. Soon after his return to Dresden he learned, much to his surprise, that his frequent requests for an assistant to relieve him of many of the added duties that had devolved upon him through the prolonged absence of Morlacchi, had at last been granted, and he lost not a minute in joyfully writing to Gänsbacher to come on to Dresden at once, as the post was now his for the taking. But the latter, weary of waiting and with hope abandoned, had just accepted the post of *Kapellmeister* of St Stephen's in Vienna. This was a sad disappointment to Weber, who had buoyed himself up for months, if not years, in the expectation of once again having his dear and lifelong friend working with him. Later on Heinrich Marschner was appointed to the post. And, last of all, on his own recommendation, he and Benedict, who had been to him almost a son, parted company, as he thought that the latter was now sufficiently advanced to enter upon an independent artistic career and that his own rapidly declining health prevented him from doing him the degree of justice his talents demanded.

As if Weber had expended all his energy and inspiration upon the creation of *Euryanthe*, it is a strange fact that immediately thereafter his creative powers came to a sudden stop, and from 19th October 1823 until 23rd January 1825 he composed nothing but one short French song, *Elle était simple et gentillette*. Benedict informs us that 'even this would not have been written but for the incessant entreaties of the author of the words, M. de Cussy.'

The year 1824 opened badly for the composer. His health was now rapidly declining, and it was not helped by the almost complete failure of the opera, which depressed him more than anything. In a letter to Danzi he wrote:

> The expectations of the masses have been puffed up to such an absurd and impossible pitch by the wonderful success of *Der Freischütz* that now, when I lay before them a simple, serious work, which only aims at truth of expression, passion and characteristic delineation, without any of the exciting elements of its predecessor, what can I expect? Be it as God will!

He was also greatly mortified by the interminable delays and obstacles that were continually being raised in connection with the Berlin production. An acrimonious correspondence with Spontini embittered him still further. But he found one great source of consolation in the production of *Euryanthe* at Dresden, with Wilhelmine Schröder in the title-part, on 31st March, after only eleven rehearsals. And, strange to say, at Dresden, of all places, it proved a conspicuous success, or, as Weber wrote to Lichtenstein, 'a brilliant triumph.'

All this time his innumerable duties were being assiduously performed; but the time came at last when he could go no farther, and he sought relaxation and recovery in a short visit to Marienbad. But there was to be no more recovery for poor Weber. The usual homesickness had also hastened his return to Hosterwitz, which actually occurred in the beginning of August. There a letter awaited him from Charles Kemble, who was then the lessee of Covent Garden Theatre in London, requesting Weber to write a new opera for his theatre and to come to England with it himself, there to produce it and conduct representations of *Der Freischütz* and *Preciosa* as well. This was not the first offer he had received for a new opera since the appearance of *Euryanthe*. There had already come several such offers from Paris, and the composer hesitated long between them. But friends intervened and strongly advised his acceptance of the London offer in preference to the others, and eventually he decided in its favour, chiefly on their advice, but also because of a strong predilection he felt for England, and out of respect for the illustrious family to which Charles Kemble belonged. Before doing so, however, he had a heart-to-heart consultation with his friend and physician, Dr Hedenus. He had at last paid up every penny of his father's debts and also of his own, contracted during his stormy sojourn at Stuttgart. This honourable conduct, combined with the more lavish mode of living necessitated by the position he occupied at Dresden, had left him with very slender means and certainly nothing to leave in the event of his death, which he himself was beginning to realize could not be long in coming. So, relating the whole of the circumstances to the doctor, he asked for a candid opinion on the matter of his health. The doctor replied: 'If you abandon all ideas of composing or conducting and spend a year at least in Italy doing absolutely nothing, you may live for another five or six years.'

'And if I do not agree?' asked Weber.

'Then,' answered the doctor, 'it can only be a question of months, or may be of weeks!'

'Ah, well,' said Weber, 'I can never expect to secure a provision for my wife and family by dragging out my life, uselessly, for a few years longer. In England there is a chance of my getting some return for my labours by which I may leave them at least some means which I could not otherwise procure. Be it as God will!'

He thereupon accepted Kemble's offer, and there ensued a rather sordid haggling over terms which, considering the sums he was then paying to Rossini, is little enough to the English-man's credit. The matter being tentatively arranged at last, however, Weber was delighted to receive from Kemble, about the middle of September, a letter permitting him to choose his own subject, but begging him to select a thoroughly German one, and suggesting either *Faust* or *Oberon* as being suitable. Weber immediately seized upon the idea of the latter and wrote to Kemble for a libretto to be sent him by return. It was, however, long in coming. But, conscientious to the last, he began to study English in order that he might the more completely be able to enter into the spirit of the English people for whom the work was to be written. Benedict remarks that 'from 2nd October 1824 till 11th February 1826 (five days before his departure for London), he took 153 lessons, with an astonishing result.' Spitta's testimony to the same effect is a little more detailed: 'So much was he in earnest that, at the age of thirty-seven, and with one foot in the grave, he began to learn English systematically, and was soon able to carry on his own correspondence in English, and when in London astonished everybody by the ease with which he spoke.'

The first and second acts of the opera libretto, which was written by a young *littérateur*, James Robinson Planché, reached him on 18th January 1825, and the third a fortnight later. On 27th February he composed the first notes of the music, Huon's grand scena in the first act, 'From boyhood trained in battle-field.' Strangely enough, after all his excitement and impatience, the work was then laid aside and not touched again for seven months. The explanation of this probably lies in the fact that new annoy/ ances and fresh vexations were again heaped upon his head.

Könneritz, the general director of the theatre, who, if no parti/ cular friend of Weber's, was at least no enemy, received a sudden transfer to the embassy at Madrid, and he was succeeded by Wolf August von Lüttichau, an adherent of the Italian school of opera, and a true disciple of Einsiedel. Whether Weber actually suffered materially from this appointment is in doubt, but it hung over his head like the sword of Damocles. The quality of pro/ duction and performance of the Italian opera in Dresden was steadily improving and the works were becoming more popular, while a performance of Spohr's *Jessonda*, magnificently sung by Wilhelmine Schröder and conducted by Weber, had fallen flat. Finally, in Paris, François Henri Joseph Blaze, better known as Castil/Blaze, a musicologist and critic of wide renown, had sud/ denly conceived the idea of reforming the condition of the operatic stage in France, and his method of doing so lay, to a large extent, in giving garbled versions of the operas of such composers as Mozart and Rossini. In course of time, when *Der Freischütz* was at the height of its popularity, he managed to procure a copy of the score, before it was even published,[1] and getting a dramatic author named Sauvage to write a new libretto in which the scene was laid in Scotland, he renamed the opera *Robin des bois, ou Les Trois Balles*, and produced it in the Odéon Theatre in Paris on 7th December 1824, with conspicuous success, and the pecuniary proceeds he shared with Sauvage and sent not a penny to the composer. Elated with this success, he obtained a piano score of *Euryanthe* and followed the same course with it, with almost equal success. But the garbled version of *Preciosa* proved a failure chiefly through

[1] In a letter of protest, dated 15th October 1825, which Weber sent to the Frenchman, he wrote: 'Vous vous procurez la partition sur un chemin tout à fait illégitime (pour légitime peut/être qu'il vous a paru), car mon opéra n'étant ni gravé ni publié, aucun maître ni marchand de musique n'avaient le droit de le vendre.'

a bad performance. Weber wrote to the management of the theatre and to Castil-Blaze himself, strongly protesting against the immorality of such conduct, but all his communications remained unanswered. To the casual reader these matters may appear to be, if not exactly trivial, at least not sufficiently vital to cause the composer any serious anxiety, but Weber was now a dying man, and his whole nervous system must have been completely deranged. He became obsessed with the aim of making enough money during the short period he now knew he had to live, to give security to his wife and family, after his death.

The beginning of the year 1825 was marked by the birth of another son, Alexander Victor Maria von Weber, to Caroline and the composer, who was now working feverishly at his duties in Dresden and probably at the *Oberon* music in his mind. The Italians, however, had gained a great victory with the production of Morlacchi's *Tebaldo ed Isolina*, the best of all his operas, whereas Weber's production of Cherubini's *Faniska* had been a failure. This depressed him enormously and in the throes of his despair he declined an offer from Count Brühl to compose the witches' music for *Macbeth*, which was then in course of preparation for the Berlin stage—a regrettable refusal.

At the beginning of April a new attack of his disease forced him to pause once again in his labours, and, acting on the advice of Hedenus, he went to Ems to take the waters there. Passing through Weimar, he met the son of Goethe, who pressed him to pay his father another visit. Much against his own inclination he yielded to pressure. Goethe, still under the influence of Zelter, somewhat heavily described himself, in relation to Weber, as no admirer of 'a talent of mushroom growth,' and when the musician called he kept him waiting interminably in an ante-room and twice sent out to inquire 'what the man's name was.' When at last he did condescend to see him, he treated him in the most insulting and unmannerly way imaginable, and dismissed him with such an affectation of hauteur as aroused Weber's ire to so great an extent as to bring on a relapse of his disease that kept him in bed for another two days, during which he was affectionately nursed by his friend Hummel and his family.

Passing through Gotha, where he was kindly treated by many old friends, he reached Wiesbaden, where he had an experience that amply consoled him for the boorish treatment he had received from Goethe. In the hotel there he met a certain Dr. Horn, a man of wide literary attainments and a great lover of music. In the course of conversation the subject of *Der Freischütz* was mentioned, and the doctor, surprised at the knowledge of it that was displayed by his unknown friend, ventured to ask his name. The composer replied that it was Weber. 'Ah, Gottfried Weber?' asked Dr. Horn. Receiving a negative reply, he said: 'Weber of Berlin?' to which the composer answered: 'He has long been dead!' Then the truth began to dawn upon the eager enthusiast: 'You don't mean to say—not—not——' The delighted composer replied: 'Yes! Carl Maria von Weber!' Dr. Horn sat speechless for a little, then, with tears in his eyes, he whispered: 'What a happiness has heaven permitted me!' And Weber himself, in recording the conversation, wrote: 'I could feel only gratitude to Providence for having given me the power to affect so deeply the heart of such a man: it was a rich reward.'

At Ems also he was overwhelmed with kindness and was especially gratified to receive there a visit from Charles Kemble and Sir George Smart, who, being on a visit to Germany, called to discuss the question of the composition and production of *Oberon*. Smart invited him to stay in his house while he was in London. He left Ems on 20th August and returned to Dresden, passing through Frankfort by the way, where, as he noted in his diary, he had the honour of being solemnly welcomed with trumpets and kettledrums during a performance of *Euryanthe*. There was now a slight improvement in his health, and, with a degree of generosity that was almost superhuman, he put Spontini's *Olympia* in rehearsal at once for the Dresden stage. And he went even farther by himself composing an important recitative for the part of the goddess Diana, with a poetical allusion to the wedding of Prince Max with a Princess of Lucca, for the celebration of which the opera was being produced. This act of disinterested generosity on the part of Weber touched Spontini's heart to such a degree that he withdrew all further opposition to the production of *Euryanthe* in Berlin. On 5th December Weber again left Dresden in order to superintend the rehearsals of the opera in the Prussian capital, and the performance took place, at last, on the 23rd. The success achieved was so tremendous that even the old antagonist Zelter was converted. For this triumphant performance Weber received 800 thaler for himself and 100 for the authoress, but even that was given grudgingly by Prince Wittgenstein, and only after strong pressure on the part of Count Brühl.

While he was in Berlin Weber received a letter from Charles Kemble informing him that the arrangements for the performance of *Oberon* at Covent Garden were at last completed, and the composer, although a dying man, devoted every spare hour to the opera and resolved to undertake the journey to London in order that his wife and children should not suffer want after his death. At this time, also, he composed the accompaniments of ten Scottish songs for the famous Edinburgh publisher, George Thompson. But the less said about these the better.[1]

---

[1] Much better would it have been if Weber had accepted an offer he received from the Zürich publisher Nägeli in June 1825, instead of Thompson's. Much water had flowed under the Elbe bridges since that May day in 1810, when he wrote to Nägeli: 'I should very much like to see a work of mine published by your respected firm, and as I have a store of compositions of every kind, I beg you will write to me and say what will best suit you.' The tables had, indeed, been turned when again, on 6th June 1825, he wrote to the same publisher: 'I gratefully acknowledge your flattering proposal, and also your kind remarks regarding myself. I am afraid it will be utterly impossible for me to promise you a pianoforte sonata this year, however. My dramatic works exclusively absorb the whole of my time. Besides, my failing health and ungenial mood, the latter no doubt the result of the former,

COVENT GARDEN THEATRE AT THE TIME OF 'OBERON'

In spite of all remonstances, to which his invariable answer was: 'It's all the same. Whether I go or remain, in one year I am a dead man. But if I go, my children will have bread when their father dies, if I remain they will starve,' Carl Maria von Weber, after a heart-rending parting from his wife and family, on 16th February 1826 set out upon the last journey he was to make. Much to Caroline's satisfaction and relief, the celebrated flautist Fürstenau, who had always been a firm friend and admirer of Weber's, arranged to accompany him. They travelled by easy stages, and reached Paris, where he originally resolved to remain incognito, on the 25th. He stayed with the music publisher Maurice Schlesinger, and in spite of his resolution soon found himself in the vortex of the musical society of the time, by every member of which he was received with almost overwhelming kindness. He called on Rossini, Berton, Catel, Paer, Auber, Onslow and Cherubini who, on two different occasions, returned his call and sincerely, and in the most enthusiastic terms, expressed his admiration for him. Considering Cherubini's brusque and somewhat disgruntled manners, this was probably one of the greatest distinctions that could possibly have fallen to any composer of that age. He visited both the Opéra and Opéra-Comique on several occasions, and at the latter house he heard the first performance of Boïeldieu's *La Dame blanche*, which delighted him to such an extent that he wrote at once to Theodor Hell: 'What a charm it has; what humour! Such a comic opera has never been composed since *Figaro*. Get the book from Schlesinger, translate it at once and make Musje Marschner put it on the stage immediately. It is a catch for our repertory!'

On the bitterly cold morning of 2nd March Paris was left behind and Calais was reached on the 4th. The sea passage was made on the same day. A strange reception awaited Weber at

---

constitute difficulties. I can therefore promise nothing whatever except my perfect willingness to co-operate with you in your new undertaking as soon as my time, strength and inclination permit.'

Dover, where his luggage was allowed to pass through the custom-house unexamined. He was delighted with the English landscapes. 'We dashed along like lightning,' he wrote, 'through a country charming beyond all description. The meadows are of the loveliest green, the gardens full of beautiful flowers, and all the houses are of an elegance and neatness that contrast, in the most incredible way, with the dirt of France.'

London was reached on the 5th and the composer was received with open arms by Sir George Smart in his beautiful and luxurious home at 91 (later 103) Great Portland Street. Here, as in Paris, every one vied with every one else to place Weber at his ease and to make his sojourn in England a memorable joy. Weber had been engaged to conduct twelve of the so-called oratorio concerts, and on 8th March he made his first public appearance in England at one of these, when the overture and a selection of pieces from *Der Freischütz* were performed. On the following day he began the rehearsals of *Oberon* and, although he wrote to Caroline that all was going well, he had not long to wait before the singers who included Ann Paton, Lucia Vestris and the veteran tenor John Braham, were performing their usual tricks, declaring their respective solos to be quite unsuited to their voices and the music generally to be more or less unsingable. It must surely have been a consequence of Weber's terrible illness that, for the first time in his career, he consented to a substitution: he wrote an entirely new scena, 'Yes, even Love to Fame must yield,' for one to which Braham objected. This, although better adapted to the singer's now somewhat jaded voice, was quite out of keeping with the general style and spirit of the opera. 'I hate the whole business,' the composer wrote to his wife, 'but what can I do? Braham is the idol of the public and so I must swallow the bitter pill.' And he added: 'But I do so love my original air, and you may be sure I shall keep it for Germany.'[1]

[1] The prayer in the second act is said to have also been specially written for Braham during the rehearsals of the opera.

Sixteen rehearsals of *Oberon* were held, and all the time Weber was fulfilling his contract with the oratorio concerts, at each of which, no matter what other works were down for performance, great chunks of *Der Freischütz* had to be rendered, until the music became so popular that every butcher's boy in London was whistling and every barrel-organ was playing the laughing chorus, the bridesmaids' chorus, the huntsmen's chorus and selections from the overture, *ad nauseam*.

On 3rd April Weber conducted the orchestra at a Philharmonic concert, but was chilled by the cold detachment of his audience. The overture to *Oberon* was completed on 9th April and Weber wrote at the end of his score: *Soli Deo gloria!* On 12th April Covent Garden Theatre was crammed to suffocation for *Oberon's* first performance. Every ticket for the first twelve performances had indeed been bought up weeks before, and now every notability, social or artistic, was present and on edge to acclaim the composer. As Baron von Weber records: 'At the last moment, fine gentlemen fought for the last places in the topmost gallery.' For the third time in his life Weber must have felt that the supreme golden hour had come to him. The great audience rose to receive him as soon as he appeared in the orchestra, and for nearly a quarter of an hour the hand-clapping and shouts of acclamation continued. It was only with difficulty that quiet was at length restored and the opera allowed to begin. The same enthusiasm persisted all through the performance. The overture was encored and every number was greeted with the noisiest demonstrations. During the whole evening Weber had the greatest difficulty in preventing a continuous series of outrages upon the dramatic proprieties. But, as usual, the critics were lukewarm and, strange as it may appear to us to-day, their principal grievance was the opera's alleged lack of melody.

Meanwhile, death was steadily creeping on, and while Weber was as eager for work as ever, the price he was paying can never be estimated. To make matters worse, the old home-sickness had him once again in its clutches. A spell of bad weather also took its fatal toll. On 18th April he wrote to Caroline:

To-day is a day enough to kill one, a thick, dark, dank yellow fog. It is almost impossible to see without candles. The sun does not shine; it is only a red patch amid the fog. It is awful. My yearning for Hosterwitz and a bright sky is indescribable. But patience! patience! Day crawls away after day.

And again:

I count the days, hours, minutes, until we meet again. We have often been parted before, and loved each other dearly, God knows! But this terrible yearning I have never known before. God grant me patience.

Private engagements did not come in such numbers as he had expected, and on the solicitation of friends he gave a concert himself, for which many of the best English singers of the day gave their services, on 26th May. He had promised the famous Catherine Stephens to set to music the words of Tom Moore, *From Chindara's warbling fount I come*, and, after reading through the whole of the poem from which they are taken, *Lalla Rookh,* he composed the song, but had not the strength to fill in the accompaniment, which he played impromptu at the concert when it was being sung. This was Weber's last composition, but, despite his now desperate condition, it is quite up to his average, so far as quality is concerned. Weber's rendering of the accompaniment to this song also constituted the last notes he ever played on the pianoforte. The audience, though small, on account of many untoward circumstances, was vociferous in its enthusiasm, but even that did not prevent his collapse immediately after the concert.

His desire for home now became almost a passion, and in spite of all that the doctors could say he fixed 6th June as the day of his departure. His sole cry was: 'I must go back to my own— I must! Let me see them once more—and then God's will be

done!' In that heart-rending cry, which arose from the very
depths of his soul, we have a complete epitome of Weber's entire
psychological make-up. On the evening of 4th June, it was
apparent to all his friends that the master was very seriously ill,
but he would allow no one to sit by his bedside. He bade all
who were present—Sir George Smart, Goeschen, Fürstenau and
Moscheles—good night, and as he was led away to his bedroom
by his host, he said: 'May God reward you all for your kind love
to me!' On reaching the bedroom, he wound up his watch,
shook hands with Smart and said: 'Now let me sleep!' These,
so far as any one can know, were the last words he ever spoke.
'After he had left their midst,' Max von Weber informs us,

For a long time the friends sat together in Sir George Smart's room,
filled with sorrowful presentiments, and earnestly consulting what means
might best be taken to prevent the journey. About midnight the party
broke up. On leaving the house, they noted that all was dark in
Weber's room. His light had been extinguished.

The rest cannot be better told than in the words of Benedict:

Early on the morning of the 5th, when Sir George Smart's servant
knocked at Weber's door, he received no answer. He knocked again
and again, but without result. Alarmed, he went to his master, who
rushed immediately to the room. Fürstenau was sent for and arrived
anticipating the worst. After repeated fruitless attempts to be heard
they burst the door open and approached the bed.[1] There the beloved
friend lay lifeless—his head resting on his hand as if in sweet slumber;
no traces of his suffering could be seen in those noble features. His
spirit had fled—home indeed!

A doctor was called and declared that he had been dead
five or six hours as the result of consumption and an ulcer

[1] After Smart had left him on the previous evening, Weber must have
got out of bed and, in accordance with his usual custom, barred the door
of his room.

in the throat. The corpse was embalmed, and, after many delays, it was interred in Moorfields Chapel,[1] where an imposing funeral service was held, Mozart's *Requiem* being sung on the occasion, by Madame Caradori-Allan, Miss Paton, Braham and Lablache.

Fifteen years later an article appeared in the German periodical *Europa*, making a fiery and fervent appeal for the restitution of Weber's remains to his native soil. Other papers took up the matter and slowly, but steadily, the agitation extended, until, in October 1844, permission was granted by all the authorities concerned for the transfer to be effected. The coffin was landed in Hamburg on 20th October 1844, but owing to the Elbe's being frozen it did not reach Dresden until nearly two months later, on 14th December, when the remains were laid in the family vault, whither his younger son, Alexander, had preceded him only a fortnight earlier, and where Caroline joined him ten years later. On this occasion Richard Wagner delivered a speech over the body of the composer with the following peroration:

There never was a more German composer than thou; in whatever distant fathomless realms of fancy thy genius bore thee, it remained bound by a thousand tender links to the heart of thy German people, with whom it wept or smiled like a believing child listening to the legends and tales of its country. Yes, it was thy child-like simplicity which guided thy manly spirit, like a guardian-angel, keeping it pure and chaste, and that purity was thy chief characteristic. . . . Till death didst thou preserve that supreme virtue. Thou couldst never sacrifice it or alienate this beautiful inheritance of thy German origin; thou couldst never betray us. Behold, the Briton does thee justice, the Frenchman admires thee, but only the German can *love* thee. Thou art his own, a bright day in his life, a drop of his blood, a particle of his heart!

In the materialistic Germany of to-day, one wonders to what extent these words would apply or be accepted. It is one of the

[1] This is the Roman Catholic Church of St Mary, situated at the corner of East Street, Finsbury Circus.

tragedies of modern social and political life that we have every-where departed so completely from the spirit of Weber, and a universal revival of his glorious and romantic compositions would, we may feel sure, do more towards the general pacification of our war-weary world than all the loud bombast of dictators or the smooth platitudes of the so-called leaders of the alleged democracies put together. But, as Weber himself inevitably would have said: 'Be it as God will!'

CHAPTER IX

THE EARLY AND MIDDLE DRAMATIC WORKS

In dealing with the musical creations of Carl Maria von Weber, two general factors must be kept constantly in mind: the essential aspects of his work are (1) its almost invariable dramatic character, and (2) its intense romanticism. It is Weber the composer of three operas, a number of overtures and two brilliant works for pianoforte who alone is known to the present generation, yet a study of these works were sufficient in itself to demonstrate the justice of my claim. But, as we have seen, Weber, in his short and busy life, created a great deal of beautiful music besides the works mentioned, and in practically all of it one or both of the two essential factors are traceable, even if, as seldom happens, they are not absolutely self-evident. It is, of course, in the operas that these aspects are most pronouncedly apparent, but there is rarely anything particularly abstruse in Weber's music, and one has not usually far to seek in order to find them in works of other kinds as well. Perhaps the most philosophical work Weber ever wrote was his comparatively early cantata, *Der erste Ton*, and we have already seen how fundamentally dramatic that was, although Spitta is inclined to discredit that view 'because the poem is narrative and not dramatic.' But that is only begging the question, and, given such a setting as Weber gave *Der erste Ton*, the dullest of narrative poems must inevitably acquire so great a dramatic power and impressiveness, as indeed this work actually does, as should raise it from its native mediocrity to a thing of rare and scintillating charm.

Yet what is this subtle dual quality that makes the music of

Weber, who, when all is said and done, was not a startlingly original composer, so full of that indefinable beauty and charm that never seems to pall? Of the incidence of drama in music little need be said. It is largely a matter of trickery, such as the piling up of effects from the softest *pianissimi* to the loudest *fortissimi*, the exaggerated use of the pause and rest and the employment of the oasis method that is so common in the works of Richard Strauss, or of its obverse, a sudden blare of cacophony in the midst of a beautiful melody. The oasis method is frequently employed by Weber, especially in his overtures, but usually more for romantic than for dramatic effect. And that brings us to the point as to what the romantic in music may be, and how it is effected.

In the Introduction to Volume VI of the *Oxford History of Music* (second edition), which deals with 'The Romantic Period,' Edward Dannreuther writes: 'Premising that music, be it vocal or instrumental, is incapable of describing matters of fact, we may speak of the romantic element in music as poetical suggestion by musical means.' But this does not help us much, even with the added 'few typical examples': 'the last eighteen bars of the second act of *Die Meistersinger*, when the moonlight peers through the streets of old Nürnberg after the riot, the forest voices in *Siegfried*, the strange chords when Brünnhilde sinks to sleep.' We reach more solid ground, however, when, after showing how touches of romantic sentiment sporadically occur in works of some of the older composers, Dannreuther demonstrates that there comes a gradual change in music running on more or less parallel lines with the literary trends of the time, until the new form of expression becomes definitely established in the music of Spohr and Weber:

Taken together the romantic movement—in so far at least as instrumental music and the orchestra is concerned—appears as an unconscious tendency towards the relaxation of the laws of structure in favour of characteristic details, an almost total rejection of organic design on self-contained lines, and, step by step, an approach to a sketchy sort of impressionism and a kind of scene-painting—a huge piling-up of means for purposes of illustration.

And he goes on to say that

No doubt it was guilty of many excesses. It was often crude, often extravagant; sometimes apparently inspired by mere defiance and bravado.

But that was later. In whatever light we may choose to regard the musical romanticism of Weber to-day, there can be no question of its having been either crude or extravagant in its conception, even at the time it was composed. In the first place it was written in absolute sincerity and completely reflected the spirit of the time; in the second place it gave a certain degree of musical expression to the racial idealism of the Germanic peoples. There can be no question of the fact that Weber was the true founder of the German national opera. As André Cœuroy has justly remarked, he combines in his music all the characteristics of *l'esprit germanique* in forms of a richer and more apparent description than Germany had ever known before, thus: 'Placé au centre de ce romantisme comme un écho sonore, Weber en résume tous les caractères: inspiration nationale, exotique, légendaire, patriotique, populaire, fantastique, chevaleresque, humoristique, champêtre, symbolique.'

With these factors kept constantly before us, then, we may, without any further preliminaries, pass *in medias res* and, considering the essential and overwhelming dramatic aspect of practically the whole of his musical output, we shall deal first of all with the music-dramas and operas.

Weber on one occasion remarked to Schubert that a composer's earliest operas were like puppies: they ought to be drowned. Whether or not he acted on that principle as regards his own works we do not know, but it is a fact that of his earliest opera, *Die Macht der Liebe und des Weins*, no trace remains, although it is tolerably certain that much of it that appeared to him to be worthy of preservation, was worked into some of his later compositions. And, as far as his second opera, the 'romantisch-komisches' *Waldmädchen*, is concerned, we are little better placed, as only two fragments of the score have survived, one being an aria sung by Mathilde, the other a trio sung by Prince Arbander, Krips the Squire of Prince Sigismund—a low-comedy character to whom Weber gave some of the best music he wrote in the later adaptation of the dumb maiden theme, which appeared under the title *Sylvana*—and Mathilde, the prince's daughter. The two fragments, which, with the rest of Jähns's fine collection of Weber autographs, are now in the Berlin State Library, consist of only 214 bars, but these are sufficient to enable us to detect at once the Weber of the later operas in embryo. What, for example, could be more Weberish than this?

And the opening bars of the trio are such as are the common stock of practically every overture he composed:

Dr Erwin Kroll remarks that the influence of Mozart is very apparent, and he particularly instances the similarity of the opening of the trio to a passage in *Die Zauberflöte*, where Monostatos, after the great duet of Papagena and Papageno, sings the warning notes:

stil - le, bald drin-gen wir in Tem - pel

ein.

Das Waldmädchen, which at different periods carried also the titles *Das stumme Waldmädchen* and *Das Mädchen im Spessartwalde*, was composed, as we have seen, at Freiberg in 1800, to a libretto written by Steinsberg, the director of a company of comedians at Carlsbad. It was originally in two acts and in that form it was rendered at Freiberg by Steinsberg's company and at Chemnitz, in the winter of 1800. It was afterwards revised by Weber and arranged into three acts, and this revision was performed in Vienna, Prague and St Petersburg four years later with a degree of success which the composer himself felt to be somewhat embarrassing, as he had already expressed the opinion that it was immature. The second act had indeed been written in ten days.

Weber's third opera, *Peter Schmoll und seine Nachbarn*, written in 1801, in spite of the fact of little more than a year having elapsed since the completion of *Das Waldmädchen*, shows a remarkable advance, so far as its musical quality is concerned; but this may no doubt be attributed to the supervision exercised over the composer by Michael Haydn while the work was in progress. Like all Weber's operas except *Euryanthe*, *Peter Schmoll* is a *Singspiel*, a musical entity defined by Edward Dannreuther as 'a play of light texture in prose or verse copiously supplied with incidental music.' Up to the time of the emergence of Wagner practically all German operas, with the exception of Weber's *Euryanthe* and Schumann's *Genoveva*, were merely enlarged *Singspiele*.[1]

The whole of the spoken dialogue of Weber's third opera has disappeared, but that loss need not grieve us at all, for thus early Weber was already demonstrating his peculiar genius for making choice of the worst possible librettos he could obtain. Happily, however, the whole of the music has survived, for with *Peter Schmoll* Weber had already begun to exert an influence upon the development of operatic form and technique. It is a fact, strongly emphasized by Philipp Spitta, that when he composed this opera Weber was woefully deficient in a knowledge of the theory of music, and especially so in that of harmonic progressions. His technical equipment was, indeed, practically non-existent. Yet, as the event proved, this was far from being detrimental to the movement which, subconsciously, he was already inaugurating. Generally speaking, music in the larger forms was still more or less hidebound by classical usage, and the hard and inflexible precepts of the 'schools,' so that, if our composer had begun his composition of operas with a greater knowledge of rules and regulations, the likelihood is that the free joyousness that characterizes practically the whole of his operas would have been curbed by the harmonic pedantry that vitiated so much otherwise creditable musical work of this character in the seventeenth and eighteenth centuries.

Bad, however, as the libretto of *Peter Schmoll* undoubtedly was, it was entirely in keeping with the romantic spirit of the times,

[1] *Oxford History of Music*, vol. vi, p. 16.

which, originating in the work of Walter Scott and Byron, had rapidly spread over the whole of Europe. And nowhere was the soil more ready to receive such influences than it was in Germany. It was indeed from Germany itself that the germs which first impregnated the mind of Scott emanated. And they were good enough, and relevant enough, to serve as a peg, or series of pegs, upon which to hang the glorious melodies with which the composer's head was everlastingly teeming.

There is such a thing as the Weberian melody, original, so far as the melodic line is concerned, distinctive and easily distinguishable by those who have steeped themselves in that composer's music, although it is not easily definable. It takes its initial inspiration from the German folksong, with which Weber was so widely and lovingly conversant, but it vastly transcends that wonderful body of national melody by means of a peculiar sweetness that invariably strikes the ear as something essentially new, yet never cloys in repetition. This quality is of course the essential ingredient of Weber's self. But it is not altogether, nor particularly, the vocal work in *Peter Schmoll* that gives it an outstanding degree of importance in the history and development of the music-drama. It was in the orchestration of this work that the composer demonstrated a wealth of originality altogether incommensurate with his age. Spitta, arguing from the academic point of view, is inclined to minimize this. 'He puts almost all he has to say into the voice parts, the accompaniments being unimportant at least as regards polyphony.' But immediately afterwards he contradicts himself in the sentence: 'There is much originality in the harmony, and the colouring is individual and full of meaning.' And that is the significant factor in *Peter Schmoll*. It was the first indication that the German *Singspiel* had begun to throw off all its indebtedness to the Italian models and to pass into the glamorous realm of music-drama.

That Weber fully recognized the value and importance of melody in opera is clearly seen in his reaction to its treatment by Rossini; but even in a *Singspiel* melody was not everything to him.

Indeed, in such a number as Agatha's scena in the second act of *Der Freischütz* there are forty bars of pure vocal recitative, from the beginning to the *vivace con fuoco*, against fifty-five bars of melody, and that, taken at random, is by no means an exceptional case. Both melody and recitative were to him pure media for enunciating the more emotional aspects of the drama or narrative. But further, about the time at which he was working on the score of *Peter Schmoll*, he stumbled, quite by accident, upon an idea which was to have far-reaching effects and ramifications. In his autobiographical sketch, he mentions that, from an article in a musical journal, said by Wilhelm Altmann to have been the *Allgemeine musikalische Zeitung*, he got the idea of 'writing in quite another fashion by bringing into use old forgotten instruments.' This was something that immediately stimulated the imagination of the young composer whose own favourite instrument was the guitar, and he lost no time in putting the suggestion into experimental effect, so that we find the instrumentation of *Peter Schmoll* even more revolutionary than that of Richard Strauss, when we take into account the respective eras in which the two composers lived. It embodied such instruments as two *flauti dolci*—a reed instrument of the recorder family—two basset horns, two bassoons in addition to strings. From the employment of these in various combinations he obtained the idea of orchestral colour which was to play so large a part in the tonal enrichment of his own operas, and of those of later composers down to our own times. The manner in which he obtained his effects may be gathered from the opening few bars from the trio, No. 14 (on opposite page).

As Spitta remarks: 'His motive was not a mere childish love of doing something different from other people, but he had an idea that these strange varieties of tone helped to characterize the situation.' And his idea, which, the *Allgemeine musikalische Zeitung* notwithstanding, must have been almost intuitive, was indeed absolutely right, as Spitta half grudgingly admits. 'In the passage named'—'Empfanget hier des Vaters Segen,' as scored above—'the peculiar combination of wind instruments does

Emp-fan-get— hier des Va - ters Segen.

produce a peculiarly solemn effect.' In the romance sung by
Minette near the beginning of the opera, to an accompaniment of
horns, bassoons, divided violas, cellos and basses, but without
violins, the tone-colours are also particularly rich and quite remarkable as the creation of so youthful a composer at such an
early period in the history of orchestral development. In this
solo he achieves a wonderful effect by means of a solo flute, which
is thus described by Spitta:

Minette sings a mournful song of a love-lorn maiden, and as the voice
ceases, the last bar is re-echoed softly by a single flute solo, a perfect
stroke of genius to express desolation, loneliness and silent sorrow, and
recalling the celebrated passage in the third act of *Euryanthe* where the
desolation of the hapless Euryanthe is also depicted by a single flute.

His further treatment of the flute may be gathered from the two following examples, the first depicting the gambols of a brisk, high-spirited maiden:

and the second from the exquisite *adagio non troppo* of the overture:

As was habitual with Weber, he afterwards used many of the themes of this opera in later works.

Peter Schmoll and his Neighbours was a comic opera of the boisterous Teutonic type, with a good deal of rough horse-play such as one finds in the scene in which Schmoll, Minette and

Hans Bast play blind-man's-buff in the dark; but it was likewise
Teutonic in the sense of its pure romanticism. I have perhaps
devoted more space to it than it actually merits, when it is judged
merely from the point of view of a music-drama, but regarded as
the first step towards the creation of a German national opera,
with all that it held in reserve of what was to follow, and
regarded also as the earliest real attempt to treat the orchestra
as something more important than a mere support to a set
of empty vocal gymnastics, the first opera into which genuine
instrumental colour had been imported as an essential part
of the orchestral scheme, its æsthetic and developmental value is
considerable.

Weber's next opera, *Rübezahl*, belongs, as we have seen, to his
Breslau period, and it is distinguished by nothing but the fact
that it was rather contemptuously dismissed by Spohr as amateurish.
The libretto was based on a legend of the Riesengebirge. Rübezahl, the ruler of the spirits, falls in love with a mortal princess who
is lured into his castle and kept a prisoner there. While she is
there she succeeds in securing his magic sceptre, by means of which
she sends him into the garden to count turnips, each of which,
at her word, turns into a human being, and while Rübezahl is
thus engaged, she calls up a griffin who carries her back to her own
home. This flimsy story was padded out to make a two-act
drama which, as such, was about as bad as any drama could
possibly be; but it contained several magic scenes that were after
Weber's own heart. All the musical numbers have completely
vanished, however, except a chorus of spirits intended to be sung
behind the scenes, a recitative and aria and a quintet for four
sopranos and one bass, and, of course, the overture, although only
eleven bars of this, in its original form, are known to be in existence. From what has survived of this opera, there is nothing to
show that the composer had made any advance on the principles
embodied in the score of *Peter Schmoll*; indeed the music is less
Weberish than any of his preceding works for the theatre that are
now known to us. Some of the passages from the quintet were

afterwards utilized, in Weber's characteristic spirit of borrowing
from himself, in the *Jubel-Ouvertüre* and in his cantata *L'accoglienza*.
And seven years after its composition he completely revised the
overture, which was published under the title of *Der Beherrscher
der Geister* (*The Ruler of the Spirits*). Although essentially
theatrical and somewhat bombastic, this overture is remarkable in
many respects. Weber himself described it in 1811 as the 'most
powerful and lucid thing I have yet written . . . a veritable park
of artillery!' A mere glance at this overture, which is scored for
one piccolo, one flute, two oboes, two clarinets, two bassoons, four
horns, two trumpets, three kettle-drums and strings, amply confirms the latter part of the description, at all events. Vogler's
influence is very apparent here, as he had already employed four
horns and three kettle-drums in his opera *Castor und Pollux* and
in the overture to *Samori*, and we can trace from it a very apparent
and definite influence on Wagner—it is so decided as to be almost
imitative—in his overture to *The Flying Dutchman*. Professor
Sir Donald Tovey comments upon the surprising number of
different themes in the overture, and he remarks, after noting how
the return of the opening bars of the second subject:

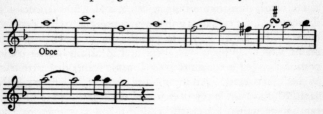

in the tonic major on the brass instruments constitutes 'one of the
most successful pieces of pioneer work in the history of orchestration,' that 'it would be impossible to guess by the sound of it that
this glorious mass of soft harmony for brass instruments was written
with the imperfect resources available in the year in which Beethoven was writing the *Ruins of Athens*.' In the sole surviving
aria from the opera one may find, in the accompaniment, the

earliest example of an harmonic progression that became typically Weberish:

Wie Bien-chen im Früh-ling, hausch! sau-sen sie hin

Reference has already been made to the manner in which Weber's fifth opera *Sylvana* was composed,[1] and taking the facts of the case, as there related, it is little wonder that it should have come down to us as a work of a very unequal character indeed. None the less, its importance is considerable, first, by reason of its being another stage in Weber's development as a composer of opera; secondly, on account of his treatment of the orchestra and his musical material generally, in delineating and individualizing the characters in the drama; and thirdly, by his employment of a new factor—the conversational use of a solo instrument—which exerted a further influence upon Wagnerian methods. Arbitrary as the 'three-period' system may too often be in estimating the work of musical composers, it occasionally does apply, and it is not without reason that Spitta remarks that with *Sylvana* we take leave of Weber's boyish compositions. '*Sylvana* and *Abu Hassan,*' he writes, 'form the middle group of Weber's dramatic works, while *Freischütz*, *Preciosa*, *Euryanthe* and *Oberon* constitute the third and last.'

The story of *Sylvana* is another variation of the *Waldmädchen* theme. The libretto was written by the young poet Franz Carl

[1] See page 37.

Hiemer, who came into Weber's life during his sojourn at the court of King Friedrich in Stuttgart. It concerns a young medieval knight, Count Rudolph von Helfenstein, who is betrothed to Mechthilde, the daughter of a neighbouring Count Adelhardt, obviously an engagement of convenience, as neither is in love with the other. The opera opens with Count Rudolph's setting out, accompanied by his squire Krips, an admirable low-comedy character, on a bear-hunting expedition, and this gives the composer an opportunity for one of his favourite opening hunting choruses. The bear-hunting, however, is only an excuse on the young noble's part to seek out a wild young maiden he had previously encountered in the forest. This girl was living under the protection of a hermit who had instructed her to pretend to be dumb in the event of her ever being addressed by strangers. The hunting-party having reached the forest, a halt is made for refreshment, and while Rudolph is in the midst of a drinking song, the dumb girl comes bounding out of the copse and into the arms of the singer, who promptly carries her off. Rudolph's betrothed, on the other hand, has fallen in love with a certain Albert von Kleeberg, a son of Count Adelhardt's deadly enemy, who had, many years before, in revenge for having been worsted in a love-affair, stormed Adelhardt's castle and carried off another of his daughters whom, it is generally supposed, he had afterwards murdered. In a vigorous duet the lady tells her father that she does not love Rudolph, but he insists that the marriage should take place at once. Following this scene between the enraged parent and his daughter, young Kleeberg, with his friend Kurt, surreptitiously gains an entrance into the apartments of Mechthilde, who is attended by her woman, Clara, which gives the composer an opportunity for the creation of a very charming piece of concerted music—a love quartet—executed in a manner that is entirely characteristic of Weber and shows his master-touch to perfection. At the same time, by a strange error of judgment, Rudolph has introduced the dumb girl into Adel-hardt's castle, where she finds herself in a perfect wonderland, however, and a pantomime scene, in which she dances before a mirror, ensues, again giving Weber an opportunity for the production of music of the most graceful character. Meanwhile the preparations for a gorgeous nuptial display are proceeding, which all add as much to the spectacular aspects of the opera as they do to the musical. The chief event in the festivities is a tournament in which Albert von Kleeberg conspicuously shines, but, on his identity being discovered, he is ignominiously ejected. Further complications ensue when the enraged Count Adelhardt discovers that a pretty young maiden has been secreted in Rudolph's apartments. His anger knows no bounds and he is about to slaughter the intruder in cold blood when Albert returns, bringing with him the hermit Ullrich, who immediately declares that Sylvana is the count's own daughter who had been confided to his care by the elder Kleeberg and brought up by him as his ward. The two pairs of lovers then unite and all ends happily in a torch dance and chorus that constitute another of the bright spots in this strange and luminous opera.

For the reasons already given, *Sylvana* is very unequal in style. The autograph copy of the overture bears the inscription: 'renovata il 23 Marzo 1809,' and this can only imply that it is the overture of his earlier work, *Das Waldmädchen*, slightly revised. It is scored for two flutes, two oboes, two horns, two trumpets, two kettle-drums, violins, violas and basses, to which, according to Jähns, two clarinets and a bass trombone were added in 1822. The opening *andante* is strongly reminiscent of Mozart's *Zauber-flöte* overture, but the quality of the music is vastly inferior. It is turgid and poverty-stricken in ideas, and the entire overture is easily the poorest that Weber composed. Mozart's influence is also apparent in the only other instance that can be established as an actual borrowing from his earlier opera: the aria 'Liegt so ein Unthier ausgestreckt,' the opening of which is identical with a surviving ritornel from *Das Waldmädchen*. This is sung by Krips, who is described by Kroll as 'the droll, swaggering young shaver bursting into the song like a descendant of Mozart's

'Osmin.' And that, indeed, is exactly what he is, as the music allotted to him clearly demonstrates to as great an extent as the actual words to which it is set. This was the idea which after-wards boiled down to the *Leitmotiv*. Weber also adopted here the musical equivalent of the Shakespearian principle of poetry for the noble and prose for the commoner. For example, when the count, Rudolph or Mechthilde have occasion to give expression to feelings of a profound and intense character, they do so in *Kunstlieder*, whereas Krips invariably makes use of the *Volkslied*. Two extracts will sufficiently demonstrate this fact. The first is taken from Rudolph's exquisite love-song, and the second is the first verse of Krips's arietta in E flat, which Spitta describes as being interesting as a specimen of the distinction between Weber's and Mozart's *vis comica* as shown in the *Entführung* and *Zauberflöte*:

fra - gen   schlägt   zärt - lich auch diess Herz für

mich   o   lass   mir die - se Aug - en   sa - gen

Ich   lie - be dich

Oboe

The wide diversity between this beautiful song and that of Krips, described by Weber's son, perhaps a little recklessly, as 'the brightest gem of the opera,' will be apparent immediately, and one can easily appreciate the popular appeal that it made, necessitating its having to be repeated on the occasion of the opera's first appearance, and setting every youth and urchin in Frankfort a-whistling, almost before the echoes of the singer's voice had died away, putting even the balloon ascent of Madame Blanchard immediately in the shade:

A Popular Song

Sah

ich sonst ein Mäd - chen be - scheid - en und

stumm, husch schlich ich ums schüch - ter - ne

Weber

Täub-chen her - um,   und   wenn es__ dann

nick - te,   die   Hän - de__ mir   drück - te!   gings

rum bi - di wi - di bum bum bum   bum bi - di wi - di bu

Especially notable in this opera also are Sylvana's dance in the first act in which Weber makes use of the oboe and flute with great skill and effectiveness:

and the famous duet between Rudolph and Sylvana, already referred to, in which the dumb girl's part is entirely pantomimic, while the musical aspect is supplied by a solo violoncello. This, as I have already said, was an innovation in musico-dramatic technique for which Wagner generally gets the credit that is undoubtedly, and solely, due to Weber:

Weber

Willst du nicht die - sen Auf - ent

halt mit ein - em freund - lich - en ver -

A Duet in 'Sylvana'

(Sylvana verneintes)

- tau - schen?

War - um denn nicht?

(Sylvana deutet an, dass ihr die Gegend lieb geworden)

With the composition of his delightful one-act opera, *Abu Hassan*, Weber's middle period ends gloriously. It is one of those works, so rarely found in German opera, that sparkle like champagne. For once, and only once, the composer had found a good libretto, and he rose to the occasion and made of it a good opera. German humour is often lacking in refinement; the tendency indeed is generally to the opposite extreme of heaviness. Weber was too good an artist to commit a breach of good taste, but, as we have seen in dealing with *Peter Schmoll*, he occasionally allowed his customary high spirits to overstep the border-line of pure fun and to become over-boisterous. But this is by no means the case with *Abu Hassan* which, when it is not reminiscent of Mozart, or Weber at its most obvious, is certainly more English than German in style. But perhaps it is more French than either. No one knew better than Weber the pangs of being dunned for money, and perhaps he appreciated the creditors' points of view more than the average debtor may be expected to do. He was never himself a debtor from choice, and when he did happen to be in funds, he usually made some effort to liquidate at least the most pressing of his debts. He probably also saw a streak of humour in one individual who, almost to the point of its becoming an obsession, was constantly clamouring for money that he did not require, even if it was his own; and in another being everlastingly pressed for money that he did not possess and could not pay. It is said that Hiemer intended the libretto to be a kind of skit on some of their joint experiences in Stuttgart. Be that as it may, it is certainly not without significance that the first number Weber composed was the creditors' chorus, 'Geld, Geld, Geld, ich will nicht länger warten.' The opera originally consisted only of the overture and eight vocal numbers, but two more were added at later dates—the duet, 'Thränen sollst du nicht vergiessen' in 1812, and the air 'Hier liegt, welch martervolles Loos,' in 1823—so that one acquires a sense of inequality of style on listening to a rendering of the score. Nevertheless it is a little operatic gem that deserves a better fate than the comparative oblivion to which it has been relegated, especially in this country.

The overture to *Abu Hassan* is from many points of view one of the best that Weber produced. It is scored for one piccolo, one flute, two oboes, two clarinets in C, two bassoons, two horns in A, two trumpets in C, one bass trombone, two kettle-drums in C and G respectively, cymbals, triangle, side-drums, first and second violins, violas, cellos and basses. This is an ideal

orchestra for the performance of the exotic music that Weber set
out to compose. It is one of the few overtures he wrote which do
not open with a slow movement, somewhat in the old Italian
style. Jähns informs us that of the 238 bars of the overture 106 are
to be found in later numbers of the opera. Thus, from the very
first note he plunges *in medias res* with the eight-bar theme of the
final chorus:

There is scarcely a phrasing sign in the whole overture. None
is required, as it is entirely built on the eight-bar or double four-bar
system and the scheme is simplicity itself. In the development of
this subject the composer employs many characteristic little
romantic touches, such as:

The second subject—another four-plus eight-bar phrase, is a very typical example of Weber's employment of the descending scale and of the haunting and brilliant effects he secures thereby:

In the development of this theme the first subject is cleverly utilized in combination, thus, for example:

and in the very exuberance of his creative joy the composer runs into this essentially Weberish phrase with its strange interruption:

This is obviously a reminiscence of an exactly similar inter-ruption in the melodic flow, which occurs in the first scene of Beethoven's *Fidelio* about forty bars from the end of the great duet of Marzelline and Jaquino. As *Fidelio* was first produced in 1805, Weber is certain to have heard it, and the curious effect of the loud and vigorous interpolation of the reiterated semitones breaking in upon the tune, with no apparent rhyme or reason, must have stuck in his sub-conscious mind and seems to have fallen quite spontaneously into the melodic stream of *Abu Hassan*. Even in the pitch there is a difference of only a semitone,

Beethoven having written C sharp and D natural, whereas Weber writes C natural and D flat, probably a mere lapse of memory on the latter's part.

In the music of this opera Weber again creates a real exotic and Oriental atmosphere, chiefly by means of tonal colour, but this is not attained by the tricks of the mere cabaret composer, who relies only upon cymbals, triangles and other percussion instruments for his effects. Weber does not, of course, despise the orchestral 'kitchen utensils,' but his favourite woodwinds are never far to seek when the real rich colour of the Orient is required. Apart from colour there is not a great deal that calls for special mention, although two harmonic incidents may be noted in passing. The first is his use of the chord of the ninth, which he had already employed in *Sylvana* as an expression of love-longing:

and the other is a bold and abrupt modulation from the key of B major to that of D major:

CHAPTER X

LATER WORKS FOR THE STAGE

MUCH as Carl Maria von Weber suffered from the effects of his vastly overworked 'evil star,' it must be admitted that there were occasions on which, as later events were to prove, the evil, serious as it may have seemed at the time it first came into action, was more apparent than real. It must have seemed to Weber, when Count Vitzthum came to him with the news that the commission he had received for the composition of a new opera had been counter-manded, and that the count, in consequence, had sent in his resignation of the directorship of the theatre, that this surely was the greatest blow that had ever fallen upon him. Yet for the future fame of the composer it was perhaps the best thing that had ever happened, or could have happened, for, as Spitta remarks:

Had *Alcindor* been written, Weber and Spontini might have been direct rivals, for Spontini's opera of that name, composed a few years later at Berlin, is drawn from the same source. Perhaps also the work on which Weber's world-wide fame rests, and which was to give him a triumph over Spontini, might have taken another form, or never have been written at all.

Elsewhere he states that 'with *Der Freischütz* Weber laid the foundation of German romantic opera.' The particular accepta-tion of the epithet 'romantic' in this sentence does not immediately concern us here, but readers who are interested may find material for thought in the long, though scarcely altogether relevant com-mentary which Spitta interpolates in his article in Grove's *Dictionary of Music and Musicians*. But *Der Freischütz* is consider-ably more than the base upon which the later German romantic opera is founded: it is the finest and noblest and most highly sustained musical work Weber ever accomplished. 'The opera, as Professor Sir Donald Tovey has said, 'has had its ups and downs in respect of fashion,' but that applies only to the literary and dramatic features of the work; the music is of such universal permanence and appeal as to raise it infinitely above all the dictates of fashion or the claims of any age or nation. Weber, as a composer of operas, has suffered inordinately from the comparative crudity of his librettos and from the superficiality of the majority of music critics who, taking the line of least resistance, fix, as one well-known writer has done, upon the melodramatic action which certain orchestral illustrations are designed to augment, and, without regard to the musical content at all, describes these illustrations by such ridiculous phrases as 'circus effects.' Such descriptions are quite unfair to the composer, and should never be accepted without very careful individual examination.[1]

[1] It must always be remembered, of course, that in opera the music can never be entirely divorced from the drama, but my point is that Weber never lowers the musical quality to accord with an inferior dramatic content. The question of development comes into quite a different category, and I think that Spitta, for once, went considerably astray when he wrote:

'Perfect as are these smaller musical forms, it must in justice be conceded that Weber did not always succeed with his larger ones, which often have a sort of piecemeal effect. The construction of a piece of music in grand, full proportions was to him a labour, and rarely a successful one. He does not so much develop from within as superimpose from without, and not infrequently the musical flow stagnates. The finale of the third act may be cited as an instance of his way of falling short in this respect. For the most part, however, this is only true of his music when considered simply as music without regard to dramatic fitness, and such defects [!] are therefore much less noticeable in performance, so accurately does he hit the appropriate musical development for each moment of the action.'

It seems to me that the last sentence of this extract completely nullifies all that goes before.

The story of *Der Freischütz* is founded on a German tradition that any forester who seeks the aid of Samiel, 'the Wild Huntsman,' may, in return for his soul, receive seven bullets which will never fail to hit the mark at which they may be aimed. Should the recipient of these bullets succeed in enticing some other victim into the demon's power, his life will be extended beyond the stipulated time, otherwise he must pay the penalty in full. On the estate of Ottokar, a Bohemian prince, two young foresters, Max and Caspar, both excellent marksmen, served under the chief ranger Cuno, who had promised to give his sanction to the marriage of Max and his daughter, who were in love with each other, should the former prove himself successful in a shooting contest that was about to take place. Caspar, who had sold himself to Samiel, saw, however, an opportunity to benefit himself, when, on the day of the contest, a peasant marksman, Kilian, was the successful competitor. By various subtle suggestions and proofs of his ability to assist him, he entices Max to meet him in the Wolf's Glen at midnight. And there, amid terrifying scenes of horror, the bullets are cast and delivered to the half-demented lover. Meanwhile Agathe, also terrified by ominous warnings, anxiously awaits her lover. She is attended by her cousin Aennchen, who endeavours by every possible means to arouse her to cheerfulness, but succeeds only partially. Presently, the prince, walking in the forest, encounters Max, now proud and confident in the possession of his silver bullets, and he asks him to shoot a dove to which he directs the forester's attention. Max fires just as the bird flies for shelter into a tree behind which Caspar is hidden, and at the same moment Agathe and her bridesmaids appear. As he fires, Caspar and Agathe simultaneously emit cries of distress and the maiden is led away by a hermit who has been watching over her. Max is immediately accused of having shot his bride, but Agathe thereupon reappears. She has been saved by a miracle and it is Caspar who has been wounded. Samiel then appears to claim his victim and Caspar dies, while the curtain falls upon a happy reconciliation, Max being forgiven on the hermit's intercession.

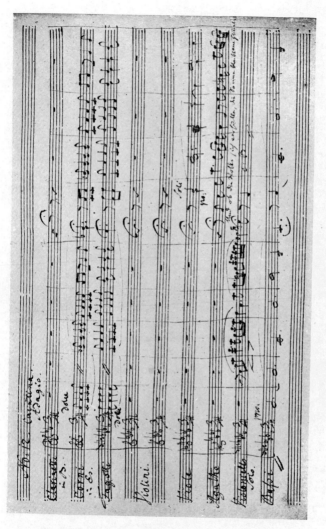

AUTOGRAPH OF AGATHE'S CAVATINA, 'FREISCHÜTZ,' ACT III

Weber had not yet quite reached the point of development at which he was to produce the first genuine grand opera, and *Der Freischütz* was still essentially in the German *Singspiel* stage; but he was rapidly approaching the point, and the great scene of the Wolf's Glen comes, in its musical treatment, as near to the grand opera idiom as anything Weber ever accomplished. Considering what he had done in preceding works of this nature, however, the *Leit-motiv* principle is strangely absent in *Der Freischütz*, although Her-mann Abert, in his introduction to Eulenburg's miniature score of the opera, makes an ingenious, though somewhat overstrained effort to demonstrate that the *Leitmotiv* is present in the system of tonality which he claims to have been consciously employed by Weber. Undoubtedly, as he remarks, 'the æsthetics of tone are treated in this opera with the greatest degree of finesse and con-sistency,' but that, I believe, was only a consequence of Weber's natural intuition as regards what constituted the fitness of things, and I am convinced that when he set the music associated with Samiel in the key of C minor, and that relating to the powers of good in the key of C major; or when he used the relative major tonality of C minor (E flat) to confer a colour which is deeply sombre but without the mystery inherent in the former, he was merely employing the most appropriate materials that lay at his disposal, without any particular consideration as to whether they should afford a key to certain underlying references or thoughts, in the manner employed so extensively by Wagner later.

Apart from the music employed in the Wolf's Glen scene, which was the portion of the work that so powerfully appealed to Beethoven by its impressiveness and originality, there is not much of the creative Weber himself in the opera. The choruses, of course, are purely Weber, so far as treatment goes, but it is here, and in one or two of the arias, that the folk element, which is so essentialy the German aspect of the opera, is apparent. Romance in literature and art was also very much in the air, and, after making every possible allowance for the composer's own profoundly romantic nature, one cannot deny that much of the romanticism embodied in the music came from without. Abert gives a long and imposing list of composers and tendencies whose influence must have gone to the creation of the work; yet, when all is said and done, Weber alone was surely capable of producing the complete and perfect—perfect, so far as Weberian opera may be regarded as such—entity, as we have it to day.

Sir Donald Tovey, writing of the overture, says that it 'is especially remarkable for the completeness with which it sums up all that music can tell of the story to be enacted,' and this must be regarded rather as a mark of the composer's genius in his ability to epitomize a complete opera in three hundred and forty three bars of instrumental music than as an indication of any degree of long windedness in the three thousand or so that follow. As Sir Donald further asserts, 'the rest of the opera proved still more convincing and revealed the real poetic power of the overture.' The impressive opening of that exquisite composition has often been described. A picture of the forest depths is introduced by an eight bar melody containing some spice of mystery, given out by the woodwinds and strings:

Adagio
Ob. Clt. Bsn. & Strs.

A lovely melody for four horns, fully harmonized, follows, and after slowly passing through fifteen bars, it merges into a series of dark tremolo chords which characterize the demon Samiel. Soon the key changes to C minor and we hear the despairing cry

of Max which, later, he emits when Samiel appears to him in the
first act:

This naturally leads to the storm music of the Wolf's Glen,
the first *tutti*, which, continuing through two and a half dozen
bars, culminates in a blast from the horns announcing a melody,
given out, *con molto passione*, by a clarinet, telling, as Tovey
remarks, 'in one of the most famous passages in romantic opera,
how Max first looks down into the awful depth of the wolf's
glen by the light of the full moon, as yet uneclipsed':

And with one other melody, the chief and frequently recurring
strain of Agathe, the overture stands thematically complete, and
the opera lies before us in a nutshell:

203

The working-out is a masterpiece of logical development and artistic concentration. As regards the details in the opera itself, the part of Max's aria in the first act set to the words 'Durch die Wälder, durch die Auen,' is pure Rossini, written probably in that style as a concession to the Italian party which, as we have seen, was predominant then at Dresden. In the second act Agathe's scene with the famous 'Leise, leise, fromme Weise' constitutes one of the greatest things in the whole realm of German opera, but Aennchen's romance in Act III, 'Einst träumte meiner sel'gen Base,' was an obvious mistake, such as Weber only made when he allowed his own perfect sense of artistic values to be subordinated to the ignorant desires of some singer or other.

Of Weber's unfinished comic opera *Die drei Pintos*, the libretto of which was adapted from a German novel entitled *Der Braut-kampf*, by Theodor Hell, little need be said, except to express agreement with Benedict in his lamentations over the loss of the bulk of the music. From the few fragments that have survived, and from what Benedict has recorded regarding it, it appears that this opera might have done more to keep Weber in the regular repertory than anything else he ever wrote. It was conceived in the spirit of *Abu Hassan* and must surely have given us a matured and even more lovable resurrection of the Weber of the earlier happy days, when *Peter Schmoll*, *Sylvana* and *Abu Hassan* first saw the light. Here is Benedict's description:

It was the privilege of the writer of these lines, not only to hear every piece of the first act as it came fresh from the brain of the author, but to become so familiar with them that he could remember every note, though they were penned in the usual hieroglyphic style of the master, who, having the whole, with all its instrumental and choral effects, perfect in his head, was satisfied with writing only the vocal parts, in many instances without even a bass, and with very scanty indications of the accompaniment. Had the task of completing the fragments been confided immediately after the death of the beloved master, or even one or two years later, to his pupil, he could have supplemented the deficiencies and omissions, and at any rate have presented a pianoforte score containing the harmonies and chief features of every number; but this was not to be.

Several attempts were afterwards made to complete the work, but without success.

Weber's next great dramatic work, Euryanthe, may be described as the greatest operatic success of his time, and the most complete operatic failure of all time. In his critical treatment of this work Spitta devotes more than half his space to a defence of the libretto which, after nine revisions, was still thoroughly bad. This was a mere ploughing of the sand. The failure of Euryanthe at the time of its production and its subsequent inability to retain the status its musical qualities undoubtedly merit are entirely due to the literary defects and narrative absurdity of the book. Paul Bekker,[1] it may be said, however, attributes its failure to another cause: 'the false effort to raise the folk opera, considered not artistic enough, to the plane of a supposedly higher art-form.' This, on the face of it, is decidedly far-fetched and, as is proved by the strange story told by Sir Donald Tovey, quite erroneous. The professor relates that

In 1922 a distinguished dramatist, Rolf Lauckner . . . undertook a thorough revision of the libretto. Previous attempts have failed through lack of appreciation of Weber's sense of form. It is no use improving the play on lines which imply that Weber's huge musical design matters less than Wagner's. Lauckner's new text alters not a single mood or contrast in the story, and by a constant process of translation from the jargon of 'das Chez' into the language of poetry, achieves a straightforward and impressive drama which perfectly follows and supports Weber's music. In the whole opera no musical addition is required beyond about forty bars, distributed in three separate scenes, the longest interpolation being in one of the recitatives, and the others being in places where the music was patchy as Weber left it. The patchiness was mainly due to the nonsensical dramatic situations, and it vanishes

---

[1] The Changing Opera, translated by Arthur Mendel, 1936, p. 104.

with their removal. . . . I own that, with all my admiration for the music of Weber's *Euryanthe*, I was astonished at the effect the new text has upon the many tragic and complex passages which suffered from their absurd original background.[1]

I have never yet known Sir Donald's taste in matters of this sort to be at fault, and on this evidence alone I should have no hesitation whatever in asserting that the failure of the opera is solely attributable to the inadequacy and absurdity of the libretto. Further on, in the essay from which the above long quotation is extracted, the professor forcibly adds:

The subject and style of *Euryanthe* admits of no nonsense; and it came as a revelation to me to find that Weber's tragic music was worthiest of Beethoven or Wagner just in those passages where the original libretto was incredible. *With a truthful text the music reveals its truth.*

In face of this pronouncement by such an authority it surely needs little argument on my part to show wherein the success of *Euryanthe* lies. 'Chivalry,' writes Niecks, 'is the predominant note of the *Euryanthe* overture,' and it is likewise that of the entire opera. Bekker, while admitting Weber's possession of a talent for naturalistic representation, and for the application of fresh spontaneity and vigour in combining rhythm and harmony in painting a picture so as to express the non-musical, visual world of a poem by musical means, in order to bring it within the scope of popular appreciation, yet attributes Weber's alleged failure to his inability to cope with the great passions constituting the fundamental basis upon which the structure of *Euryanthe* rests. But throughout the whole of his argument, which runs through more than one of his works on the German opera, Bekker displays a strange misconception of Weber's artistic character and of the fundamental aspect of that much abused and greatly misunderstood quality, chivalry. With all his love for the glamour and trappings of the stage, Weber never lost sight of the true nature of

[1] *Essays in Musical Analysis*, vol. iv, p. 56.

chivalry. It was no high-falutin conception such as the medieval writers of the decadence had invented and evolved that he employed, but a thing of simple grace, courtesy and dignity. And, with the perfect intuitive sense of the fitness of things that never failed to keep his work on correct and absolutely artistic lines, he gave us, even in *Euryanthe*, the real thing. But the outstanding success of this opera lies in the fact that it constitutes the first experiment in a new style of German opera which was destined to revolutionize the whole idea of operatic form and idiom and to be the precursor of music-drama conceived on completely new lines of development and achievement. It is in the treatment of his melodies in relation to the harmonies and general accompaniments that Weber most clearly demonstrates his creative genius, and two examples should alone suffice to indicate his use of the *Leitmotiv*: the Euryanthe and Adolar themes respectively:

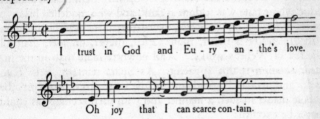

I trust in God and Eu-ry-an-the's love.

Oh joy that I can scarce con-tain.

but a third, the Eglantine motive, must also be instanced, since it establishes the principle as it was adopted and applied by Wagner more firmly than it had ever been done, either by Weber or by any of his predecessors:

From the new character of the work also recitative is employed to a greater extent, and carried to a higher point of effectiveness, than it had probably ever reached before. The opera is less melodic than *Der Freischütz*, but the dramatic qualities of the music are more sustained, and there can be no doubt whatever that Wagner took *Euryanthe* as a model for the creation of *Lohengrin*. The similarities these two operas bear towards each other are as clearly marked as are those of Wagner's *Fliegende Holländer* overture to Weber's *The Ruler of the Spirits*. Schumann, another critic whose taste was seldom at fault, and who modelled his own opera *Genoveva* on *Euryanthe*, stated that there was no question that '*Euryanthe* is richer, more varied, deeper, grander, than all the rest of Weber's works.' And nowhere more than in the instrumentation is this apparent. As Spitta remarks, it is 'both bold and *spirituel*.' And further, the latter writer sums up the whole matter in such a manner and with such accuracy as could never be excelled:

In many passages, and particularly in the scena and cavatina in the third act, where Euryanthe is abandoned in the wilderness, the colours are used with masterly skill. The long wailing notes of the solo bassoon, and the solitary flute wandering aimlessly about, incline one to reecho Schumann's words: 'What a sound comes from the instruments! they speak to us from the very depths of all being.' The accompaniment to 'Hier dicht am Quell,' consisting only of the string quartet and one bassoon, but producing the most extraordinary effect of sound, is a striking example of what genius can do with small means. Quite different again is the colouring of Euryanthe's narrative in the first act; four muted solo violins, whose longsustained notes are supported by quivering violins and violas, also muted, with stifled moans from low flutes, suggest a spectral form, only half visible in the moonlight, hovering overhead and muttering words which die away indistinctly on the breeze.

And Schumann's last word, as it must always be the first, in connection with *Euryanthe*, stands thus:

It is his noble heart's blood; the opera certainly cost him a piece of his life, but through it he has also attained immortality!

Although Weber himself chose the subject of his last opera, *Oberon*, and accepted the libretto supplied to him by Planché, he did so with certain reservations. The English opera of the period differed from the German *Singspiel* in so far as the former was merely a play with songs, generally designated as a ballad opera, whereas the German opera, although interspersed with speaking dialogue, which in the later forms would be set to recitative, is essentially a musical entity. Weber himself, in a letter to Planché, explains the difference as follows:

I must repeat that the cut of the whole is very foreign to all my ideas and maxims. The intermixing of so many principal actors who do not sing, the omission of the music in the most important moments—all deprive our *Oberon* of the title of an opera and will make him unfit for all other theatres in Europe.

Although greatly superior to that of *Euryanthe*, the libretto of *Oberon* is far from being satisfactory. There are too many changes of scene and not sufficient scope is given to sustained dramatization. But the fairy scenes offered great opportunities to such a composer as Weber for the creation of light and beautiful chorus and dance tunes, of which he made the most. Had the work been set by a French composer, the ballet would no doubt have received more attention, yet the melodies, harmonies and orchestral colour of the fairy music are so perfectly in keeping with what one expects for such a purpose, yet so paradoxically unexpected, and so fresh and original in every sense of these terms, that one is constrained to admit that this great swan-song of Weber's is in many respects the greatest song of them all. The story is another of glamorous magic and chivalry, and tells how the fairy King Oberon, having quarrelled with Titania, had left her, swearing

> Never to meet in love, till some fond pair,
> Through weal and woe, 'mid flood and chains and fire,
> Should keep their plighted faith inviolate.

Puck immediately finds a subject for experiment in Sir Huon the Bold, who, for having in fair fight killed the son of Charlemagne, is commanded to leave the court, proceed to Bagdad and, in the Caliph's hall in the midst of high festival, slay whomsoever he may find seated at the right hand of Haroun and then claim the Caliph's daughter as his bride. By the assistance of Oberon and a magic horn which the fairy king gives him, he succeeds in his task, and by his fidelity to Rezia, his bride, in the course of numerous incredible difficulties and trials, invented for the testing of his faith and that of the abducted lady by the fairy king himself, incidentally liberates Oberon from his vow. Many adventures have to be endured before this is achieved, however, and Oriental scenery and effects come very much into the picture. And here we have the most complete employment of the *Leitmotiv* that is to be found in any of Weber's works. The overture opens with the 'horns of Elfland faintly blowing,' three notes, *adagio sostenuto*:

dolce

which recur through every act and scene of the opera whenever it is necessary to evoke a picture of the Orient. Curiously enough, however, on its first appearance after the overture, in the Elves' chorus (No. 1), we have it in reversed order:

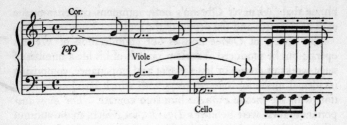

Then we have it constantly appearing throughout the opera until at last, in the grand finale (No. 22), it forms a figure upon which the entire accompaniment and dance are based. And, as in *Der Freischütz*, the overture comprises a complete epitome of the opera, with fairy music, storm music, love music and even the reminiscent air which Braham, the tenor, so stupidly despised and rejected in favour of the rather banal and appallingly conventional 'Oh, 'tis a glorious sight,' composed by Weber as a substitute. The mermaids' song is one of the most beautiful numbers and, generally, the most popular in the opera, but the great moment is undoubtedly Rezia's scena, 'Ocean, thou mighty monster,' which I have no hesitation in ranking with 'O don fatale' from Verdi's *Don Carlos* and 'Celeste Aida' from the same composer's *Aida*, as one of the three greatest operatic scenas since Mozart. And the duet 'On the banks of sweet Garonne' is a number that Mozart himself might have written. Weber's instrumentation in this opera is essentially characteristic and, like the vocal numbers, shows a growing power and a greater command of colour rather than any falling off such as, considering the state of his health, might easily have been noted and excused. The succeeding passages for horns, muted strings and woodwinds respectively, in the opening bars of the overture, are a real stroke of genius. In little over a dozen bars they conjure up in the mind's eye a series of pictures, of magic, fairy influence and the gorgeous pageantry of medieval Europe and the Orient. The essential aspect of this amazing opera may be summed up in Sir Donald Tovey's happy phrase that 'whatever Oberon's horn summons comes from the ends of the earth and the depths of the soul.'

This review of *Oberon* finishes our consideration of Weber's operas; but he produced at various periods of his life a number of stage works of greater or lesser extent and importance, comprising incidental music for different plays with which his close connec, tion with the theatre brought him into contact. The most im, portant of these were Schiller's *Turandot*, for which, in the autumn of 1809, he composed his *Chinese Overture* and six pieces; and P. A. Wolff's *Preciosa*, which consists of an overture and eleven numbers, written at the request of Count Brühl after the completion of *Der Freischütz* in 1820. The overture to the former is based on a bizarre Chinese melody which is very cleverly worked up to a rich and effective orchestral climax. No. 3 is a military march and No. 7 is a funeral march in which the woodwinds are employed in characteristic style. The music is of an Oriental cast.

Preciosa, on the other hand, was written at the time when Weber, under the influence of Tieck, was flirting with the idea of composing a complete opera, which *Preciosa* is not, on a Spanish subject. Had all gone well, we should have had *Die drei Pintos* shortly afterwards, and the question as to whether *Euryanthe* or the *Cid* was to be the work for Vienna still hung in the balance. And, as *Preciosa* demonstrates, he obviously possessed an in, tuitive sense of the Spanish gypsy idiom. The overture to this work, unconformably to his usual custom, was written first. Its instrumentation has all the colour and jingle that one associates with works of this character and his orchestra is replete with all the old familiar instruments that gave *Sylvana* and *Abu Hassan* their particular and individual charm, even to all the 'kitchen utensils' of the period. Once again the overture completely summarizes what is to follow, and the *Leitmotiv* principle is here utilized in its crudest and most obvious manner. The bulk of the drama is spoken recitative enunciated by two aged females and one male, with four-part chorus and instrumental numbers, dances, marches, etc., interspersed. There is only one solo part, the soprano role of Preciosa.

Other plays for which Weber from time to time wrote incidental music are Kotzebue's *Der arme Minnesinger* (four songs for solo voices with guitar accompaniment—one with four-part male chorus); Gubitz's patriotic play *Lieb und Versöhnen* (one song for baritone with three-part male chorus and orchestra; and one for tenor and orchestra); Reinbach's *Gordon und Montrose* (one ballad); Castelli's *Diana von Poitiers* (one romance with guitar accompaniment); a festival play, *Der Weinberg an der Elbe* (one vocal number); A. Müllner's *König Yngurd* (ten short instrumental numbers and one vocal); Moreto's *Donna Diana* (a short guitar piece); Kind's *Das Nachtlager von Granada* and Holbein's *Die drei Wahrzeichen* (one song each); Hell's *Das Haus Anglade* (a scena for tenor solo, chorus and orchestra); Eduard Gehe's *Heinrich IV* (eight numbers, several of which he later incorporated in his own *Euryanthe* and *Oberon* respectively); Grillparzer's *Sappho* (a chorus and a melodrama with harp accompaniment); Kind's *Der Abend am Waldbrunnen* (a song for guitar); Rublack's *Lieb' um Liebe*, Count von Blankensee's *Carlo*, Houwald's *Der Leuchtturm* and Shakespeare's *The Merchant of Venice* (one or more numbers in each). Erwin Kroll also mentions that, as recently as September 1932, a first performance of Kleist's *Käthchen von Heilbronn* was given with about sixteen musical numbers which had been established as compositions written for that work by Weber, over the Ostmarken Radio of Königsberg. An inspection of the score was not allowed, however, and all information regarding the derivation of the music was refused. But Kroll declares that after a further hearing he was able to identify most of the numbers with those said to have been composed for several of the works mentioned above. There is no doubt that Weber also occasionally contributed songs and other musical numbers to fill gaps in the works of other composers, but the majority of these were usually good-naturedly lent from works of his own.

CHAPTER XI

VOCAL, INSTRUMENTAL AND LITERARY WORKS

CARL MARIA VON WEBER composed, apart from the arias in the operas, about a hundred and fifty songs in various forms and styles. As a composer of *Lieder* he was indeed a pioneer and a direct forerunner of Schubert and Schumann. The editor of the third edition of Grove's *Dictionary of Music and Musicians*,[1] in referring to his fame as a song-writer, states 'that it has suffered somewhat from the circumstance that many of his best songs are in his operas.' Weber invariably brought his philosophic mind to bear on his creative work, and the principles he applied in the writing of vocal music were those he enunciated in a letter to young Friedrich Wieck, which he wrote in acknowledgment of his eight Songs (Op. 7): 'In the composition of songs I have always striven strenuously to apply a true and correct declamation to the poem, and to give many new melodic forms where necessary. . . . Your declamation is sometimes very loose, thereby breaking the continuity of the meaning,' and elsewhere, he completes the proposition with the remark that 'any vocal music that alters or effaces the poet's meaning and intention is a failure.' He naturally began to compose the earliest of his songs in the style that was typical of the eighteenth century, but a clear step in advance of that style was noticeable in *Die Kerze* and *Umsonst*, written at Hamburg in 1802. The poets also were, of course, producing a new style of verse, freer in form and less stilted in diction; and that must have had a clear and broadening effect on the composers as well. Weber nevertheless had his own rapidly developing ideas as to what the musical setting of a song ought to be;

[1] Vol. v, p. 71, col. i, article on 'Song.'

but his real tragedy as a song-writer lay in the fact that the development of the *Kunstlied* was proceeding too rapidly to allow of his songs attaining the popularity they undoubtedly merited, before they were eclipsed by the works of the more dynamic song-composers who followed fast upon his tracks. But no one ever excelled him in the writing of such songs as the *Schwertlied* and *Lützows wilde Jagd*, which embodied the very fundamental spirit of the German people, and of the nation's youth of that period. His canons and choruses also were invariably a rousing success wherever they were sung.

He composed a number of songs, duets and arias with orchestral accompaniment in the Italian style, and modern singers may, if they will, find a genuine mine of gold in his vocal productions, well worthy of exploration even to-day. His territory is the entire realm of human emotions. As Erwin Kroll so charmingly describes it:

There runs the small urchin; there grows the bright little rose; the colt lover with looks askance upon some skittish filly; the mother singing to sleep the darling of her heart; the beggar dancing and singing; the maiden seeking her beloved; and the pious woman secure in the knowledge of her own unctuous rectitude.

When he chooses, or the subject demands, Weber, in his songs, as indeed in all his creations, can be picturesque, tragic, sentimental, archly humorous or merely ingenuous.

Of Weber's larger vocal works much the same may be said as of the songs. His earliest cantata, *Der erste Ton*, I have already dealt with in the chapter devoted to his early dramatic works, as I consider its dramatic qualities far in excess of its merely vocal character. The final chorus terminates, like the final chorus of Verdi's *Falstaff*, in a vocal fugue, a daring enough experiment on the part of Verdi at eighty, but an amazing piece of effrontery in Weber at twenty-two, yet one surely more than pardonable by reason of its complete success. And *Leier und Schwert*, although generally described as a cantata, is really only a cycle of four-part songs for male voices, which may be regarded as having come under treatment in the preceding paragraph of this chapter.

In 1812 Weber wrote *In seiner Ordnung schafft der Herr*, a hymn for mixed choir, solo quartet and orchestra, in praise of God and His righteousness. This is a work of considerable merit, although a little inconsistent in style and development. It opens in a fine devotional spirit and culminates in a very effective incorporation of the chorale, 'Befiehl du deine Wege,' the work ending with a glorious fugue, which Kroll, however, describes as being 'less devotional than theatrical.' Benedict, on the other hand, justly says of the cantata: 'A noble and dignified work, which like many others from the same pen has not yet found recognition such as it deserves. The final fugue belongs to the best written by Weber.'

After *Der erste Ton*, the most notable of Weber's cantatas, and the crowning example of his patriotic productions, came his truly great [1] setting of Wohlbrück's *Kampf und Sieg*. Although it was composed to celebrate the overthrow of Napoleon at the battle of Waterloo, and the consequent liberation of Germany, the work was not acceptable to several of the upstart rulers who owed their status to the grace of the French emperor himself, and were probably not too sure of their position under a new regime. But with this work Weber succeeded where Beethoven had failed with his *Battle of Vittoria*. The music is largely of a military cast and, generally speaking, of no greater value than the sentiments expressed in the words; but the melody of *Lützows wilde Jagd* is effectively employed as a setting to the words:

> O Himmelsluft in Todesdrang,
> Das ist Freundes mutiger Schlachtengesang.

The tune of *God save the King* is impressively blared out by all the brass, with an accompaniment of scales of rushing demi-

---

[1] I employ the epithet 'great' here only in relation to the fact that the setting was so completely adapted to the spirit of the poem.

semiquavers played by the strings, and the work ends on a highly exalted note, 'Herr, Gott, Dich loben wir,' sung to a chorale-like tune by the full unaccompanied choir, which, however, is presently joined by the full orchestra; then a prayerful theme, 'Gieb und erhalte den Frieden der Welt,' with an insinuating violin strain creeping in, and the work proceeds to a triumphant close through one of Weber's favourite fugues, based on the original theme. In the composer's collection of literary works there appears an analytical essay on this work, which was 'written for my friends' in Prague.

After *Kampf und Sieg* a series of cantatas were written, unconnectedly and spasmodically, for birthdays and marriage days of members of the royal and ducal families with which Weber was professionally connected. *L' accoglienza* for six solo voices, chorus and orchestra, was written in a fortnight under very distracting conditions, and it is not surprising that several old numbers from *Peter Schmoll* and *Rübezahl* were borrowed and adapted for this work. Later on he borrowed some of the material here utilized to fill up blanks in his last opera, *Oberon. L' accoglienza* has never been published.

The year 1818, again, saw the composition of two cantatas, *Natur und Liebe*, a charming little work for solo sopranos, tenors and basses (two of each) and chorus, which would well repay anybody with sufficient enterprise to revive it, and the *Jubel-Cantate* for solo voices, chorus and orchestra, another exalted work, 'Erhebt den Lobgesang,' by the neglect of which modern music-lovers lose a great deal. Finally, two fine cantatas are *Du, bekränzend unsre Laren* for solos and chorus with piano and flute accompaniment, containing eight graceful numbers, one of which is a canon for four solo voices; and *Wo nehm' ich Blumen her*, for three solo voices (all soprano) with piano accompaniment. The finale of the former is incorporated in the finale to the first act of *Euryanthe*, 'Fröhliche Klänge, Tänze, Gesänge.'

In addition to the various cantatas Weber composed three masses. Considering his mother's deeply religious character and his own personal leanings towards the Roman Catholic Church, augmented by the teaching of Michael Haydn, it is scarcely a matter for surprise to find the young musician making his earliest attempt in choralism, apart from the three juvenile operas, with the composition of a Grand Mass. Weber long maintained that this work had been destroyed by fire, either accidentally or intentionally, and the fact that no trace of it could be found for a hundred years after his death had long ago convinced all who had ever heard such a work had existed that Weber had been right. But, one day, in the year 1925, Constantin Schneider of Vienna, grubbing among the piles of old music in the City Museum, 'Carolino Augusteum,' of Salzburg, discovered a bundle of manuscript music in score, bearing on the first page the following title: 'Missa solenne à 4 voci, 2 Violini Viola 2 Oboe 2 Corni 2 Trombe Timpani, Violone e Violoncello, con Organo. di Carlo Marie di Weber,' and a loose sheet between two of the pages carried the following dedication:

Hochwürdigster Reichsfürst, gnädigster Fürst und Herr. Euer hochfürstliche Gnaden geruhen als grosser Beschützer und einsichtsvoller Kenner schöner Wissenschaften beikommende Messe von meiner geringen Arbeit gnädigst anzunehmen.

Um gnädigste Nachsicht bittend in tiefer verschammender [*sic*] Ehrfurcht Euer hochfürstlicher Gnaden unterthänigster Carl Marie B. v. Weber. 3ter. Mai 1802.

Although, in his autobiography, Weber ascribes the composition of this Mass to the year 1799 or 1800, I have little hesitation in asserting that he made a mistake. The reference in the autobiography, written eighteen years later (1818), runs thus: 'I wrote under the eyes of my teacher an opera, *Die Macht der Liebe und des Weins*, a grand *Mass*, several *Piano sonatas, Variations, Violin Trios, Songs,* etc., which later became a prey to the flames.'

Weber's mother died in 1798, and the impressionable boy

would at once turn his thoughts into religious channels. Knowing his methods of composition, we can easily assume that he was mentally engaged upon the music during the earlier years, but it was not committed to paper till later, and having, in the confusion that prevailed at Salzburg during the Webers' sojourn there in 1802, doubtless mislaid the score, which he never saw again, looking back upon his life in 1818 he would naturally conclude that its destruction had taken place with the other works of his musical infancy in 1799 or 1800. But how it got into the City Museum is a mystery.

It is a mere platitude to state that in the *Jugendmesse* the influence of Michael Haydn is apparent. Of course it is—Michael Haydn was, next to Vogler, the teacher who exercised the greatest influence upon Weber's choral style—and in most of his works of that nature it should not be difficult to detect a similar influence. But if there are to be found traces of the Haydn teaching, the Mass is by no means a mere student's exercise, and it is as distinctly Weberish as any work of the kind he composed at any later date. It is indeed a significant fact that, not only does the style persist in his later masses, but that themes employed in the *Jugendmesse* are actually used again in the later works. One example will suffice. The opening solo in the *Jugendmesse* is repeated note for note in that of the E flat major Mass, and we have a distinct approach to an inverted rendering of it in the G major:

E FLAT MAJOR MASS
Solo

Ky - ri - e e - le - i - son, e - le - i - son, e-

-le - i - son, e - le - i - son.

G MAJOR MASS
Soprano Solo

Ky - ri - e e - le - i - son, Ky - ri - e e - le - i - son.

Ky - ri - e e - le - - - - i - son.

In the *Jugendmesse*, Weber's setting of the Gloria is in the older form, in which the choir begins with the words: 'Et in terra pax,' after the celebrant has intoned the 'Gloria in excelsis.' In the later settings the newer form is employed. In none of the published scores was the offertorium printed. So far as we know none was composed for the *Jugendmesse*, but for the E flat major Dresden Mass one was specially written for the famous *castrato* Sassaroli, with a four-part chorus. It is naturally of a florid character and contains such ornaments as a trill on E flat extending through four bars and a sustained high B flat for the soloist. A similar offertorium was separately composed for the G major Dresden Mass, in which the soprano is required twice to finish a run on high C. There can be little doubt that Weber wrote the E flat Mass with the *Jugendmesse* in his mind, but there is some difference in style and treatment between it and the G major. In one respect, however, they are alike: in their theatrical and dramatic qualities, and their use and popularity has grievously suffered on that account. Pope Pius X, to my mind, did incalculable harm to the cause of music and very little, if any, good to religion by the issue of his *Motu proprio* banning for liturgical use all settings of the mass and similar works except those of Gregorian plainsong or of a close approximation thereto. The mass itself is one of the most dramatic works in existence and Weber, being essentially a dramatic composer, naturally wrote his music in the style in which his best work could alone be accomplished. That did not signify any lack of reverence on his part, but rather the contrary. It is the story of *Le Jongleur de Notre-Dame* all over again. Although both the later works were composed for special occasions, we know that Weber was then working under the heavy burden of his wife's illness and that his deeply religious nature, added to the serious views with which he always regarded his art, would inspire him with the purest and noblest of intentions in writing such works as these. Further, he was then working seriously on *Der Freischütz*, and in the orchestration and solo work of the E flat Dresden Mass we have occasional suggestions of the music of that opera, especially of the beautiful and tender themes of the virginal Agathe.

It was as a composer for the pianoforte that Weber first appeared in print, and this is hardly a matter for astonishment when one considers the long and intensive training he had undergone as an executant. His own performing powers were virtuosic, and although, from the erratic manner of his training, somewhat lacking in finesse, yet sufficient to place him in the front rank of the great pianists of his time. But he was no close specialist in any branch of his art, so that, while he never went unrecognized as a great master of the instrument when he did give recitals, he never attained the European or even national fame that many a lesser artist acquired. It was the same with his instrumental compositions. As André Cœuroy remarks, 'this is because they are isolated and meagre examples of various species; instead of being grouped into solid "cycles," like the sonatas of Beethoven or of Mozart, they fritter themselves away in variations, sonatas, concertos, rondos, polonaises, waltzes, dance movements and pieces for four hands.' Yet, he continues, Weber, Beethoven and Schubert are the only composers, at the beginning of the nineteenth century, whose pianoforte works are of genuine interest. His style was to some extent determined by the formation of his own hands with their abnormal stretch and sensitivity of touch. 'For these very hands,' he writes in his *Tonkünstlers Leben,* 'these accursed keyboard fingers, which by dint of everlasting practice and exercising at last acquire a kind of independence and wilful reason of their own, are unconscious tyrants and despots of our creative forces,' and so it is not uncommon to find such phrases as this scattered throughout his solo pianoforte works:

The first seven publications, numbered respectively Op. 1 to 7, comprise pieces for pianoforte, all solo except Op. 3, which contains *Six petites pièces faciles pour le pianoforte à quatre mains.* Four of the works are variations and, from Op. 1 to Op. 7, there is a steady rise in quality, which perhaps is not surprising since their dates run from 1798 to 1807. By the latter year the composer had got well into his stride, and it was Op. 7, the *Sept Variations pour le pianoforte sur l'air 'Vien quà, Dorina bella,'* dedicated to the Queen of Westphalia, that first gave Weber renown as a serious composer for the pianoforte. The treatment of Bianchi's beautiful and romantic theme in every variation, each of which bears a special character of its own, is entirely in keeping with the spirit of the inspiring strain, and it becomes more intense as it proceeds. In the composition of his later works for this medium there is a steady growth of imaginative invention and increase of virtuosity, as set after set appeared. In Op. 9, for example, *Variations sur un thème original,* the former aspect is demonstrated in No. 4, 'Spagnuola,' and in No. 6, a clever 'Fantasia,' but invention seems to have deserted him for the most part in the *Variationen über ein*

Zigeunerlied (Op. 55). The most difficult of them all are the *Variationen über die Romanze aus Méhuls 'Joseph'* (Op. 28); and the longest are the *Variations sur un air russe—'Schöne Minka'* (Op. 40). The latter set is unique in being preceded by an introduction of twenty-five bars before the theme is set forth. In No. 7, the theme is given in the bass and the upper parts in semi- and demi-semi-quavers, in broken time, played *adagio con espressione*, are highly effective.

Weber composed only four sonatas for pianoforte solo, but they cannot be regarded as by any means the best of the work he accomplished for that instrument. This, keeping in view the freedom of style and form that the romantic composers invariably reserved for themselves, is not to be wondered at. Even Beethoven, although he wrote most of his work for the pianoforte nominally in sonata form, seldom kept to it with the degree of strictness that professors of the classics demand, and Weber never really made any pretence of writing even in binary form and, so far as development is concerned, the outstanding aspect of his sonatas is that they are formless in the purely academic sense of the term. None the less, they contain much fine music, and they deserve a better fate than the general neglect which is, at present, their lot. Like most of his works for the pianoforte they were written for the performance at his own recitals, and his own marvellous virtuosity was the measure of their playability. The first (Op. 24) is a work of considerable interest, teeming, as Benedict says, 'with surprising and nearly always happy innovations,' and 'only inferior perhaps to Beethoven.' There is an element of grandeur and broadness in the first movement, and the *Adagio* which follows is well in the Beethoven slow-movement tradition, yet it stands alone in originality. The minuet is less satisfactory, as Weber's minuets generally are in comparison with other forms, and the Rondo, *perpetuum mobile*, once a prime favourite with pianists everywhere, and now quite undeservedly neglected, still contains all the elements of assured popularity.

Sonata No. 2, in A flat major, is in many respects the

composer's masterpiece amongst the works he wrote for this instrument. It is more in the nature of a tone-poem than a formal sonata, and is the most romantic of the four, 'de ce romantisme rêveur apparenté à Schubert,' as Cœuroy says. The first movement is of great length, *Allegro moderato, con spirito ed assai legato*, and it is followed by a crisp little *Andante* in C minor. In the third movement, *Menuetto capriccioso*, Weber, for once, makes a success of the dance form, but the reason probably lies in the fact of its being a great deal less minuet than *capriccioso*, and he uses it as a medium for the indulgence of the musical humour of which he was so complete an adept, when the mood had taken him. And the last movement is a beautiful piece of musical tapestry, blazing with colour and glittering with curious little *bizarreries*. The interpolation of a phrase from the bridesmaids' chorus in *Der Freischütz* in this movement, and the fact, noted by Benedict, that the distinctive features of the whole sonata 'might perhaps be traced to this special period of Weber's career, when his whole soul was wrapt up in the love of his future partner for life, Caroline Brandt,' convinces me that he had a definite programme in mind when he composed this glowing and illuminating work. In the more romantic episodes of the rondo, also, we have a distinct foretaste of the Schumann of the *Novelletten*, both in style and in sentiment.

The third Sonata (Op. 49), generally known by the epithet of 'Demoniac,' starts off with a movement of a savage and rugged character, marked *allegro feroce*, in D minor. It is a movement of great power, but rich in melody withal. The second movement, *andante con moto*, makes a charming contrast to the preceding one, and it might easily be mistaken for a work of Mendelssohn, as indeed might also be the fate of the fiery rondo that follows. This movement, often performed apart from its context, under the title of *Allegro di bravura*, is a remarkable piece of musical interlacing. It consists of three subjects which appear each separately but become gradually intertwined in the most ingenious and effective manner. The Sonata ends with this movement. A fourth movement, whatever its nature, would have been a complete anticlimax.

The fourth and last Sonata (Op. 70), in E minor, is entirely different from any of the preceding ones, and is the most 'Weberish' of the four, although it must not be forgotten that the second is universally acknowledged to be the best. The fourth is particularly characterized as the 'Programme Sonata,' although I think that each contains intrinsic evidence of having been written to a programme of one sort or another. The work is a picture of melancholy and despondency, which runs through all the psychological stages of hope and despair, culminating at last in mental and physical exhaustion and death. The first movement is introduced by an old trick of Weber's, a series of descending scales, in various modes and rhythmical arrangements, which appear persistently to the end of the movement, with frequent episodical material reminiscent of Beethoven and Clementi. The second movement, a minuet, *presto vivace ed energico* (surely a contradictory tempo direction for a minuet), with its very charming trio, is essentially a Weber composition. The remaining movements, respectively *andante (quasi allegretto) consolante* and *prestissimo*, are adequately described by the programme the composer had in mind and they call for no special comment.

With the exception of the last, the sonatas suffer from a certain lack of continuity, and there is a great qualitative divergence between the various movements. It ought to be remarked that Weber himself, in his diary, constantly refers to the minuets as scherzos, which goes far to explain the fact that they are not minuets at all. Again, Weber, as an executant virtuoso, was not greatly interested in the development of a particular theme; it was rather the immediate effect and appeal of a beautiful melody or dramatic episode that he valued most and this may account for the lack of classical purity and form that is so immediately apparent to all who have studied these none the less truly notable works.

During the twenty years that elapsed between 1798, when he published his Opus 1, *Sechs Fughetten* for piano solo, to 1819, when the *Rondo brillante*, the *Aufforderung zum Tanz (Invitation to the Dance)* and the *Polacca brillante* appeared, Weber composed a large number of dances and characteristic pieces, large and small, and good, bad and indifferent, including about a score for four hands. The most notable are the three composed in 1819, mentioned above, and two earlier works, the *Momento capriccioso* (Op. 12) and the *Grande Polonaise* (Op. 21) (both dated 1808). All these works are concert pieces and extremely virtuosic in character.

The *Aufforderung zum Tanz* we know, on the authority of the composer's wife, to have been frankly programmatic. When Weber played it to her, he accompanied his playing with the following commentary:

First approach of the dancer (bars 1–5); the lady's evasive reply (5–9); his pressing invitation (9–13—the short *appoggiatura* C and the *appoggiatura* A♮ are very significant); her consent (13–16); they enter into conversation—he begins (17–19), she replies (19–21), he speaks with greater warmth (21–23), she sympathetically agrees (23–25). Now for the dance! He addresses her with regard to it (25–27), her answer (27–29), they draw together (29–31), take their places, are waiting for the commencement of the dance (31–35).—The dance.—Conclusion: his thanks, her reply, their retirement. Silence.[1]

Professor Niecks is inclined to go even farther than this, and to detect a subsidiary programme in the dance itself.

The smaller compositions for pianoforte are more or less mediocre and of practically no account, but there are some interesting little pieces among the duets. Weber also composed several concertos, the most remarkable of which was his famous *Concertstück* for pianoforte and orchestra (Op. 79). Of this work Sir Donald Tovey writes that it

is the origin of the post-classical concerto form established by Mendelssohn and followed by Saint-Saëns, and by Max Bruch in his best-known violin Concerto. No composer since 1850 would deny the full title of concerto to a work of this range. Like Spohr's *Gesangsscene*

---

[1] *Programme Music*, by Frederick Niecks, 1906, p. 138.

Concerto, it exemplifies the essentially dramatic, not to say operatic, character that underlies, historically and æsthetically, the concerto as an art-form.[1]

Like the *Invitation to the Dance*, the *Concertstück* has a definite programme, which Weber himself divulged to Julius Benedict immediately after he had written the last pages of the work, on the morning of the day on which *Der Freischütz* was to receive its first performance:

The lady sits in her tower: she gazes sadly into the distance. Her knight has been for years in the Holy Land; will she ever see him again? Battles have been fought; but no news of him who is so dear to her. In vain have been all her prayers. A fearful vision rises to her mind— her knight is lying on the battle-field deserted and alone; his heart's blood is ebbing fast away. Could she but be by his side!—could she but die with him! She falls exhausted and senseless. But hark! What is that distant sound? What glimmers in the sunlight from the wood? What are those forms approaching? Knights and squires with the cross of the Crusades, banners waving, acclamations of the people, and there!—it is he! She sinks into his arms. Love is triumphant. Happiness without end. The very woods and waves sing the song of love; a thousand voices proclaim its victory.[2]

The musical treatment of this somewhat tawdry novelette is one of the greatest achievements that Weber ever effected, and those who feel themselves influenced by the ignorant and uncritical pronouncements on Weber it has recently become the fashion to make in the musical press and elsewhere, too often by writers who appear to know no more about music than they know about Weber, will be well advised to read the essay by Professor Tovey already cited. The finale of the *Concertstück* is indeed one of the greatest things in music, and of it Sir Donald writes: 'the nearest classical parallel to the mood, as well as the "programme," of his finale is the finale of Beethoven's *Lebewohl* Sonata'; and

---

[1] *Essays in Musical Analysis,* by Donald Francis Tovey, vol. iv, p. 61.
[2] *Weber,* by Sir Julius Benedict. Fourth edition, 1896, p. 66.

again: 'We must go to Beethoven for any deeper glow of joy.'
But best of all:

As to the finale, I frankly confess that it thrills me. Weber's range
of harmony is hardly wider than Gluck's; and when he gets beyond
tonic and dominant his changes are really as grand in effect as in intention. As for the pianoforte writing, it conclusively proves Weber to
have deserved his reputation as one of the greatest players ever known
on any instrument. Every detail of it must have been discovered during
extemporization at full speed: there is no other means of guessing that
such passages lie well for the hand at all.

And that, from Tovey, ought to be the last word on Weber's
Concertstück.

Two other pianoforte concertos were early compositions, Op. 11,
approved by Vogler, and effective enough (a strange omission
from Weber's orchestra is that of clarinets here), but of no outstanding importance; and Op. 32, composed two years later,
a characteristic and difficult work with many fine moments.
The *Adagio* with its divided and muted violins is one of the high
lights of musical romance, even in the Weber output, and the
concluding rondo is a movement of scintillating brilliance.

Weber, as we have seen, experimented to a considerable extent
in the production of orchestral colour, and he naturally made use
of the woodwinds, especially the clarinet, flute and bassoon, in this
respect. His association with Bärmann was the means of inducing him to explore the possibilities of the clarinet as a solo
instrument even more widely that he might otherwise have done.
A *Duo* for clarinet and pianoforte (Op. 48) is indeed one of the
happiest efforts that Weber ever made in the realm of concerted
music. This, and two other works, a Quartet for pianoforte,
violin, viola and violoncello (Op. 18) and a Trio for pianoforte,
flute and violoncello (Op. 63), constitute the only chamber
music compositions on a large scale he ever attempted. The
Quartet, although rich in good thematic material, is marred by a
certain degree of stiffness, due largely to Weber's weakness in

development already referred to in connection with the pianoforte sonatas. But the Trio is a work of high merit and romantic beauty. It is conceived in the spirit of a pastoral drama which opens with a serious and contemplative *allegro moderato*. This is followed by an idyllic 'Shepherd's Plaint,' the theme of which is a variation of the popular German folksong, 'In einem kühlen Grunde,' rendered on the piano by the left hand, while the right hand and the other two instruments seem to improvise an intricately simple accompaniment. This work is a real masterpiece in its way.

Weber's compositions for violin, viola or violoncello and piano, with the exception of *Nine Variations on a Norwegian Air*, are of no great value, being mostly of a showy character adapted for effect on the concert platform, and although this applies, to a certain extent, to his two clarinet Concertos, his bassoon Concerto and his *Concertino* for horn, the orchestral background seemed invariably to inspire him to impart a deeper æsthetic content even to the firework solo effects. But Weber, as we have already seen, had a great liking for wind instruments, especially the woods, and he probably felt more in his element, particularly in his younger days, when writing for them. It is all the more surprising therefore that his first Symphony—he composed two, both in C major, when he was only twenty years of age—contains no part for clarinets at all. Apart from the overtures, the majority of which have been dealt with in our consideration of the dramatic works, and the concertos, these were the only works of any importance that Weber composed for full orchestral performance, and they conclusively prove that his genius was not symphonic. They show the same defects as we noticed in the pianoforte sonatas: lack of continuity throughout the various movements and an almost complete absence of sonata form and thematic development. The influence of Haydn is powerfully in evidence in so far as the melodic content goes, and as individual musical numbers most of the movements might pass. The overtures, on the other hand, succeed because of their essentially dramatic character and purpose, and because Weber was the greatest dramatic composer of his time.

This is a biography of Weber, one of the 'Master Musicians,' and it might be argued that a glance over the literary activities of a master musician is entirely irrelevant in such a book, and quite unnecessary to enable one to form a general estimate and to obtain a correct view of the man and his work. This can never be so in the case of Weber, however. His literary work was almost as much a part of what went to constitute him a master musician as his musical compositions and his administrative and concert and opera directorship activities themselves. Although there was a time when he seriously contemplated abandoning the career of a professional musician and devoting his life entirely to literature, there never was any real danger of his abandoning his master-musicianship. With a single exception, a short essay on Baden-Baden, everything he ever wrote, so far as can be gathered from his published work, had a greater or lesser musical bearing. The most extensive of his writings, if we leave out of account his letters, which in a more complete sense than the letters of any other musician were *Kunstbriefe* of the richest possible quality, is his unfinished novel *Tonkünstlers Leben* and, as Spitta remarks, it is a pity that he never lived to finish it, 'for as he himself was the musician whose life he described, we should have gained an artistically drawn autobiography of inestimable value.' But enough was written to enable us to estimate his talents as a pure *littérateur* and a judge of artists and their art. In his manner of using literature as a handmaid and accessory to his musical aims and achievements, he was, in the literary sense, as much the forerunner of Schumann and Wagner as he was in the musical. His most productive period in literature was the decade from 1809 to 1818. During these years he wrote sketches, reviews of books and music, concert and opera criticisms, descriptions of new inventions of musical instruments and material, and even poems, all of them of real significance and of genuine importance as contributions towards the best interests and furtherance of the art of music. And he was too good and too honest an artist to write merely to please a publisher or producer. If a work was bad, neither fear nor favour prevented him from saying so, but if it was good he was equally candid, and private enmities or prejudices were never at any time allowed to encroach upon his critical judgments. Weber had many vices, but jealousy was never one of them, and even while himself suffering from the jealousies and oppressions of others, he not infrequently went out of his way to further the interests of musicians who were not always too favourably disposed to work on his behalf. His generous attitude towards the works of Meyerbeer, Spohr, Spontini and Marschner are notable cases in point. In whatever medium he worked, he was unfailingly a great artist, because he was essentially a great man. Even in his most frivolous moods, paradoxical as it may seem, his art was inspired by the 'high seriousness' that Matthew Arnold postulated as the essential and invariable element of genius, while, as his son recorded, he was a veritable priest of his art, and it was clearly not without an inner consciousness of his own high artistic principles that he himself expressed a wish that there should be inscribed upon his tomb:

Here lies a man who has loved man and art in all sincerity and purity.

APPENDICES

APPENDIX A

CALENDAR

(Figures in brackets denote the age reached by the person mentioned during the year in question.)

Year	Age	Life	Contemporary Musicians
1786		Carl Maria von Weber born Dec. 18, at Eutin near Lübeck, son of Franz Anton von Weber (52), a town musician, formerly director of music to the Bishop of Lübeck and Eutin.	Bishop born, Nov. 18; Sacchini (51) dies, Oct. 7. Auber aged 4; Bach (C. P. E.) 72; Beethoven 16; Boccherini 43; Boïeldieu 11; Cherubini 26; Cimarosa 37; Clementi 34; Dibdin 41; Dittersdorf 47; Dussek 25; Field 4; Gluck 72; Gossec 52; Grétry 45; Haydn 54; Hummel 8; Kozeluch 32; Lesueur 26; Méhul 23; Monsigny 57; Morlacchi 2; Mozart 30; Paer 15; Paisiello 45; Piccinni 58; Reichardt 34; Righini 30; Salieri 36; Sarti 57; Schenk 25; Spohr 2; Spontini 12; Umlauf 30; Viotti 33; Vogler 37; Wanhal 47; Weigl 20; Winter 31; Zelter 28; Zingarelli 34; Zumsteeg 26.
1787	1	The family leads a wandering life with a theatrical company.	Gluck (73) dies, Nov. 15.
1788	2		Bach (C. P. E.) (74) dies, Dec. 15.

232

Year	Age	Life	Contemporary Musicians
1789	3	Having a diseased hip-bone, W. has not yet learnt to walk.	
1790	4	Itinerant theatrical life continued.	
1791	5	His father, anxious to make a musical wonder-child of him, teaches him singing and piano.	Czerny born, Feb. 20; Hérold born, Jan. 28; Meyerbeer born, Sept. 5; Mozart (35) dies, Dec. 5.
1792	6	Makes some progress in music, but not enough to satisfy his father's ambitions.	Rossini born, Feb. 29.
1793	7	To his father's disappointment, W. is not yet ready to make public appearances.	
1794	8	Wandering theatrical life still continues. W.'s mother (26), *née* Genofeva von Brenner, appears as Constanze in Mozart's *Entführung* at the theatre in Weimar managed by Goethe (45), June 16. Goethe cancels the Webers' engagement and they go to Erlangen, Sept.	
1795	9	Not satisfied with his progress in music, his father (61) makes him turn to drawing and painting, with even less success.	Marschner born, Aug. 16.
1796	10	Removal to Hildburghausen, where W. becomes a pupil of the oboist Johann Peter Heuschkel (23), who teaches him piano and theory. The lessons are	Loewe born, Nov. 30; Umlauf (39) dies, June 8.

233

Year	Age	Life	Contemporary Musicians
		interrupted on the family's removal to Salzburg, where W. enters the training school for choristers directed by Michael Haydn (59).	
1797	11	Training at Salzburg continued.	Donizetti born, Nov. 29; Schubert born, Jan. 31.
1798	12	Michael Haydn (61) offers to teach him composition for nothing, Jan. Death of W.'s mother (30), March 13. Visit to Vienna with his father (64), where he hears Haydn's(66) *Creation*, April. 6 Fughettas (Op. 1) for piano finished, Sept. 1. Removal to Munich, where he becomes a pupil of Valesi (63), autumn. His father abandons the stage and resumes a military career.	
1799	13	Lessons with Valesi (64) continued. He also becomes a pupil of Kalcher (33) for composition and begins to make progress at last. He is by this time a good enough pianist to play at concerts.	Dittersdorf (60) dies, Oct. 24; Halévy born, May 27.
1800	14	Opera, *Die Macht der Liebe*, sonatas and variations for piano, songs, etc., composed (all destroyed). He engraves a set of Variations on an original theme for piano (Op. 2) dedicated to Kalcher (34), having learnt en-	Piccinni (72) dies, May 7.

Year	Age	Life	Contemporary Musicians
		graving from Senefelder (29). Removal to Freiberg (Saxony), where Chevalier Steinsberg, the manager of a theatrical company, gives W. the libretto of *Das Waldmädchen*, which is produced Nov. 24. It has little success, but is better received at Chemnitz, Dec. 5.	
1801	15	W. and his father (67) settle at Chemnitz, but return to Salzburg later in the year, where he resumes lessons with Michael Haydn (64). Opera, *Peter Schmoll und seine Nachbarn*, and piano pieces (Opp. 3 and 4) composed.	Bellini born, Nov. 1; Cimarosa (52) dies, Jan. 11; Lanner born, April 11.
1802	16	Mass (*Jugendmesse*) in E flat major, May 3. Visit to North Germany with his father, summer. A fortnight spent at his birthplace, Eutin, Oct. Visit to Hamburg, Oct., where he composes the songs, *Die Kerze* and *Umsonst*, and 6 Écossaises for piano, dedicated 'to the fair sex of Hamburg.' After a visit to Coburg, W. and his father stay some time at Augsburg, Nov., where he studies musical treatises by C. P. E. Bach, Kirnberger and others collected during the journey.	Sarti (73) dies, July 28; Zumsteeg (42) dies, Jan. 27.

Year Age	Life	Contemporary Musicians
1803 17	*Peter Schmoll* produced at Augsburg. Departure for Vienna, spring, where he makes the acquaintance of Vogler (54), under whose guidance he analyses the works of the great masters. He meets Haydn (71) and Beethoven (33).	Adam born, July 24; Berlioz born, Dec. 11; Glinka born, May 20 / June 2; Lortzing born, Oct. 23.
1804 18	Variations on a theme from Vogler's (55) *Castor und Pollux* for piano (Op. 5) composed and another set for piano with violin on a theme from the same composer's *Samori* (Op. 6). Friendship with Johann Baptist Gänsbacher (26). Arrival at Breslau, June, where he has been appointed conductor at the theatre on Vogler's recommendation. He takes up his duty, autumn, and the leader of the orchestra, Joseph Schnabel (37), resigns, refusing to serve under so young a conductor.	Benedict born, Nov. 27; Strauss (J. i) born, March 14.
1805 19	He makes himself unpopular with the singers and orchestra by tactlessness and with the management by insisting on costly new departures, but the director, Prof. J. G. Rhode, favours him and writes the libretto of *Rübezahl* for him. He	Boccherini (62) dies, May 28.

Year	Age	*Life*	*Contemporary Musicians*
		becomes a skilful guitar player and writes many songs with guitar accompaniment. *Overtura chinesa* (see 1809) for orchestra composed.	
1806	20	W. drinks by mistake some nitric acid, which makes him ill for some time and causes the loss of his singing voice. He resigns his conductorship at the theatre, spring, but remains at Breslau as a music teacher. Invitation by the Duke Eugen of Württemberg to the castle of Carlsruhe in Silesia, summer. He remains there as domestic musician, together with his father (72), whom he still supports. Composes among other things a *Romanza siciliana* for flute and orchestra, a horn Concerto (Op. 45), Variations for viola and orchestra and a Cantata (Op. 43) to words by Theodor Körner (15) in memory of Prince Louis Ferdinand of Prussia (34), who has fallen in the battle of Saalfeld.	
1807	21	Two Symphonies composed, Jan. After a Napoleonic victory, Duke Eugen is obliged to dismiss his musicians, but recommends W. as private secretary to his	

Year	Age	Life	Contemporary Musicians
		brother, Duke Ludwig of Württemberg, at Stuttgart, Feb. But W. first goes on a concert tour. Arrival at Stuttgart, July 17. He cultivates his mind and reads philosophy at court, but also takes part in its dissipations, being, as a nobleman, admitted to its circles. Friendship with the conductor of the court opera, Franz Danzi (44), who introduces him to the company, some members of which lead him farther astray. Attachment to the singer Margarethe Lang. Meeting with Spohr (23), who visits Stuttgart, and friendship with the poet Matthisson (46) and the sculptor Dannecker (49). Variations for piano on Bianchi's (*c.* 55) *Vien quà, Dorina bella* (Op. 7).	
1808	22	Polonaise for piano (Op. 21) finished and dedicated to Margarethe Lang, June 4. Composition of the opera, *Sylvana* (on the same subject as *Das Waldmädchen, see* 1800), begun. The librettist is Franz Carl Hiemer, a member of the merry fraternity called 'Fausts Höllenfahrt,' to which W. belongs. Variations on an original	Balfe born, May 15.

Year	Age	Life	Contemporary Musicians

theme for piano (Op. 9); *Der erste Ton*, poem by Rochlitz (39), for recitation with accompaniment and final chorus (Op. 14); *Momento capriccioso* for piano (Op. 12), dedicated to Meyerbeer (17).

1809 23 W.'s father (75) arrives at Stuttgart, spring, and once more becomes a drag on him. Piano Quartet (Op. 18) composed, also music for Schiller's version of Gozzi's *Turandot* (Op. 37), including the *Overtura chinesa* (*see* 1805). W. incurs the displeasure of King Friedrich II of Württemberg (55) by sending into his room an old woman who had asked for the court washerwoman.

Haydn (77) dies, May 31; Mendelssohn born, Feb. 3.

1810 24 At the court theatre, where *Sylvana* is about to be put into rehearsal, W. is arrested by order of the king, Feb. 9. He is accused of having accepted money to procure a court appointment for a young man anxious to avoid military service. His innocence is established and he is released, Feb. 26, but banished from the kingdom. He goes to Mann-

Chopin born, Feb. 22; Nicolai born, June 9; Schumann born, June 8.

Year	Age	Life	Contemporary Musicians

heim. He receives the libretto of *Abu Hassan* from Hiemer of Stuttgart, March 29. In April he removes to Darmstadt, where he studies with Vogler (61) again and is constantly in the company of his fellow‑students, Meyerbeer (19) and Gänsbacher (32). *Sylvana* produced at Frankfort o/M., with Caroline Brandt (*c.* 25) in the title part, Sept. 16. Concert at Mannheim, where W. plays the new piano Concerto in C major (Op. 11) and conducts the revised *Peter Schmoll* overture, Nov. 19. W. and Alexander von Dusch plan an opera on Apel's story of *Der Freischütz*, the latter to write the libretto.

1811 25 Comic opera, *Abu Hassan*, finished, Jan. 12. W. leaves Darmstadt to go on a concert tour, Feb. 14. He meets Sterkel (61) at Aschaffenburg and E. T. A. Hoffmann (35) at Bamberg. Concertino for clarinet (Op. 26) performed by Heinrich Bärmann (27) in Munich, April 5, and *Abu Hassan* produced there, June 4. Clarinet Concertos (Opp. 73 and 74) composed for

Hiller born, Oct. 24; Liszt born, Oct. 22.

Year	Age	Life	Contemporary Musicians

Bärmann. Tour in Switzerland, Aug.–Nov. Overture, *Beherrscher der Geister*, a revised version of the *Rübezahl* overture, first performed in Munich, Nov. 11. Bassoon Concerto (Op. 75) composed for F. G. Brandt of the Munich court orchestra. Visit to Prague with Bärmann, Dec. Visits to Dresden and Leipzig, late Dec. Meeting with Rochlitz (42) at Leipzig.

1812 26 W. goes to Gotha at the invitation of Duke Emil Leopold August of Saxe-Gotha, Jan. 17. Meeting with Spohr (28), with whom he gives a concert at court, Jan. 24. He visits Goethe (63) at Weimar with Spohr, but the poet receives them coldly, end of Jan. Visits to Dresden and to Berlin, where he stays with Meyerbeer's (21) parents, Feb. Production of *Sylvana* in Berlin, July 10, in spite of the opposition of Righini (56) and Bernhard Anselm Weber (46). Death of W.'s father, Franz Anton von Weber (78) at Mannheim, April 16. Return to Gotha, Sept. 6, where he soon begins to find attendance on

Dussek (51) dies, March 20.

Year Age	*Life*	*Contemporary Musicians*
	the duke hampering. Visit to Weimar, Oct., where he gives lessons to the Grand Duchess Maria Pavlovna and has some pleasant inter-course with Wieland (79), but is still snubbed by Goethe. Piano Sonata, C major (Op. 24), dedicated to the Grand Duchess of Saxe-Weimar; Variations for piano on a theme from Méhul's (49) *Joseph* (Op. 28); piano Concerto in E flat major (Op. 32).	
1813 27	The Concerto performed by W. at a Gewandhaus con-cert in Leipzig, where he also gives the Hymn, *In seiner Ordnung*, for solo voices, chorus and orchestra (Op. 36), Jan. 1. Departure for what is intended to be a long European tour, Jan 10. He goes to Prague first and finds the conductorship at the theatre vacant by the re-signation of Wenzel Müller (46). It is offered to him and he decides to accept it and to give up his tour. Visit to Vienna to find new singers for Prague, March 27. He hears Hummel (35) and Moscheles (19) play there. He returns to Prague with a new company, including	Dargomizhsky born, Feb. 2/14; Grétry (72) dies, Sept. 24; Heller born, May 15; Verdi born, Oct. 10; Wagner born, May 22; Wanhal (74) dies, Aug. 26.

Year	Age	Life	Contemporary Musicians
		Caroline Brandt (*c.* 28), who had sung in *Sylvana* at Frankfort o/M (*see* 1810), April. He shows great genius for organization and directs the stage management as well as the music in the operatic performance, which he opens with Spontini's (39) *Fernand Cortez*, Sept. 10. Friendship with Ludwig Tieck (40) and Clemens Brentano (35) and love affair with Therese Brunetti, a minor actress in the company.	
1814	28	W. falls in love with Caroline Brandt and, cutting himself off from Therese Brunetti, becomes engaged to her, spring. All the operas produced by him are newly studied from every point of view; he is completely exhausted at the end of the season and goes to the baths of Liebwerda, July 8. Visits to Berlin and Gotha during the summer. His engagement as conductor to the Berlin Court Opera in succession to Himmel, who has died on June 8, is considered; but he returns to Prague, Sept. 25. Brentano (36) begins a libretto for him on the subject of the	Reichardt (62) dies, June 17; Vogler (65) dies, May 6.

Year	Age	Life	Contemporary Musicians
		Tannhäuser legend, but abandons it. Song cycles for voice and piano (Op. 41) and male voices (Op. 42) on poems from Körner's *Leyer und Schwert* completed. Owing to the young poet's death in the Napoleonic wars they are very successful.	
1815	29	Greatly troubled by the caprices of his betrothed, Caroline Brandt (*c.* 30), who cannot make up her mind to marry him, and discovering that derogatory rumours about their relationship begin to circulate, he urges an immediate marriage, but insists that she should leave the stage. She objects to this condition and the engagement is broken off. W. leaves Prague for the summer and goes to Munich. Cantata, *Kampf und Sieg*, composed there to celebrate the battle of Waterloo. On receiving a letter from Caroline suggesting that they should part for ever, he finds he cannot live without her and returns to Prague, early Aug. On seeing him again, she once more changes her mind and agrees to marry him on his conditions.	Franz born, June 28.

Year	Age	Life	Contemporary Musicians
		Quintet for clarinet and strings (Op. 34).	
1816	30	During a visit to Berlin in the summer, Count Brühl (44) endeavours to secure him an appointment at the Court Opera, but in vain. He resigns his post at the Prague Opera, Sept. 30, and returns to Berlin, where Caroline has to fulfil an engagement, Oct. On the point of starting for Hamburg and Copenhagen, he is informed of his appointment as conductor to the Dresden Opera by Frederick Augustus of Saxony (66), Dec. 25. He goes and takes up his new duties at once. Piano Sonatas in A flat major and D minor (Opp. 39 and 49); song cycle, *Die vier Temperamente* (Op. 46); *Grand Duo concertant* for clarinet and piano (Op. 48).	Paisiello (75) dies, June 5.
1817	31	W. gives a German translation of Méhul's (54) *Joseph*, Jan. 30, the first venture of its kind at Dresden, where Italian opera has so far flourished exclusively. The Italian company, under Morlacchi (33), is secretly but strongly opposed to him. Meeting with Friedrich Kind (49), who writes the	Gade born, Feb. 22; Méhul (54) dies, Oct. 18; Monsigny (88) dies, Jan. 14.

Year	*Age*	*Life*	*Contemporary Musicians*

libretto of *Der Freischütz*, based on Apel's story, for him, Feb. He nearly resigns his post because he is not given the title of *Kapell-meister*, which Morlacchi holds. Friedrich August (67) confers it on him, re-luctantly, having no liking for him owing to the in-trigues set on foot against him. Although the or-chestra is excellent, he has immense difficulties to over-come with inferior singers, and he goes to Prague to induce Therese Grünbaum, the prima donna there, to come to Dresden, March. Caroline is still there and a marriage is arranged for the autumn. Return to Dresden after a concert at Leipzig, April. He receives an offer from the Berlin Court Opera and begins to nego-tiate, but the Berlin theatre is destroyed by fire, July 31. The king confirms his ap-pointment for life, with a share in the musical direc-tion in the Chapel Royal, Sept. Cantata, *L'accoglienza*, for the marriage of the Grand Duke Leopold of Tuscany (20) to Princess Maria Anna Caroline of

Year	Age	Life	Contemporary Musicians
		Saxony, Oct. Visit to Prague, where he marries Caroline Brandt (*c.* 32), Nov. 4. Their honeymoon takes the form of a concert tour. Return to Dresden, Dec. 20.	
1818	32	W. works at *Der Freischütz*, but puts off its completion, April. Morlacchi (34) and the Italian company grow more and more hostile. Fiftieth anniversary of the accession of Frederick Augustus (68) to the Saxon throne, for which W. has composed the *Jubel-Cantate* (Op. 58). The king forbids its performance, but the *Jubel-Ouvertüre* (Op. 59) is given. Scena and aria composed for Anna Milder-Hauptmann (33) for interpolation into Cherubini's (58) *Lodoiska*. Mass in E flat major (Op. 75A). Incidental music to Gehe's *Heinrich IV* and Grillparzer's (27) *Sappho*. Daughter born, Dec. 22. W. is beginning to show signs of ill-health.	Gounod born, June 17; Kozeluch (46) dies, May 7.
1819	33	Mass in G major (Op. 76) finished, Jan. 4. Death of W.'s infant daughter, April 28. W. is asked to write an opera for the marriage of	Offenbach born, June 21.

Year Age	Life	Contemporary Musicians
	Prince Frederick Augustus of Saxony (22) to the Archduchess Caroline of Austria and chooses the subject of Alcindor from the *Arabian Nights*, but the commission is withdrawn, June 28, and given to Morlacchi (35). During a summer holiday at Hosterwitz near Pillnitz W. composes 8 pieces for piano duet (Op. 60), the *Rondo brillante* for piano (Op. 62), the Trio for piano, flute and cello (Op. 63), the *Aufforderung zum Tanz* (Op. 65) and *Polacca brillante* for piano (Op. 72) and some of the songs (Opp. 64, 68 and 71). Visit of Marschner (24) to Dresden and W.'s acceptance of his *Heinrich IV und Aubigné* for production there, Aug. 18. W. at last begins to work continuously at *Der Freischütz*, Sept. 17. Meeting with Loewe (23), who visits Dresden. W.'s illness progresses.	
1820 34	Composition of *Der Freischütz* completed, May 13. Incidental music to Wolff's play, *Preciosa*, finished for the Berlin Court Theatre, July 15, and comic opera, *Die drei Pintos*, begun. W.	Serov born, Jan. 11/23; Vieuxtemps born, Feb. 20.

Year	Age	Life	Contemporary Musicians
		and his wife start a concert tour, which takes them to Halle, Göttingen, Hanover, Bremen, Oldenburg and Hamburg. He leaves Caroline there and goes alone to Copenhagen, after a visit to Lübeck and his birthplace, Eutin, Sept. Arrival in Copenhagen, Sept. 24. Concert before the court at the castle of Frederiksborg, Oct. 4, and public concert at the Theatre Royal, Oct. 8. He rejoins his wife at Hamburg, where they give another concert, and they return to Dresden, Nov. 4.	
1821	35	Hummel (43) brings Benedict (17) to W. and the latter becomes his pupil. Performance of Wolff's *Preciosa* in Berlin, with W.'s incidental music, March 14. Arrival in Berlin for the production of *Der Freischütz*, May 4. There is great anxiety lest this German opera should fail to assert itself against the Italian rule of Spontini, whose *Olympia* is produced with great success in a revised form, May 14. Mendelssohn (12) is introduced to W., June. *Concertstück* for piano and	

Year	Age	Life	Contemporary Musicians

orchestra (Op. 79) finished in Berlin on the morning of the production of *Der Frei-schütz*, June 18. Heine (*c.* 21), E. T. A. Hoffmann (45) and Mendelssohn are in the audience. The work has an immense success. W. plays the *Concertstück* for the first time, June 25. Return to Dresden, July 1. W. recommends Spohr (37) for an appointment at the court of Cassel, which he has nearly accepted him-self, Sept. Composition of the opera, *Euryanthe*, to a libretto by Helmine von Chezy, commissioned by Barbaja (43), manager of the Kärnthnerthor Theatre in Vienna, begun, Dec. W. abandons *Die drei Pintos* in its favour.

1822	36	*Der Freischütz* is first per-formed in Dresden, Jan. 26, Prague, Feb. 14, and Vienna, 18. In the latter place, where he has not supervised it him-self, it is badly done and he is anxious to conduct it him-self, which he does on March 9. He meets Hel-mine von Chezy, with whom he discusses altera-tions in the libretto of *Eury-anthe*; also Schubert (25),	Franck born, Dec. 10; Raff born, May 27

Year	Age	Life	Contemporary Musicians
		Salieri (72), Gyrowetz (59), Grillparzer (31), Castelli (41) and Caroline Pichler (53). He is invited to settle in Vienna as conductor of the German Opera, but the plan does not materialize. He is ill with throat trouble and returns to Dresden, March 26. Birth of son, Max Maria von Weber, March/April. *Euryanthe* nearly completed during a summer holiday at Hosterwitz near Pillnitz. Piano Sonata, E minor (Op. 70).	
1823	37	W. gives Beethoven's (53) *Fidelio* for the first time at Dresden, April 29, with Wilhelmine Schröder (19) in the title part. He has been in correspondence with Beethoven on the subject, and visits him at Baden, Oct. 5, with his pupil Benedict (19), during his visit to Vienna for the production of *Euryanthe*, which takes place on Oct. 25. Henriette Sontag (17) sings the title part. It has only a moderate success and W. quarrels with Schubert (26), who has criticized the work adversely. Return to Dresden after a visit to Prague, Nov. 10. Marsch-	Lalo born, Jan. 27; Steibelt (58) dies, Sept. 20.

Year	Age	Life	Contemporary Musicians

ner (28) becomes second conductor under W.

1824 38 First Dresden performance of *Euryanthe*, March 31. It is more successful there than elsewhere, but W. is much depressed by its poor reception in various towns. He ages prematurely and suffers from bad health. A cure at Marienbad proves unavailing and he spends the rest of the summer at Hosterwitz again. There he finds a letter from Charles Kemble (49), the lessee of Covent Garden Theatre in London, who proposes that W. should come to conduct there and also suggests his composing an English opera on the subject of Wieland's *Oberon*. He begins to take lessons in English to equip himself for this task, Oct.

Contemporary Musicians (1824): Bruckner born, Sept. 4; Cornelius born, Dec. 24; Reinecke born, June 23; Smetana born, March 2; Viotti (71) dies, March 3.

1825 39 Birth of second son, Alexander Victor Maria von Weber, Jan. 6. Composition of *Oberon*, to an English libretto by James Robinson Planché (29) begun, Jan. 23. W. has violent attacks of his throat disease and his doctor tells him that while a year in Italy might preserve him for another five or six years, a visit to Eng-

Contemporary Musicians (1825): Salieri (75) dies, May 7; Strauss (J. ii) born, Oct. 25; Winter (70) dies, Oct. 17.

Year	Age	Life	Contemporary Musicians

land and the completion of *Oberon* will be fatal, April. He is ordered a cure at Ems, on the way to which he visits Weimar, early July. He is warmly received by Hummel (47), but once again so coldly by Goethe (76) that he is taken ill with vexation. At Ems he is admitted into the circle of the Crown Prince of Prussia (30), afterwards Frederick William IV. Charles Kemble (50) and George Smart (49) come from London to discuss the *Oberon* production with him. After his return to Dresden, Schumann's (15) father asks him to instruct his son in music, but he gives an evasive answer. Although very seriously ill, he conducts the first Berlin performance of *Euryanthe*, which has been delayed by Spontini's (51) wilful neglect, Dec. 23.

1826 40 In spite of his serious illness W. is determined to undertake the journey to London in order to keep his family from want. After a heartbreaking parting with his family, he leaves for London, in the company of the

Auber aged 44; Balfe 18; Beethoven 56; Bellini 25; Benedict 22; Berlioz 23; Bishop 40; Boïeldieu 51; Bruckner 2; Catel 53; Cherubini 66; Chopin 16; Clementi 74; Cornelius 2; Czerny 35; Dargomizhsky

Year	Age	Life	Contemporary Musicians

flute player Anton Bernhard Fürstenau (34), Feb. 16. Arrival in Paris after a journey made by easy stages, Feb. 25. He meets Cherubini (66), Rossini (34), Berton (58), Catel (53), Paer (55), Auber (44) and Onslow (42). Berlioz (23), on the other hand, tries in vain to see him. The management of the Opéra is anxious that he should conduct *Euryanthe* there, but he is unable to stay. Departure for London, March 2, and arrival there, March 5. He stays at the house of George Smart (50). After a concert at which he conducts selections from *Der Freischütz*, March 8, rehearsals of *Oberon* begin at Covent Garden, March 9. Two new arias composed for Braham (*c.* 52), who is too old to sing those originally assigned to Sir Huon. W. conducts works of his own at a Philharmonic concert, April 3. Production of *Oberon* at Covent Garden, April 12. With Braham, Ann Paton (24) and Lucia Elizabeth Vestris (29) are in the cast. Although feeling increasingly ill, he conducts

13; Donizetti 29; Field 44; Franck 4; Glinka 23; Gossec 92; Gounod 8; Halévy 27; Hérold 35; Hummel 48; Liszt 15; Loewe 30; Lortzing 25; Marschner 31; Mendelssohn 17; Meyerbeer 35; Paer 55; Rossini 34; Schenk 65; Schumann 16; Smetana 2; Spohr 42; Spontini 52; Verdi 13; Wagner 13; Weigl 60; Zelter 68.

Year Age	Life	Contemporary Musicians
	the next twelve perform-ances and appears at half a dozen concerts during May. He also gives a concert of his own, at which Catherina Stephens (32) sings his song, *From Chindara's warbling fount*, from Thomas Moore's (47) *Lalla Rookh*, May 26. He is worn out by ill-health and overwork and hasty preparations for his return home are made, early June. At Smart's house he goes to bed exhausted, June 4, and is found dead in bed in the morning, June 5. A medical examination shows that he suffered from con-sumption and an ulcer of the throat.	

APPENDIX B

CATALOGUE OF WORKS

The following catalogue of Weber's compositions is based upon that in the third edition of Grove's *Dictionary of Music and Musicians*, but the latter has not been slavishly followed and the list has been greatly augmented, chiefly from the *Reliquienschrein* compiled by Dr Leopold Hirschberg to celebrate the hundredth anniversary of the composer's death. This catalogue I believe to be now the most complete in existence.

I. OPERAS

1. *Die Macht der Liebe und des Weins.* 1798. (No longer in existence.)
2. *Das Waldmädchen.* 1800. (Only two numbers have survived—an aria and a trio—both printed in the *Reliquienschrein* published in 1926, the centenary year of the composer's death.)
3. *Peter Schmoll und seine Nachbarn.* 1801. (2 acts.) (Unpublished.)
4. *Rübezahl.* 1804–5. (Only three numbers have survived, a quintet published many years ago, a chorus of Spirits and a recitative and aria for bass and chorus, printed in the *Reliquienschrein.*)
5. *Silvana.* 1810. (3 acts.)
6. *Abu Hassan.* 1811. (1 act.)
7. *Der Freischütz.* 1820. (3 acts.)
8. *Die drei Pintos.* 1821. (3 acts.) (Unfinished.)
9. *Euryanthe.* 1823. (3 acts.)
10. *Oberon.* 1826. (3 acts.)

II. OTHER DRAMATIC WORKS

1. *Der erste Ton.* Orchestral music for declamation with final chorus. 1808. Op. 14.

2. Music to Schiller's *Turandot*. 1809. (Overture and six short instrumental pieces.) R.[1] Op. 37.

3. Music to Adolph Müllner's *König Yngurd*. 1817. (Ten short instrumental pieces and one song.) R.

4. Music to Gehe's *Heinrich IV, König von Frankreich*. 1818. (Eight instrumental pieces. Only six are given in R. The second piece, 'Tanz,' was arranged as a pianoforte duet by Weber, and is included in his Op. 60. No. 5 was used as an episode in *Oberon*, and thirty-six bars of No. 6 as a *pas de cinq* in *Euryanthe*.)

5. Music to Rublack's play *Lieb' um Liebe*. 1818. (Four vocal pieces, one march and one melodrama.) R.

6. Music to Houwald's tragedy *Der Leuchtthurm*. 1820. (Two short melodramas and two interludes for harp.) R.

7. Music to Wolff's *Preciosa*. 1820. (Overture, four choruses, one song, three melodramas and three dances.)

8. Music to a festival play by Ludwig Robert, *Den Sachsensohn vermählet heute*. 1822. (Instrumental movement and five choruses.) Choruses only in R.

9. *Rondo alla Polacca* for tenor, 'Was ich da thu' das fragt er mich,' in Haydn's opera *Der Freybrief*. 1809.

10. Four *Lieder* for single voice and guitar in Kotzebue's *Der arme Minnesinger*. 1811. (Three are included in Op. 25, Nos. 2, 3 and 5.) *Goswins Lied*, 'Rase, Sturmwind, blase,' with guitar, only in R.

11. Two *Lieder*, 'Mein Weib ist capores' and 'Frau Liserl juhe' for baritone, from Anton Fischer's *Der Travestirte Aeneas*. 1815. R.

12. Two *Lieder*, 'Wer stets hinter'n Ofen kroch' and 'Wie wir voll Gluth uns hier zusammenfinden,' from Gubitz's *Lieb und Versöhnen*, for baritone and tenor respectively. 1815.

13. Ballad for single voice and harp, 'Was stürmt die Haide herauf?' from Reinbach's tragedy *Gordon und Montrose*. 1815.

14. Arietta to Huber's *Sternenmädchen im Maidlinger Walde*. 1816.[2]

15. Romance for voice and guitar, 'Ein König einst gefangen sass,' from Castelli's *Diana von Poitiers*. 1816.

---

[1] R. signifies that all the works thus indicated are previously unpublished pieces now appearing in the *Reliquienschrein* referred to above.

[2] Probably the *Lied ohne Worte* in R. *See under* V. Vocal Solos, etc. No. 58.

16. *Lied*, 'Hold ist der Cyanenkranz,' from Kind's festival play *Der Weinberg an der Elbe*. 1817.
17. Chorus and melodrama from Grillparzer's tragedy *Sappho*. 1818. R.
18. *Lied* for single voice and guitar, 'Ein Mädchen ging die Wies' entlang,' from Kind's *Der Abend am Waldbrunnen*. 1818.
19. Chorus for female voices, with wind instruments, 'Agnus Dei,' from Graf von Blankensee's tragedy *Carlo*. 1820. R.
20. *Lied* for three female voices and guitar, 'Sagt woher stammt Liebeslust' ('Tell me where is fancy bred'), from Shakespeare's *Merchant of Venice*. 1821. R.
21. Music and recitative for Spontini's *Olympia*. 1825. R.
22. Recitative and rondo for soprano and orchestra, 'Il momento s' avvicina.' 1810. Op. 16.
23. *Scena ed aria* for soprano and orchestra, 'Misera me,' from *Atalia*. 1811. Op. 50.
24. *Scena ed aria* for tenor, men's chorus and orchestra, 'Qual altro attendi.' 1811. R.
25. *Scena ed aria* for tenor, two choruses and orchestra, 'Signor se padre sei,' for *Inez di Castro*. 1812. Op. 53A.
26. *Scena ed aria* for soprano and orchestra, 'Ah, se Edmondo fosse l' uccisor,' for Méhul's *Hélène*. 1815. Op. 52.
27. *Scena ed aria* for soprano and orchestra, 'Non paventar, mia vita,' for *Inez di Castro*. 1815. Op. 51.
28. *Scena ed aria* for soprano and orchestra, 'Was sag' ich? Schaudern macht mich der Gedanke,' for Cherubini's *Lodoiska*. 1818. Op. 56.
29. Three duets for two sopranos and pianoforte, 'Se il mio ben'; 'Mille volte' and 'Va, ti consola.' 1811. Op. 31.
30. Music to Moretto's *Donna Diana*. 1817. R.
31. Music to Theodor Hell's *Das Haus Anglade*. 1818. R.
32. Music to *Oberon*, unprinted. 1826. R.

III. CANTATAS

1. Hymn, *In seiner Ordnung schafft der Herr*, for four solo voices, chorus and orchestra. 1812. Op. 36.
2. *Kampf und Sieg*, for four solo voices, chorus and orchestra. 1815. Op. 44.

3. *L' accoglienza* for six solo voices, chorus and orchestra. 1817. (Still unpublished.) [1]
4. *Natur und Liebe,* for two sopranos, two tenors, two basses and pianoforte. 1818. Op. 61.
5. *Jubel-Cantate,* 'Erhebt den Lobgesang,' for solo voices, chorus and orchestra. 1818. Op. 58.
6. *Du, bekränzend unsre Laren,* for solo and chorus with pianoforte and flute. 1821.
7. *Wo nehm' ich Blumen her,* for three solo voices and pianoforte. 1823. R.

IV. MASSES

1. *Grosse Jugendmesse,* E flat major, for four solo voices, chorus and orchestra. 1802.
2. *Missa Sancta,* E flat major, for four solo voices, chorus and orchestra. 1818. Op. 75A.
3. *Offertorium,* E flat major, to No. 2, for soprano solo, chorus and orchestra. 1818. R.[2]
4. *Missa Sancta,* G major, for four solo voices, chorus and orchestra. 1818–19. Op. 76.
5. *Offertorium,* C major, to No. 4, for soprano solo and chorus. 1818. R.[2]

V. VOCAL SOLOS, PARTSONGS, ETC.

1. *Die Kerze,* 'Ungern flieht das süsse Leben. 1802. (For solo; also a setting for four voices, in R.)

---

[1] The opus number 57 has never been allotted to any work and it is possible that Weber intended *L' accoglienza* to take that number. Other opus numbers without allocations are 67, 69 (see note to IV, 5), 77 and 78.

[2] Op. 69, to which no work has been allotted, was probably intended to embrace the Dresden *Agnus Dei* and these two offertories, as one collection.

2. *Canon,* 'Mädchen, ach meide.' 1802. R.
   Liebeszauber, 'Mädel, schau mir.' 1807.
   Lied, 'Sanftes Licht.' 1809.   Op. 13.
   'Die Schäferstunde.' 1810.
   'Wiegenlied.' 1810.
   'Die Zeit.' 1810.

3. *Six Songs.* Op. 15.
   'Meine Lieder, meine Sänge.' 1809.
   'Ein steter Kampf ist unser Leben.' 1808.
   'Ach wenn ich nur ein Liebchen hätt.' 1809.
   'Was zieht du deinem Zauberkreise.' 1809.
   'Ich sah ein Röschen am Wege stehn.' 1809.
   'Ein Echo kenn' ich.' 1808.

4. *Six Songs.* Op. 23.
   'Meine Farben.' 1808.
   'Rhapsodie.' 1809.
   'Maienblümlein.' 1811.
   'Sonett.' 1812.
   'Heisse stille Liebe schwebet.' 1812.
   'An eine Freundin.' 1812.

5. *Five Songs.* Op. 25.
   'Liebe-Glühen.' 1812.
   'Ueber die Berge mit Ungestüm.' 1811.
   'Lass mich schlummern.' 1811.
   'Bettlerlied.' 1812.
   'Umringt vom mutherfüllten Heere.' 1811.

6. *Tre Canzonette.* Op. 29. 1811.
   'Ah dove siete.'
   'Ninfe se liete.'
   'Ch' io mai vi possa.'

7. *Six Songs.* Op. 30.
   'Wiedersehen.' 1804.
   Lied, 'Es stürmt auf der Flur.' 1813.
   'Unbefangenheit.' 1813.
   'Minnelied.' 1813.
   'Reigen.' 1813.
   Lied, 'Sind es Schmerzen, sind es Freuden.' 1813.

8. *Leyer und Schwert.* Op. 41. 1814. (Four Songs.)

'Gebet während der Schlacht.'
'Abschied vom Leben.'
Trost, 'Herz, lass dich nicht zerspalten.'
'Was ist des Sängers Vaterland.'

9. *Leyer und Schwert*. Op. 42. 1814. (Six Songs.)
   'Reiterlied I.'
   'Lützows wilde Jagd.'
   'Gebet vor der Schlacht.'
   'Männer und Buben.'
   'Trinklied vor der Schlacht.'
   'Schwertlied.'

10. *Leyer und Schwert*. Op. 43. 1816. (One Song.)
    'Düst're Harmonieen hör' ich klingen.'

11. *Die Temperamente beim Verluste der Geliebten*. Op. 46. 1816.
    (Four Songs.)
    'Der Leichtmüthige.'
    'Der Schwermüthige.'
    'Der Liebemüthige.'
    'Der Gleichmüthige.'

12. *Six Songs*. Op. 47.
    'Die gefangenen Sänger.' 1816.
    'Die freien Sänger.' 1816.
    Ballade, 'Was stürmet die Haide herauf.' 1815.
    'Der Jüngling und die Spröde.' 1816.
    'Mein Verlangen.' 1816.
    'Gebet an die Geliebte.' 1814.

13. *Five Partsongs for Men's Voices*. Op. 53B.
    'Lebenslied am Geburtstage.' 1814.
    'Zwei Kränze zum Annen-Tage.' 1817.
    'Schöne Ahnung ist erglommen.' 1818.
    'Schmückt das Haus mit grünen Zweigen.' 1818.
    'Singet dem Gesang zu Ehren.' 1818.

14. *Seven Songs*. Op. 54.
    'Die fromme Magd.' 1818.
    'Quodlibet.' 1817.
    'Liebeslied.' 1817.
    'Abschied.' 1817.
    'Alte Weiber.' 1817.

   Volkslied, 'Wenn ich ein Vöglein war'.' 1818.
   Volkslied, 'Weine, weine.' 1818.

15. *Eight Songs*. Op. 64.
   Volkslied, 'Mein Schatzerl ist hübsch.' 1818.
   'Mailied.' 1817.
   'Heimlicher liebe Pein.' 1818.
   'Gelehrtheit.' 1818.
   'Abendsegen.' 1819.
   'Liebesgruss aus der Ferne.' 1819.
   'Ei, ei, ei, wie scheint der Mond so hell.' 1818.
   Volkslied, 'Herzchen, mein Schätzchen.' 1819.

16. *Six Songs*. Op. 66.
   'Das Veilchen im Thale.' 1817.
   'Rosen im Haare.' 1818.
   'Ich denke dein.' 1806.
   'Lebensansicht.' 1812.
   'Der Lethe des Lebens.' 1809.
   'Wunsch und Entsagung.' 1817.

17. *Six Partsongs for Men's Voices*. Op. 68.
   'Das Turnierbankett.' 1812.
   'Ermunterung.' 1819.
   'Freiheitslied.' 1819.
   'Schlummerlied.' 1822.
   'Gute Nacht.' 1819.
   'Husarenlied.' 1821.

18. *Six Songs*. Op. 71.
   'Triolett.' 1819.
   'Bach, Echo, Kuss.' 1818.
   'Das Mädchen an das erste Schneeglöckchen.' 1819.
   'Umsonst.' 1802.
   'Lied der Hirtin.' 1818.
   'Das Künstlers Abschied.' 1810.

19. *Six Songs*. Op. 80.
   'Lied von Clotilde.' 1821.
   'Sehnsucht.' (*Weinachtslied*.) 1819.
   'Elfenlied.' 1819.
   'Schmerz.' 1820.

'An Sie.' 1820.

'Der Sänger und der Maler. 1820.

20. *Grablied*, 'Leis' wandeln wir, wie Geisterhauch.' (2 tenors and bass.) 1803.

21. *Serenade*, 'Horch, leise horch!' (One voice with guitar.) 1809.

22. *Romanze*, 'Die Ruinen.' 1809.

23. Duet, 'Dich an dies Herz zu drücken,' for soprano and tenor. (First used in *Peter Schmoll* and afterwards much altered in Haydn's *Der Freybrief*.) 1809.

24. *Canzonetta*, 'Italiänisches Ständchen.' 1810.

25. Canon, 'Die Sonate soll ich spielen.' (3 voices.) 1810. R.

26. Three-part Canon, 'Canons zu zwei sind nicht drey.' 1810. R.

27. *Romanze*, 'Um Rettung bietet ein güld'nes Geschmeide.' 1812. R.

28. *Schwäbisches Tanzlied*, 'Geiger und Pfeiffer,' partsong for treble, two tenors and bass. 1812.

29. *Canon*, 'Zu dem Reich der Töne schweben.' (4 parts.) 1814. R.

30. *Canon*, 'Scheiden und leiden ist einerlei.' 1814. R.

31. *Dreistimmige Burleske*, 'Drei Knäbchen lieblich ausstaffieret.' (A musical frolic based on themes from Mozart's *Zauberflöte*.) 1815. R.

32. *Romanze*, 'Leise weht es.' 1818.

33. Duet, 'Sei gegrüsst, Frau Sonne, mir,' for tenor and bass. 1818. R.

34. Double Canon for 4 voices, without words. 1819. R.

35. 'Das Licht im Thale,' ballad with pianoforte. 1822.

36. *Romance*, 'Elle était simple et gentillette.' 1824.

37. *Schützenweihe*, 'Hörnerschall, Ueberfall.' (4 parts.) 1825.

38. *Zehn Schottische National Gesänge*. Preludes, accompaniments, etc., for pianoforte, flute, violin and violoncello added by Weber. 1825.

'The Soothing Shades.'
'The Troubadour.'
'O Poortith Cauld.'
'Bonnie Dundee.'
'Yes, thou may'st walk.'
'A soldier am I.'
'John Anderson, my Jo.'
'O my Love's like the Red, Red Rose.'
'Robin is my joy, my dear.'
'Whar hae ye been a' day.'

39. *Kriegseid,* 'Wir stehn vor Gott.' 1812. R.
40. 'From Chindara's warbling fount I come.' 1826. R.
41. 'Ein neues Lied.' 1810. R.
42. *Lied,* 'Entfliehet schnell von mir.' 1803. R.
43. 'Herz, mein Herz, ermanne dich.' 1820.
44. *Lied,* 'Ich sah sie hingesunken.' 1804. R.
45. *Trinklied,* with chorus, 'Weil es Gott also gefügt.' 1809. R.
46. *Reiterlied,* 'Hinaus, hinaus, zum blut'gen Strauss.' (4 parts.) 1825. R.
47. *Terzetto* for soprano, tenor and bass, 'Ein Gärtchen und ein Häuschen drin.' 1803. R.
48. 'Hörst du der Klage dumpfen Schall,' for mixed chorus and wind instruments. 1811. R.
49. *Canon,* 'Leck' mich im Angesicht.' 1810.
50. *Sextett,* 'Lenz erwacht und Nachtigallen.' 1812.
51. *Canon,* 'Weil Maria Töne hext.' 1816. R.
52. 'Strafpredigt über die französische Musik.' 1801. R.
53. 'Brief an Danzi.' 1808. R.
54. Quartet without words for Danzi. 1809. R.
55. *Canon* for 34 voices, 'Prost Neujahr' (without words). 1811. R.
56. *Canon,* 'Leise kömmt der Mond gezogen.' (4 voices.) 1814. R.
57. *Gebet an Amor,* 'Alles in mir glühet zu lieben.' 1814. R.
58. *Lied* in 'Das Sternenmädchen' (without words). 1816. R.[1]
59. *Lied in der Fremde,* 'Einsam? einsam? nein.' 1817(?). R.
60. *Solfeggien* (4). 1818. R.
61. 'Den König segne Gott,' 'Heil, Dir im Siegerkranz,' and 'Musik zum Prolog des 11,' to the tune of 'God save the King.' Four-part harmonizations for men's voices by Weber. 1818(?). The Prologue with instrumental accompaniment. 1819. R.
62. Double Canon for 4 voices. 1819. R.
63. 'Deo Rosa.' 1821. R.
64. *Vatergruss,* 'Du gute, gute Mäzze.' 1823. R.

---

[1] See under II, 14.

Appendix B—Catalogue of Works

VI. Instrumental Works

(a) Symphonies, Overtures and other purely Orchestral Works

1. *Grande Ouverture à plusieurs instruments.* 1807. Op. 8.[1]
2. *Sinfonia in C, No. 1.* 1807. Op. 19.
3. *Ouvertüre zum 'Beherrscher der Geister.'* 1811. Op. 27.
4. *Jubel-Ouvertüre.* 1818. Op. 59.
5. *Sinfonia in C, No. 2.* 1807.
6. *Kleiner Tusch von zwanzig Trompeten.* 1806. R.
7. *Overture, E flat major.*[2] 1809(?). R.
8. Waltz for wind instruments. 1812. R.
9. *Deutscher* for full orchestra, D major. 1815.
10. *Tedesco* for full orchestra, D major. 1816. R.
11. *Marcia* for 10 trumpets, D major. (Used in *Euryanthe*.) 1822. R.
12. Fragment from an unknown work. 1823. (Also used in the original production of *Euryanthe*.) R.
13. March for wind instruments, C major. 1826.
    (*Overtura chinesa,* see II, 2: music to Schiller's *Turandot*.)

(b) Concertos, Concerted Works and Chamber Music

1. *Grand Concerto,* C major, for piano, No. 1. Op. 11. 1810.
2. *Grand Quatuor* for piano, violin, viola and cello. 1809. Op. 18.
3. *Grand Pot-pourri* for cello and orchestra. 1808. Op. 20.
4. Nine Variations on a Norwegian Air for piano and violin. 1808. Op. 22.
5. *Six Sonates progressives* for piano and violin obbligato. 1810. Op. 17.

---

[1] This is the overture to the unpublished opera, *Peter Schmoll und seine Nachbarn.* In this section I do not mention overtures which are published with their respective operas.

[2] The authorship of this overture is not absolutely established, but so great a consensus of opinion as regards the likelihood of its having been composed by Weber prevails that Dr Leopold Hirschberg risked inserting it in the *Reliquienschrein*.

6. *Concertino* for clarinet and orchestra. 1811. Op. 26.
7. *Grand Concerto*, E flat major, for piano, No. 2. 1812. Op. 32.
8. Seven Variations for clarinet and piano on a Theme from Weber's *Silvana*. 1811. Op. 33.
9. *Grosses Quintett*, for clarinet, violins, viola and cello. 1815. Op. 34.
10. *Andante e Rondo Ongarese*, for bassoon with orchestral accompaniment. 1813. Op. 35. (Originally composed in 1809 for viola.)
11. *Divertimento assai facile*, for guitar and piano. 1816. Op. 38.
12. *Concertino* for horn and orchestra. 1806. (Rescored 1815.) Op. 45.
13. *Grand Duo concertant*, for piano and clarinet. 1816. Op. 48.
14. Trio for piano, flute and cello. 1819. Op. 63.
15. Concerto for clarinet, No. 1, F minor. 1811. Op. 73.
16. Concerto for clarinet, No. 2, E flat major. 1811. Op. 74.
17. Concerto for bassoon. 1811. Op. 75.
18. *Concertstück* for piano and orchestra. 1821. Op. 79.
19. *Romanza siciliana*, for flute, with accompaniment for small orchestra. 1806.
20. Variations for cello. 1810. (The greater portion of this work, No. 9 of Weber's posthumous works, had already been used in Opp. 9 and 20.)
21. *Adagio and Rondo*, for harmonichord (or harmonium), with orchestral accompaniment. 1811.
22. Six Variations for viola on the folksong 'A Schüsserl und a Reind'rl.' 1806. R.

(c) *Pianoforte Music*

1. *Sechs Fughetten*. 1798. Op. 1.
2. Six Variations 'fürs Klavier oder Pianoforte,' on an original theme. 1800. Op. 2.
3. *Six petites pièces faciles*, for piano (4 hands). 1801. Op. 3.
4. *Douze Allemandes*. 1801. Op. 4.
5. Eight Variations 'air de ballet,' from Vogler's *Castor und Pollux*. 1804. Op. 5.

6. Six Variations for piano, with violin and cello accompaniment, *ad libitum*, on the air of Naza, 'Woher mag dies wohl kommen?' from Vogler's opera *Samori*. 1804. Op. 6.

7. Seven Variations on Bianchi's air 'Vien quà, Dorina bella.' 1807. Op. 7.

8. *Thème original varié* (7) *pour le pianoforte*. 1808. Op. 9.

9. Six Pieces for piano (4 hands). 1809. Op. 10.

10. *Momento capriccioso*. 1808. Op. 12.

11. *Grande Polonaise*. 1808. Op. 21.

12. Sonata No. 1, C major. 1812. Op. 24.

13. Seven Variations on the romance from Méhul's opera *Joseph*, 'A peine au sortir de l'enfance.' 1812. Op. 28.

14. Sonata No. 2, A flat major. 1816. Op. 39.

15. *Air Russe* ('Schöne Minka'), 9 variations. 1815. Op. 40.

16. Sonata No. 3, D minor. 1816. Op. 49.

17. Seven Variations on a gypsy song. 1817. Op. 55.

18. Eight Pieces for piano (4 hands). 1818–19. Op. 60.

19. *Rondo brillante* ('La Gaieté'). 1819. Op. 62.

20. *Auffordernung zum Tanz (Invitation to the Dance)*.[1] Rondo brillant. 1819. Op. 65.

21. Sonata No. 4, E minor. 1822. Op. 70.

22. *Polacca brillante* ('L'Hilarité'). 1819. Op. 72.

23. Six Écossaises. 1802.

24. Piano arrangement of Vogler's opera *Samori*. 1804.

25. *Favorit-Walzer der Kaiserin von Frankreich, Marie-Louise* (18). 1812.

26. *Melodie*. 1811(?). R.
    (Only thirty-two bars of unaccompanied melody, with repeats.)

27. *Sächsischer Zapfenstreich*. 1818(?).[2]

---

[1] Usually translated *Invitation to the Waltz*.

[2] Dr Hirschberg prints this composition in R. with the remark that, although it appeared in the *Album des Marches internationales* as a production of Weber's, its authenticity is more than doubtful.

APPENDIX C

PERSONALIA

Aiblinger, Johann Caspar (1779–1867), Bavarian composer, mainly of church music, was musical director of the Munich Opera in 1819–23.

Bader, Karl Adam (1789–1870), German tenor and organist, in the latter capacity succeeding his father at Bamberg Cathedral in 1807. He took to the stage in 1811 and became first tenor at the Berlin Court Opera in 1820.

Bärmann, Heinrich Joseph (1784–1847), German clarinet player and composer for this instrument, member of the Court Orchestra in Munich.

Bassi, Luigi (1766–1825), Italian baritone singer, appeared in soprano parts at the age of thirteen and went to Prague in 1784, where he made a great reputation and sang the title-part of Mozart's *Don Giovanni* for the first time.

Benedict, Julius (1804–85), English composer and pianist of German birth, pupil of Weber, settled in England in 1835, later became a naturalized Englishman and was knighted in 1871.

Berner, Friedrich Wilhelm (1780–1827), German organist, theorist, cellist, clarinettist and pianist, founded a Singakademie at Breslau on the model of that in Berlin.

Berton, Henri Montan (1767–1844), French composer, mainly of comic opera, violinist at the Paris Opéra from 1782, professor at the Conservatoire from 1795 and conductor at the Opéra-Comique from 1807.

Böttiger, Karl August (1760–1835), German archæologist, appointed rector of the Gymnasium at Weimar, where he entered the circle of great literary men, and went to Dresden with a court appointment in 1814.

Boucher, Alexandre Jean (1778–1861), French violinist, appeared in public at the age of six, was court violinist at Madrid in 1787–1805 and toured Europe from 1820 to 1844 with sensational success.

Braham, John (1777–1856), English tenor singer and composer of popular songs.

Appendix C—Personalia

Brentano, Clemens (1778–1842), German romantic poet and novelist.

Caradori-Allan, Maria Caterina Rosalbina, née de Munck (1800–65), English soprano of Italian birth, made her first appearance in London in 1822.

Carafa di Colobrano, Michele Enrico (1787–1872), French composer of Italian birth, settled in Paris in 1822 and composed many operas.

Castelli, Ignaz Franz (1781–1862), Austrian dramatist, librettist and minor poet, editor of the *Allgemeiner musikalischer Anzeiger* 1829–40.

Castil-Blaze (François Henri Joseph Blaze) (1784–1857), French critic of music and drama, translator of opera librettos for the Parisian stage and author of several books on music. Critic of the *Journal des Débats* before Berlioz.

Catel, Charles Simon (1773–1830), French composer and professor of music, accompanist at the Paris Opéra, 1790–1802, and professor at the Conservatoire from its foundation in 1795. Published his famous treatise on harmony in 1802.

Chezy, Wilhelmine (or *Helmine) Christine von, née von Klencke* (born 1783), German dramatist and novelist born in Berlin and settled in Vienna.

Clement, Franz (1780–1842), Austrian violinist, first appeared at the age of nine, was appointed conductor of the Theater an der Wien in Vienna and was the first to perform Beethoven's violin Concerto, which was written for him.

Dalayrac, Nicolas (1753–1809), French composer of a great number of comic operas.

Danzi, Franz (1763–1826), German composer and cellist, pupil of Vogler (q.v.), was a member of the band of the Elector Palatine at Mannheim and, from 1778, in Munich. *Kapellmeister* at the court of Württemberg at Stuttgart, and from 1808 at Carlsruhe.

Démar, Jean Sébastien (1763–c. 1832), French organist and composer of Bavarian birth, settled at Orleans as conductor and music publisher from 1806.

Devrient, Gustav Emil (1803–72), German actor, nephew of Ludwig Devrient (q.v.), made his first appearance at Brunswick in 1821. His brother, Karl August Devrient (1797–1872), married Wilhelmine Schröder (q.v.) in 1823.

Devrient, Ludwig (1784–1832), German actor, uncle of the preceding, made his first appearance at Gera in 1804. He was afterwards at Dessau, Breslau and Berlin.

Donzelli, Domenico (*c.* 1790–1873), Italian tenor, made his first appearance in Italy in 1816, Vienna in 1822, Paris in 1824 and London in 1829.

Eberwein, Karl (1786–1868), German violinist and composer, pupil of Zelter (q.v.), was in the court orchestra at Weimar, his native place, from 1803, and through Zelter's influence was much esteemed by Goethe, who showed no appreciation of Schubert and Weber.

Eichendorff, Joseph von (1788–1857), German romantic poet and novelist, studied law and lived in Vienna until 1813, when he fought with the Prussian army against Napoleon. In 1816 he accepted a judicial office at Breslau, and later held similar posts at Danzig, Königsberg and Berlin. He retired in 1844.

Fioravanti, Valentino (1764–1837), Italian composer, mainly of comic operas, and church music written after his appointment as choirmaster at St Peter's, Rome, in 1816.

Fischer, Anton (1777–1808), Austrian composer of operettas and comic operas, conductor in Vienna.

Fodor-Mainvielle, Joséphine (1789–1870), French operatic soprano, first appeared at the Paris Opéra-Comique in 1814.

Fröhlich, Joseph (1780–1862), Bavarian composer and teacher, who founded an institute at Würzburg in 1804 which became a royal school of music in 1820.

Fürstenau, Anton Bernhard (1792–1852), German flute player, in the court orchestra at Dresden from 1820. He wrote two methods and many pieces for his instrument.

Gänsbacher, Johann Baptist (1778–1844), Austrian composer, pupil of Albrechtsberger and Vogler (q.v.), appointed *Kapellmeister* of St Stephen's Cathedral, Vienna, in 1823.

Grätz, Joseph (1760–1826), Bavarian pianist, composer and theorist in Munich.

Grillparzer, Franz (1791–1872), Austrian poet and dramatist, appointed poet to the Hofburgtheater in Vienna in 1818, the year in which he produced *Sappho*.

Haydn, Michael (1737–1806), Austrian composer and organist, brother of Joseph Haydn. Boy chorister at St Stephen's in Vienna, appointed musical director to the Bishop of Grosswardein in 1757 and in 1762 became conductor to the Archbishop of Salzburg, where he was afterwards organist.

Appendix C—Personalia

Heuschkel, Johann Peter (died 1853), German oboe player and organist, appointed to the court chapel of Hildburghausen in 1794.

Hoffmann, Ernst Theodor Amadeus (originally *Wilhelm*) (1776–1822), German romantic novelist and amateur composer, became operatic conductor at Bamberg in 1808.

Houwald, Christoph Ernst von (1778–1845), German dramatist, cultivated an inferior form of drama known as 'fate tragedy' as an amateur while he lived on his family estate.

Humboldt, Alexander von (1769–1859), German naturalist and traveller.

Hummel, Johann Nepomuk (1778–1837), Austro-Hungarian pianist and composer, pupil of Mozart, at one of whose concerts in Vienna he made his first appearance in 1787. His most important appointment was that of *Kapellmeister* at Weimar in 1820.

Isouard, Nicolo (1775–1818), French composer born at Malta, produced his first opera at Florence in 1795, settled in Paris in 1799, where he produced 33 French comic operas. He was often called Nicolo only.

Jean Paul. See *Richter*.

Kalcher, Johann Nepomuk (1766–1826) Bavarian organist and composer, appointed to the Munich court in 1798.

Kemble, Charles (1775–1854), English actor, made his first appearance at Sheffield in 1792.

Kind, Johann Friedrich (1768–1843), German playwright and novelist resident at Dresden from 1814.

Kleist, Bernd Heinrich Wilhelm von (1777–1811), German poet, dramatist and novelist, first served in the army, then studied law, but began to devote himself entirely to a literary career in 1801.

Körner, Theodor (1791–1813), German poet, published his first volume of verse in 1810 and fell in the Napoleonic wars.

Kotzebue, August Friedrich Ferdinand von (1761–1819), German playwright, obtained an appointment at St. Petersburg, was arrested and sent to Siberia in 1800. A comedy secured his return, when he obtained the directorship of the German theatre at St Petersburg.

Kreutzer, Conradin (1780–1849), German composer and conductor, pupil of Albrechtsberger in Vienna, where he was conductor at the Kärnthnerthor and Josephstadt Theatres 1825–40.

Lablache, Luigi (1794–1858), Italian bass singer of French and Irish descent, made his first appearance at Naples in 1812.

Milder, Pauline Anna (1785–1838), German soprano, made her first

271

stage appearance in Vienna in 1803. Married in 1810 and from that time appeared under the name of Milder-Hauptmann.

Moreto y Cavana, Agustín (1618–61), Spanish dramatist, published a first volume of plays in 1654.

Morlacchi, Francesco (1784–1841), Italian composer, produced his first comic opera at Verona in 1807 and was appointed conductor of the Dresden Italian Opera in 1810.

Moscheles, Ignaz (1794–1870), German pianist and composer, long settled in London.

Mosel, Ignaz Franz von (1772–1844), Austrian composer and author, from 1820 theatrical manager and from 1829 librarian in Vienna.

Müller, August Eberhardt (1767–1817), German organist and composer, held appointments at Magdeburg, Berlin and Leipzig, where he became cantor at St Thomas's church in 1804. In 1810 he became court *Kapellmeister* at Weimar.

Müller, Wilhelm (1794–1827), German poet who served as volunteer in the Prussian army. Father of the philologist Max Müller.

Nägeli, Hans Georg (1773–1836), Swiss music publisher, composer and teacher, began to publish works by old masters in 1792 and contemporary piano music, including Beethoven, in 1803.

Naumann, Johann Gottlieb (1741–1801), German composer, studied in Italy and was appointed court composer of church music at Dresden in 1763.

Nicolo. See *Isouard*.

Niebuhr, Barthold Georg (1776–1831), German statesman and historian, who after holding various appointments became professor at the University of Berlin in 1810.

Onslow, George (1784–1853), Anglo-French composer living at Clermont-Ferrand and Paris.

Paer, Ferdinando (1771–1839), Italian opera composer settled in Paris in 1807 as *maître de chapelle* to Napoleon.

Paton, Mary Ann (1802–64), Scottish soprano, who appeared as a child at concerts playing the harp, piano and violin and made her first stage appearance in London in 1822.

Pichler, Caroline (1769–1843), Austrian novelist and minor poetess.

Planché, James Robinson (1786–1880), English dramatist, librettist and critic.

Polledro, Giovanni Battista (1781–1853), Italian violinist, made his first appearance at Turin in 1797 and, after touring extensively, was concert master at Dresden 1814–24.

Radziwill, Anton Heinrich, Prince (1775–1833), Polish-German amateur composer, cellist and singer.

Rastrelli, Joseph (1799–1842), German conductor and composer, became assistant conductor at the Dresden Opera in 1829 and first conductor in 1830.

Reissiger, Karl Gottlieb (1798–1859), German composer and conductor, succeeded Marschner as director of the German Opera at Dresden, the post formerly held by Weber, in 1827.

Richter, Jean Paul Friedrich (1763–1825), German romantic novelist known under the pen-name of 'Jean Paul.'

Righini, Vincenzo (1756–1812), Italian composer, pupil of Martini at Bologna, went to Prague as opera singer in 1776 and produced three operas there; held appointments at various German courts.

Ritter, Peter (1763–1846), German cellist and composer, from 1784 first cellist and from 1803 conductor of the Mannheim orchestra.

Rochlitz, Johann Friedrich (1769–1842), German music critic, editor of the *Allgemeine musikalische Zeitung* in Leipzig and an occasional poet.

Romberg, Bernhard (1767–1841), German cellist and composer, first appeared at the age of fourteen, toured widely and was court conductor in Berlin 1815–19. He wrote several operas.

Salieri, Antonio (1750–1825), Italian composer who settled in Vienna in 1766, studied under Gassmann, produced his first opera there in 1770 and succeeded Bonno as court musical director in 1788.

Schelling, Friedrich Wilhelm Joseph von (1775–1854), German philosopher.

Schnabel, Joseph Ignaz (1767–1831), German composer, violinist and conductor, settled at Breslau in 1797 and held various appointments there.

Schröder, Wilhelmine (1804–60), German dramatic soprano, made her first appearance at Vienna in 1821 and married the actor Karl Joseph Devrient (1797–1872) in 1823, thereafter calling herself Schröder-Devrient.

Schubert, Franz Anton (1768–1824), German conductor who directed the Italian Opera at Dresden.

Senefelder, Alois (1771–1834), German inventor of lithography.

Smart, George Thomas (1776–1867), composer and conductor in London.

Sontag, Henriette Gertrude Walpurgis (1806–54), German soprano, appeared at Prague at the age of fifteen as deputy for a *prima donna*.

Stephens, Catherine (1794–1882), English soprano, first appeared in Italian opera in 1812 and at Covent Garden in 1813.

Sterkel, Johann Franz Xaver (1750–1817), German secular priest and pianist, famous as an improviser.

Tieck, Ludwig (1773–1853), German poet, novelist and critic, one of the chief figures of the German romantic school.

Tiedge, Christoph August (1752–1841), minor German romantic poet.

Thibaut, Anton Friedrich Justus (1774–1840), German writer on music, professor of law at the University of Heidelberg.

Valesi, Johann Evangelist (real name *Wallishauser*) (1735–1811), German singer first appointed to the episcopal court of Freising, travelled much and became chamber singer to the Duke of Bavaria at Munich in 1756, where he had many pupils.

Vestris, Lucia Elizabeth, née Bartolozzi (1797–1856), English actress and operatic soprano of Italian descent, made her first appearance as a singer in 1815.

Vogler, Georg Joseph (1749–1814), German composer, teacher and theorist, pupil of Martini at Bologna and of Mysliweček, court chaplain to the Elector Palatine at Mannheim from 1775.

Voss, Johann Heinrich (1751–1826), German poet and translator, lived at Göttingen, where he was a member of an intellectual circle and became rector of the Gymnasium at Eutin in 1782.

Wallishauser. See *Valesi.*

Weber, Aloysia (1760–1839), German soprano, second daughter of Fridolin Weber (q.v.), first appeared at the electoral court of Mannheim and Munich, and was engaged for Vienna in 1780, where she married the actor Josef Lange. Mozart fell in love with her in 1778.

Weber, Bernhard Anselm (1766–1821), German conductor and composer who, after studying law and theology and managing theatrical companies, toured with Vogler (q.v.), his master, in 1790 and became *Kapellmeister* in Berlin in 1793.

Weber, Fridolin (1733–79), German singer and violinist, member of the electoral chapel at Mannheim, father of Aloysia Weber (q.v.), Josefa Weber (q.v.) and Mozart's wife, Constanze Weber.

Weber, Gottfried (1779–1839), German composer and theorist, settled at Mannheim from 1802 as lawyer and Government employee.

Weber, Josefa (1758–1820), German soprano, eldest daughter of Fridolin Weber (q.v.), does not appear to have sung in public until after 1780 in Vienna, where she appeared at Schikaneder's theatre from about 1789, in which year she married the violinist Franz Hofer.

Weigl, Joseph (1766–1846), Austrian composer, son of Joseph Weigl (1740–1820), a cellist under Haydn at Esterház. The younger Weigl was a pupil of Albrechtsberger and Salieri (q.v.). Wrote his first opera in 1782.

Wieck, Friedrich (1785–1873), German pianist and teacher at Leipzig, father of Clara Schumann (1819–96).

Winter, Peter von (1755–1825), German composer at Mannheim and Munich, composer of operas produced all over musical Europe.

Zelter, Carl Friedrich (1758–1832), German composer, conductor and teacher in Berlin, friend of Goethe, many of whose poems he set to music. Conductor of the Berlin Singakademie.

APPENDIX D

BIBLIOGRAPHY

Allekotte, H., 'C. M. von Weber's Messen.' (1913.)

Barbedette, H., 'Charles Marie de Weber: sa vie et ses œuvres.' (Paris, 1862.)

Benedict, Julius, 'Weber.' (London, 1926, new edition.)

Chop, Max, 'Carl Maria von Weber: "Der Freischütz," geschichtlich, szenisch und musikalisch analysiert.' (Leipzig, 1926.)

Cœuroy, André, 'Weber.' (Paris, 1925.)

Degen, Max, 'Die Lieder von Carl Maria von Weber.' (Freiburg i/B., 1924.)

Gehrmann, H., 'Weber' ('Berühmte Musiker'). (Berlin, 1899.)

Georgii, W., 'Weber als Klavierkomponist.' (Leipzig, 1914.)

Gumprecht, O., 'K. M. von Weber.' (Leipzig, 1866.)

Hefode, F., 'Die Vorfahren K. M. von Webers.' (1926.)

Hell, Theodor, 'Hinterlassene Schriften von C. M. von Weber,' 2nd edition. (1850.)

Jähns, F. W., 'Carl Maria von Weber in seinen Werken.' Chronological Thematic Index with Notes. (Berlin, 1871.)

—— 'Carl Maria von Weber: eine Lebensskizze.' (Leipzig, 1873.)

Jullien, Adolphe, 'Weber à Paris en 1826.' (Paris, 1877.)

Kaiser, Georg, 'Beiträge zu einer Charakteristik Carl Maria von Webers.' (Berlin, 1910.)

—— (edited by), 'Briefe an den Grafen Karl von Brühl.' (Leipzig, 1911.)

Kapp, Julius, 'Carl Maria von Weber: eine Biographie.' (Leipzig, 1930, 5th edition.)

Kleefeld, W., 'Carl Maria von Weber.' (Bielefeld, 1936.)

Kroll, Erwin, 'Carl Maria von Weber.' (Potsdam, 1934.)

—— 'Carl Maria von Weber: sein Leben in Bildern.' (Leipzig, 1936.)

Listl, Paul, 'Weber als Ouvertürenkomponist.' (Würzburg, 1936.)

Lobe, H., 'Gespräche mit Weber.' (Leipzig, 1853.)

Appendix D—Bibliography

Nohl, Ludwig, 'Musikerbriefe.' (Letters to Gänsbacher.) (Leipzig, 1867.) English translation by Lady Wallace (London, 1867; 2nd edition, augmented, 1873.)

Pfitzner, Hans, 'Was ist uns Weber?' (Augsburg, 1926.)

Reissmann, A., 'C. M. von Weber: sein Leben und seine Werke.' (Berlin, 1883.)

Reiter, E., 'Carl Maria von Webers künstlerische Persönlichkeit aus seine Schriften.' (Leipzig, 1926.)

Rudorff, E., 'Briefe von C. M. von Weber an Heinrich Lichtenstein.' ('Illustrierte deutsche Monatshefte.' Brunswick, Oct.–Dec. 1899.)

Sundt, A., 'Karl Maria von Webers Opern in ihrer Instrumentation.' (Frankfort, 1932.)

Servières, G., 'Weber: biographie critique.' (Paris, 1907.)

Skalla, F., 'Carl Maria von Weber.' (Prague, 1895.)

Waltershausen, Hermann von, 'Der Freischütz.' (Munich, 1920.)

Watzlik, H., 'Die romantische Reise des Herrn Carl Maria von Weber. A novel. (Leipzig, 1932.)

Weber, Carl Maria von, 'Ausgewählte Schriften.' Edited by Wilhelm Altmann. (Ratisbon, 1937.)

—— 'Gesammelte Schriften.' Edited by G. Kaiser. (Berlin, 1908.)

—— 'Reise-Briefe an seine Gattin Caroline: herausgegeben von seinem Enkel.' (Leipzig, 1886.)

—— 'Siebenundsiebzig bisher ungedruckte Briefe.' Edited by L. Hirschberg. (Hildburghausen, 1926.)

Weber, Max Maria von, 'Carl Maria von Weber: ein Lebensbild.' New edition by Rudolf Pechel. (Berlin, 1912.)

—— 'Carl Maria von Weber.' English translation of the above by J. P. Simpson. (London, 1865–8.)

Weber, Waldemar, 'Wie Gera den Komponisten des "Freischütz" erlebte.' (Gera, 1936.)

INDEX

INDEX

Index

Index